THE GOLDEN DOOR

HISTORIES BY ISAAC ASIMOV

Ancient

THE GREEKS

THE ROMAN REPUBLIC

THE ROMAN EMPIRE

THE EGYPTIANS

THE NEAR EAST

THE LAND OF CANAAN

Medieval

THE DARK AGES

THE SHAPING OF ENGLAND

CONSTANTINOPLE

THE SHAPING OF FRANCE

Modern

THE SHAPING OF NORTH AMERICA

THE BIRTH OF THE UNITED STATES

OUR FEDERAL UNION

THE GOLDEN DOOR

ISAAC ASIMOV

THE GOLDEN DOOR

The United States from 1865 to 1918

Houghton Mifflin Company Boston 1977

12040

Joel Davis and George Scithers,
and the new venture.

Maps by Eliza McFadden

Library of Congress Cataloging in Publication Data

Asimov, Isaac, 1920–
    The golden door.

    Includes index.
    SUMMARY: Traces United States history from the
Reconstruction through World War I.
    1. United States—History—1865-1921—Juvenile
literature. [1. United States—History—1865-1921]
I. Title.
E661.A74   973.8   77-21385
ISBN 0-395-25798-0

w 10 9 8 7 6 5 4 3 2 1

CONTENTS

THE GOLDEN DOOR

1

AFTERMATH OF WAR

LINCOLN VERSUS CONGRESS

The Federal Union had survived!

For four years a bitter and costly war had raged in the southeastern quarter of the United States. Eleven states had ranged themselves in skillful and determined war against the rest of the nation, and had lost—but not before 620,000 men had died on the two sides and 375,000 men had been wounded. A million casualties had been suffered out of a total population of some 33 million.*

Large sections of the erstwhile Confederacy had been badly scarred by the war, particularly in those states, like Virginia and Tennessee, where most of the battles had been fought; and in those states, like Georgia and South Carolina, where toward the end the Union armies had swept through with deliberate devastation.

* The story of this tragic episode in American history and of the events that led up to it are narrated in my book *Our Federal Union* (Houghton Mifflin, 1974).

But the Union had survived. The United States ended the war with its territory intact, every square inch of it, and with its economy, as a whole, stronger than ever. The states of the victorious Union-side had profited economically, their manpower losses made up for by immigration and by a high birth rate.

Then, too, the erstwhile Confederate States, having put up a most magnificent fight against great odds, proved even more unusual in defeat than in war, for, by and large, they accepted the decision. They returned to the fold, and while the scars of war remained for decades, and the reverent memory of the "lost cause" and the men who fought for it never vanished, the states never again attempted to leave the Union; nor, in any future crisis, did they ever give any cause for suspicion against their loyalty.

As the war wound down to its close, however, there was no way of foreseeing this Confederate acceptance of the verdict. Some members of the Union government felt hatred for the states whose armies had humiliated the Union in many battles. Some feared the rise once again of rebellious feelings and were sure this could be prevented only by harsh control. Some were anxious to make sure that the disgrace of slavery would be lifted from the United States and felt that the former slave-masters could not be trusted to do this.

For all these reasons, and also out of political considerations, a section of the Republican party became particularly vengeful toward the former Confederate States. This section of the party was called "Radical Republican."

Opposed to them was the Republican president, Abraham Lincoln, who had steered the Union through the dangerous years of war. Lincoln held that since secession was illegal, the states of the Confederacy had never left the Union. It was just a group of willful men, he maintained, who had levied war. Once those men were driven from power and once enough of the population of a rebellious state had declared their loyalty to the Union, that state was, in his view, reinstated as a member of the Union, with the full rights and privileges of a state.

Because he was far-sighted and anxious to avoid a future in which a group of states would forever harbor a grievance, would forever long for independence, would forever strike again and again for it—and perhaps eventually succeed—Lincoln labored to make the return as easy as possible for the rebellious states. He was generous in his amnesties and he asked an oath of loyalty from no more than 10 percent of the voters of any state that had been taken over by Union forces. One other important step had also to be taken—the state had to agree to abolish slavery.

In 1864, even while the war was still on, enough loyalty-oaths were obtained in Arkansas and Louisiana to satisfy Lincoln's standards. Both states were recognized by Lincoln as having been restored to the Union, both formed state governments, and both elected senators and representatives to Congress.

The Radical Republicans, however, were strong in Congress and they would not accept the elected representatives from Arkansas and Louisiana. They thought Lincoln's conditions were unbearably soft. In fact, they didn't want the president to be in charge of the reconstruction of the Union at all. For twenty years before the Civil War, the United States had been governed by weak presidents, and Lincoln's wartime powers, which made him powerful and Congress weak, were considered exceptional. Once peace came, the Radical Republicans expected that the president would return to his customary weakness and Congress would take over.

With this in mind, the Radical Republicans set up a plan of "Congressional Reconstruction" as opposed to Lincoln's "Presidential Reconstruction." The Radicals felt that 10 percent loyalty was not enough; they demanded that fully 50 percent of a state's voters must swear loyalty. What is more, the oath had to be retroactive; not only must those who took the oath swear to be loyal in the future, but they must also swear that they had never been disloyal in the past (something just about impossible to expect of half the population unless there were wholesale perjury).

A bill to this effect was put through Congress on July 4, 1864. Sponsoring it was Senator Benjamin Franklin Wade of Ohio (born in Feeding Hills, Massachusetts, October 27, 1800), an ardent reformer who was not only vigorously opposed to Black slavery, but was also prolabor and prowomen's rights. In the House of Representatives, the sponsor was Henry Winter Davis of Maryland (born in Annapolis, August 16, 1817). From a slave state, he was nevertheless fiercely loyal to the Union and had been a key figure in keeping Maryland from attempting secession.

Lincoln knew that under the Wade-Davis Bill no state of the Confederacy could possibly qualify for reentry into the Union for years; the conditions were unreasonably severe. The Radical Republicans were, of course, aware of this; they had no illusions in that respect. Some of them felt sufficiently vengeful to consider this justified; others felt it would be a good way of insuring the domination of the United States by the industrial northeast for a long time.

Lincoln, however, had no vengefulness in him, nor was he interested in assuring the ascendancy of any part of the nation over the whole. Since Congress was on the point of recessing, he simply put the bill to one side ("in his pocket," figuratively speaking). By not signing it, he killed it till the next session—an example of a "pocket veto."

The Radical Republicans were furious over this and made motions as though to dump Lincoln and nominate a candidate of their own for the 1864 presidential elections that were then upcoming. Lincoln outwaited them, and military victories made him sufficiently popular to show the Radical Republicans they would get nowhere by opposing him. They supported Lincoln, grumblingly, and he was reelected.

But on April 14, 1865, five days after the Confederate general Robert E. Lee had surrendered at Appomatox Courthouse in Virginia, ending the Civil War, Abraham Lincoln was assassinated. Stepping into his shoes was the vice-president, Andrew Johnson, who thus became the seventeenth president of the United States.

ANDREW JOHNSON

Andrew Johnson was born in Raleigh, North Carolina, on December 29, 1808. He was apprenticed to a tailor at the age of twelve, retaining his tailoring skills to the end of his life and showing pride in them. (And why not?) He moved to eastern Tennessee in 1826 and lived in that state the rest of his life.

He never spent a day in school but, after he married in 1827, his wife taught him to read and write. Eastern Tennessee was a land of poor farmers who were out of sympathy with the slave-holding aristocracy of the western part of the state and who preferred the rough, knockabout virtues of Johnson. His lack of education was actually an advantage and his raucous homespun style of debating was admired.

He rose steadily in government and served as governor of Tennessee from 1853 to 1857. He then entered the Senate, where he maintained an unswerving pro-Union stand. He was the only senator from a seceding state to remain in the Senate over the protests and vilification of his own constituents. It was an act of great political courage, but Johnson always maintained his views with the utmost stubbornness.

In 1862, when Union armies were in control of most of Tennessee, Lincoln rewarded Johnson for his stand by making him military governor of the reconquered state. Johnson served ably in this post for two years.

Then, in 1864, when Lincoln was running under the banner of the "Union Party" (consisting of Republicans, together with those "War Democrats" who were committed to victory), it seemed important to nominate a War Democrat for vice-president and Johnson received the nod.

At Lincoln's second inauguration on March 4, 1865, Johnson, of course, took part. Feeling ill, he took a slug of liquor to steady himself. It wasn't a good idea. Johnson didn't carry liquor well, and it unsteadied him. He seemed clearly drunk at the ceremonies, something those who opposed him never allowed the public to forget.

Once Lincoln was assassinated, Johnson was president.

Opposed to the slave-holding aristocracy, he nevertheless felt sympathy for the states of the Confederacy. He adopted Lincoln's generous attitude toward the ex-Rebels and proceeded as rapidly as he could to reconstruct the state governments of the former Confederate States.

Of course, it was necessary to put an end to slavery. Much of the emotions of the Civil War had been over the slavery issue, and when the slave-holders were defeated, there was no way in which slavery could survive.

In fact, the various states of the Union were voting on a constitutional amendment that would formally make slavery illegal in the United States. By December 18, 1865, the necessary three quarters of the states had voted in favor of this, and it became part of the

Constitution as the Thirteenth Amendment. Thus, half a year short of the ninetieth anniversary of the birth of the United States, slavery finally came to an end in the nation that had consistently looked upon itself as "the Land of the Free."

Yet though slavery was abolished as a legal system, and the once-slave-states had to accept that fact, it seemed natural for them to take other measures to make sure that the Blacks remained the equivalent of slaves—a pool of cheap labor without any political rights and scarcely any human rights.

To be sure, the Blacks faced problems. There were four million "freedmen" in the former slave states who, because of the servile position into which they had been chained, were now uneducated, unsophisticated, inexperienced in freedom and often frightened of it. If it were an ideal world, they would have been helped and taught and, in particular, their children would have been educated into freedom and equality from the beginning.°

Unfortunately, it is not an ideal world. The belief in Black inferiority was too strong in the former slave states (and in the rest of the Union as well, for that matter) and there was also the constant dread of Black revolts. It was a dread the Blacks did not deserve, for never was there a group of people so oppressed and downtrodden for so long, who nevertheless showed so little appetite for revenge. Yet the dread was there and it was a contributing factor to what happened.

The various former slave states therefore set up systems of laws, as soon as they could, designed to prevent the Blacks from changing their social status merely because they were no longer legally slaves. The first of these "Black Codes" was established by Mississippi on November 24, 1865, even before the Thirteenth Amendment abolished slavery.

The Black Codes varied in severity from state to state, but, in general, they limited the rights of the Blacks to very little more than they possessed as slaves. They could now legally marry and could own

---

° This is not an impossible dream. Second-generation immigrants of all sorts have taken their equal place in American life. My parents brought me to the United States from the Soviet Union when I was three years old. My father was without an education and could do no more than be a small retail merchant all his life. But the American educational system was open to me, and I became a writer, a scientist, and a college professor as a result. And if that were permitted me, why not others as well?

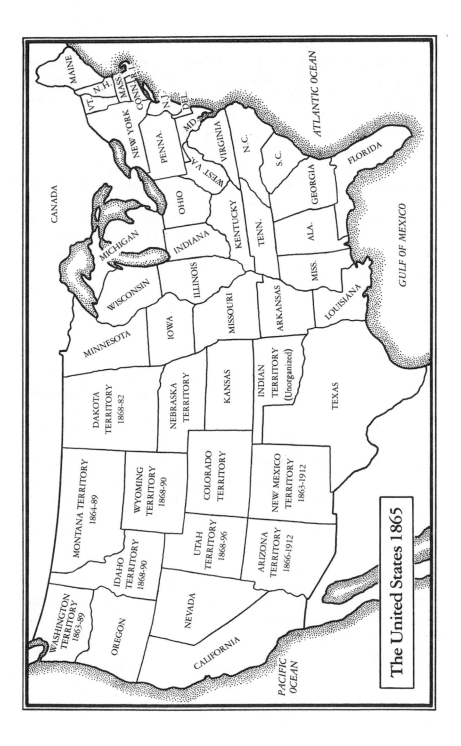

The United States 1865

limited amounts of land, but they could not vote, nor could they serve as witnesses in court. Their right to work was limited to certain menial occupations, and they could be forcibly apprenticed to some job under conditions indistinguishable from slavery if they were "vagrant." No opportunity was lost to impress upon each Black his status as an absolute inferior in every respect to any White.

We can suppose that Lincoln, had he lived, would have opposed the Black Codes, not only out of his deep humanity, but out of a shrewd understanding that the victorious states would see this as Southern cruelty and villainy and that this would make the task of true conciliation much harder. Whether Lincoln could have prevented the Black Codes and insured a reasonable compromise, North and South, is uncertain, but we can be sure he would have tried.

Johnson did not. He had no feelings of sympathy whatever for the Blacks. Slavery was abolished and that was that. He would not move an inch beyond that and he accepted the Black Codes with equanimity.

Not so the Radical Republicans in Congress who, angered by what they saw as Johnson's willingness to allow the former slave states to reverse the verdict of the war, moved into stern and implacable opposition. Leading them in this fight was the stern and implacable Congressman Thaddeus Stevens of Pennsylvania (born in Danville, Vermont, on April 4, 1792).

Stevens was born club-footed and had an impoverished childhood. Both facts may have contributed to his fanatical sympathy for the downtrodden and, in particular, for the Black slaves. He was for every kind of underdog; in fact, he is supposed to have had a Black mistress and when he was dying, he ordered that he be buried in a cemetery among Blacks so that even in death he might demonstrate his devotion to equality.

His great flaw was that he was a towering hater who could neither forgive, forget, nor compromise. To him the conquered states of the Confederacy were occupied areas with no rights. He wanted the estates of the slave-holders cut up and given to the ex-slaves who had worked them.

To the Radical Republicans, and to Stevens in particular, the Black Codes were clear evidence that the ex-Confederate States were unregenerate; that nothing had happened to cure them of their previous views. The Black Codes, and Johnson's support of them, they insisted, would remove the name of slavery, but not the shame of it from the United States. The ex-Confederate leaders, unchastened and unashamed, would be allowed by Johnson's policies to run their states and treat their Blacks as slaves still.

Stevens controlled the "Joint Committee of Fifteen," a group of six senators and nine representatives, all Radical Republicans, and they began to push forward legislation that would safeguard the rights of the Blacks. Such legislation was vetoed by Johnson, who maintained that it violated states' rights—the same argument that the former slave states had used to protect slavery and justify secession. This further infuriated the Radical Republicans, and some of the legislation was passed over Johnson's veto.

Most of all, Stevens drove relentlessly toward another amendment to the constitution; one that was designed to make the Black not merely a nonslave, but a full American citizen. This new amendment was passed by Congress on June 16, 1866, and was presented to the states, three fourths of which would have to vote their approval before it could become part of the Constitution.

The amendment declared every person born in the United States, or duly naturalized, regardless of color, to be citizens of the United States and of the state in which he or she resided. The states were forbidden to pass laws abridging the rights of any of their citizens. Ex-Confederate officials (military or civilian) who had formerly held national office and had thus betrayed their trust were disqualified from participating in political life, and it was forbidden to pay any of the Confederate war debts. In this way, the Blacks were brought forward into political life, the most important Whites were retired, and those who had invested in the Confederacy were penalized by the permanent loss of their investment.

Congress further decreed that no ex-Confederate State could be represented in Congress unless it accepted the new amendment. Tennessee was the only one that did, voting it in on July 19, 1866. On July 24, therefore, it was formally readmitted into the Union by congressional vote. The ten remaining ex-Confederate States, with misplaced optimism and with Johnson's support, refused to accept the amendment and waited for the 1866 congressional elections, hoping for the emergence of a more moderate Congress.

Johnson did his best in this regard, attacking the Radical Republicans vehemently and trying to establish a new party of Moderates. He did this so unskillfully, however, that he ended by finding his only allies among those Democrats who, during the War, had been in favor of a peace granting the Confederate States independence, and who were called "Copperheads" by those favoring victory.

Johnson tried further to support the cause of moderation by going about the nation on a speaking tour between August 28 and September 15, 1866. He could scarcely have done anything more disastrous to his cause. He brought to the large cities of the Union those tactics that had worked in the backwoods of East Tennessee—and they served only to provoke laughter and make him seem ridiculous. When he was heckled, he lost his temper and let himself be drawn into undignified vituperation.

The Radical Republicans, meanwhile, banged the drums of patriotism and played upon the still strong hatreds toward the erstwhile Rebels. The hotheads in the defeated states played into Radical hands by indulging in race riots in such cities as Memphis and New Orleans. Blacks were killed brutally and indiscriminately and the Southerners succeeded in painting themselves in the color of unregenerate villains.

The result of all this was a clearcut and resounding victory for the Radical Republicans. In the new fortieth Congress, the Republicans outnumbered the Democrats 42 to 11 in the Senate and 143 to 49 in the House. There were enough Radicals among the Republicans to make up the two-thirds majority necessary to override Johnson's vetoes.

IMPEACHMENT

The fortieth Congress prepared to run the country in defiance of Johnson and to put through its own version of Reconstruction. To do so, they needed only to pass the necessary bills, wait for the inevitable Johnson veto, then muster the necessary two-thirds vote in each house to override the veto and make the bills law.

This they proceeded to do. On January 8, 1867, for instance, Blacks were given the vote in the District of Columbia, over Johnson's veto. On March 1, Nebraska was admitted to the Union as the thirty-seventh state, and, since it was sure to be Republican in sympathies, it had to be admitted over Johnson's veto. (When the territory became a state, its capital, Lancaster, was re-named Lincoln after the dead president, and it has kept that name ever since.)

Then, Congress passed a hard-line Reconstruction bill and when Johnson vetoed it on March 2, 1867, they passed it over his veto on the very same day. By this Reconstruction Act, the ten ex-Confederate states that were not yet readmitted to the Union (all but Tennessee) *were* treated as conquered provinces.

They were divided into five military districts: (1) Virginia; (2) North and South Carolina; (3) Georgia, Alabama, and Florida; (4) Mississippi and Arkansas; and (5) Louisiana and Texas. Each was to be ruled by a military governor.

In order to get out from under this, the individual states would have to call a new constitutional convention, elected by all men of voting age, including Blacks. The new constitutions would have to accept the new amendment granting Blacks citizenship. Ex-Confederates of importance were excluded from government, and Congress reserved for itself the right to review all the acts of the states and to decide when they could reenter the Union. Later Reconstruction Acts hardened requirements still further.

Johnson recognized the new acts as law and conscientiously enforced them. He appointed military governors and did everything else that was necessary; but he interpreted every action as narrowly as he could and delayed every step as long as he could. Every bit of presidential foot-dragging further heightened Radical Republican anger and made them more intent than ever on having every bit of their way.

The Whites of the occupied states made matters worse by refusing to take part in political affairs. They hoped, apparently, that by nonparticipation they would make it impossible for the military to govern and that the attempts to liberalize the states' institutions would be abandoned in frustration.

It was a bad miscalculation. Since the local Whites held aloof, political leadership in the military districts fell into the hands of people who moved in from the rest of the nation. Some of these newcomers were idealists who wanted to help the Blacks and to turn the ex-Confederate States into more democratic paths. Others were out for what they could get, judging that in the midst of chaos the pickings would be rich. And this was so. Many of the newcomers, working under the rule of military men abundantly lacking in political know-how, could so manipulate matters as to enrich themselves at the expense of the state. It was, of course, these corrupt outsiders who tainted the entire group with a disrepute that has never been removed.

The people of the former Confederate States viewed these men from other states as interlopers intent on loot, one and all; men so poor and no-account that they came in with all their miserable store of belongings in a single bag. In those days, cheap travel-bags were made out of carpet material, and the interlopers were therefore called "carpetbaggers."*

The military governors, pressed to produce results, had no choice but to deal with these carpetbaggers and with those local Whites who were willing to cooperate. (These latter were called "scalawags" by the passive resisters, and the term carried the same significance attached to "quisling" today.)

The carpetbaggers took over the state governments, including the governorships of several of the states. They forced through new state constitutions much more democratic than the old. The new constitutions repealed the Black Codes, allowed Blacks to vote, established universal free education, abolished imprisonment for debt, and even moved in the direction of women's rights.

All this was admirable in the abstract, but, unfortunately, the interest in Black votes was often not a true interest in Black welfare but was carried through to allow for a pool of votes that could be easily manipulated in the interest of the carpetbaggers.

Blacks were elected to the state legislature and performed with astonishing credit in many cases. They never pushed for any punitive

---

* This term has been used ever since to characterize a political opponent who is more closely identified with some state other than the one in which he is seeking office.

action against the Whites, nor did they attempt to increase their own social status past what was conceivable in those days, say, by attempting to permit intermarriage. The Black record was, however, destroyed by the fact that their votes could be manipulated, when advantage was taken of their inexperience, by the carpetbaggers.

The use of the Black vote and of the military governors made it possible for the carpetbaggers to increase the state debts many times. Not all of it was the result of personal graft. There were some legitimate expenses involved in the repair of war damage, in the building of new roads and buildings, and so on.

Yet there was graft, too. A particularly notorious carpetbagger was H. C. Warmouth, for instance. He had been a Union officer of doubtful value during the Civil War and became governor of Louisiana for four years, during which period he managed to pile up a personal fortune of half a million dollars (worth far more in those days than now) at the expense of the state.

Not all the Whites of the former Confederacy were entirely passive. On December 24, 1865, a group of ex-Confederate army officers formed a social group, which they called *Kyklos*—a Greek word meaning "circle"—and since many of them were of Scotch-Irish descent, they thought of themselves as a clan, which they misspelled as "klan" for the sake of alliteration. The name quickly became "Ku Klux Klan" and the ex-Confederate cavalry leader, Nathan Bedford Forrest, who had never been defeated in battle, became the first Grand Master.

Once the military rule fastened on the ex-Confederate States, the Ku Klux Klan began to view itself as guerrilla resistance, and a kind of Robin Hood legend grew up about the organization on the part of those people who sympathized with their aims.

The fact is, though, that although the Klan considered itself as a heroic band of die-hard resisters, they did not aim their actions against the powerful occupying force, either military or political. They took action instead against the uneducated, powerless Blacks. By a combination of psychological and physical attack (dressing in white sheets served to frighten the Blacks and protect the klansman's anonymity), by destroying property and beating individuals, the Blacks were finally forced out of political life. What the Klan did was to help destroy whatever good might have come out of the new movement in the direction of freedom and racial tolerance.

The Radical Republican majority in Congress, having thus totally defeated President Johnson where Reconstruction was concerned, next went on to make the presidency altogether subservient to Congress. Since Andrew Jackson's time in the 1830s, there had not been a colorful, popular, and strong president (except for Lincoln's exceptional wartime powers), and Congress did not want another one to arise.

In order to make sure of this, and to prevent Lincoln's wartime powers from serving as a precedent, Congress set about limiting Johnson's powers in several arbitrary ways. The most notorious of these was the Command of the Army Act and the Tenure of Office Act, both passed on March 2, 1867.

By the Command of the Army Act, Johnson was required to issue all military orders through the General of the Army. This happened to be Ulysses S. Grant (see *Our Federal Union*), who was felt to be safely Radical in his views. Johnson was thus effectively deprived of his constitutional office as Commander-in-Chief of the armed forces.

By the Tenure of Office Act, Johnson was forbidden to remove any official who had required senatorial approval for appointment, without seeking senatorial approval for the removal as well. This was an attempt to keep in office those holdovers from Lincoln's administration who were pro-Radical and anti-Johnson. In particular, this was intended to save Edwin McMasters Stanton (see *Our Federal Union*) who was Johnson's holdover secretary of war. He was an excellent secretary of war, but his sympathies were with the Radical Republicans, and to the Radicals he was an effective spy in the enemy camp.

Johnson was convinced these measures were unconstitutional and he intended to violate them in order to set up a test before the Supreme Court. He chose the Tenure of Office Act as the easier one to violate spectacularly. On August 5, 1867, therefore, Johnson asked for the resignation of Secretary Stanton. He then appointed General Grant to the job, thinking that this might be a popular enough appointment to range the public on his side against Congress.

Stanton, however, cited the Tenure of Office Act and insisted that he was secretary until the Senate said otherwise. He barricaded himself in his office and Grant, no politician, and always in awe of Congress, dared not force the barricade.

The Radical Republicans, who did not yet control the Supreme Court and who knew that the Act would be judged unconstitutional, had no intention of allowing the matter to come to the test. Instead, they set about removing Johnson from office.

To do so, there was the consitutional recourse of "impeachment," which was the accusation that some public officer had misbehaved in a fashion that made his removal from office necessary. It was borrowed from Great Britain, where the House of Commons could impeach an official, who could then be tried by the House of Lords and, if convicted, would be removed from office.

In the Constitution, the grounds for impeachment are "treason, bribery, or other high crimes and misdemeanors." The catch-all reference to "other high crimes and misdemeanors" is sufficiently vague to allow great latitude, and the Radical Republicans decided that the violation of the Tenure of Office Act was grounds for impeachment.

There were few cases of impeachment prior to this. Impeachment proceedings had been brought against judges on a number of occasions, though conviction rarely followed. The most important example had been the impeachment of Supreme Court Justice Samuel Chase in 1804—and he had been acquitted. There had never before been even a hint of impeachment against any president, but now that was exactly the intention of the Radicals. Thaddeus Stevens drew up eleven charges of "high crimes and misdemeanors" against Johnson—all of them really trivial—and presented them to the House.

On February 24, 1868, the House of Representatives voted 126 to 47 to impeach the president. On March 13, the trial of President Johnson opened, with Chief Justice Salmon Portland Chase of the Supreme Court as judge and the Senate of the United States as jury. Chase (no relative of the earlier Chase) was a Radical Republican, but he disapproved of the impeachment and maintained strict judicial procedures through a trial lasting two and a half months.

If the judge was reasonably impartial, the jury was not. There were 54 senators, of whom 42 were Republicans and 12 were Democrats, and almost every senator was prepared to vote his prejudice, for or against conviction, regardless of the evidence.

In fact, if Johnson were to be convicted, there was no vice-president to succeed him,° and next in line would be the elected presiding officer of the Senate, who happened to be Ben Wade, one of the leading Radicals.

Wade did not disqualify himself as a juror, but, quite disregarding the fact that he could not conceivably be impartial when he stood to gain so enormously by conviction, he proceeded to serve on the senatorial jury and to vote. So confident was he that he was about to become president, partly through his own vote, that he even chose his cabinet.

A two-thirds vote was required for conviction—36 votes. To escape conviction, then, Johnson needed 19 votes. The 12 Democratic senators were certain to vote in his favor, but he needed at least seven Republican votes in addition, and those would be hard to get with the Radicals brutally intent on conviction at all costs.

After all, if one of their own, Ben Wade, was to become president, and if he were then reelected in 1868, he would surely have the chance to appoint Supreme Court Justices—Radical Republican ones—and with that the congressional domination of the government would be complete. Never was the American system of government so in danger of being overwhelmed by the legislative branch, and never again was it to be.°°

The case against Johnson was ridiculously weak. Whatever his insufficiencies and lack of judgment, the president had not violated the Constitution nor committed any impeachable crime. Johnson had able lawyers pleading his case, and it was quite obvious that those senators who would vote to convict would do so out of partisan political motivation rather than out of any principled consideration of the merits of the case.

Six Republicans, to be sure, found themselves forced to follow their conscience toward acquittal. A seventh was needed. Thirty-five Re-

° Not until 1967, was there any constitutional provision for electing or appointing a new vice-president when an old one had succeeded to the presidency.

°°When, over a century later, a similar danger arose, it was from the executive branch, and then it was another impeachment attempt, justified on this occasion, and the forced resignation of a president, that saved the constitution.

publicans were sure to vote conviction, but there remained one last Senator, Edmund G. Ross of Kansas, who was undecided. Despite enormous pressure, he refused to say how he would vote and when on May 26, 1868, the senatorial jury was polled, everyone knew it would be 35 to convict, 18 to acquit, and 1 vote, that of Ross, was uncertain. His was the deciding vote.

Suspense rose as name after name was called and Ross's turn approached. Finally, his turn came and he voted—for acquittal. Johnson obtained the necessary nineteenth vote so that by one vote, he, and the Constitution, were saved. Johnson remained president for the remainder of his term, while Secretary Stanton resigned and stepped down.

The Radical Republicans were chagrined and furious and made sure that the seven Republicans who had voted for acquittal, especially Ross, were hounded out of public life. Yet they had won at least a partial victory. The presidency had been humiliated and weakened, and Congress would more or less dominate the president for another two thirds of a century.

And, of course, congressional Reconstruction under hard lines continued. On June 25, 1868, over Johnson's inevitable veto, ex-Confederate States began to be readmitted to the Union under carpetbagger governments. By 1870, all the states had been readmitted under those conditions—though their local White population still considered themselves in bondage.

MEXICO AND ALASKA

While the United States was absorbed in the attempt to repair the damage of the Civil War and in the simultaneous battle between Congress and the president, the outside world still existed. Problems there still had to be faced, and beyond the borders, the chief problem existed in Mexico.

In 1861, Mexico had come under the liberal rule of Benito Pablo Juárez. He was the first Mexican president of Indian descent and also the first civilian to rule the nation. He had come to power after a civil war that had destroyed European-owned property, however, and his administration lacked the money to pay damages or debts. Great Britain, France, and Spain, taking advantage of American preoccupation with the Civil War, landed troops in Mexico in 1862 to collect the debts.

Great Britain and Spain soon removed their troops, but France was under the rule of Emperor Napoleon III, who had a fatal knack for ill-judged adventures. Napoleon strongly favored the cause of the Confederacy, and it seemed to him that the United States was on the point of disintegration. It seemed an opportune time to set up a French-dominated kingdom in Mexico.

Ignoring the bitter protests of the momentarily helpless United States, Napoleon sent thirty thousand troops to Mexico and, on June 7, 1863, just as Lee was invading Pennsylvania and as the Civil War was coming to its turning point at the Battle of Gettysburg (see *Our Federal Union*) the French occupied Mexico City and drove out Juárez.

Napoleon needed a puppet ruler of Mexico and for that purpose he persuaded a younger brother of Emperor Francis Joseph of Austria to come to Mexico. This was the Archduke Maximilian, a naive young man of vaguely liberal views, who was under the impression that the Mexican people would greet and love him. On June 10, 1864, he was named Emperor of Mexico, and his wife, Carlota (the daughter of King Leopold I of Belgium), became the Empress.

Maximilian proceeded to carry through a policy of liberal reform that antagonized the conservative elements who would have supported him, without mollifying the Juárez liberals who were carrying on a guerrilla war in the countryside. Maximilian was kept in office only by the French army, though he himself may not have recognized that fact.

Once the American Civil War ended, with the Union triumphant, the United States turned grimly toward Mexico. The protests against the French occupation were now repeated with a growing edge of impatience and 50,000 hardened veterans of four years of fighting, under the able general Philip Sheridan (see *Our Federal Union*) took their place on the Mexican border.

Napoleon III was in a bad position. The French intervention was getting nowhere. The whole scheme had turned into a quagmire that was costing the French money without producing any indication that the Mexican people would ever reconcile themselves to foreign rule. And it was not beyond the realm of possibility that the United States might even welcome a foreign war as a way of helping to reunite the nation.

Napoleon III had no stomach for such a fight and, considerably bedraggled, agreed to leave Mexico. On March 14, 1867, the last French soldier was out of the land.

Maximilian, still convinced somehow that he was popular with the Mexicans, refused to go with them. The result was sad, but inevitable. The forces of Juárez quickly reoccupied Mexico City and, despite pleas by foreign governments for clemency, executed Maximilian on June 19.

Napoleon III's Mexican venture was over, and it had served only to weaken his government further and to help prepare the ground for its ultimate destruction by the Prussians in 1870. For the United States, the dénouement served to prove to the world that the Civil War had ended and that the United States was itself again.

In the far north, there was an even more spectacular event that redounded to American advantage; one that carried no tragic overtones at all.

The great northwestern North American peninsula of Alaska had been under Russian control ever since the time of the American Revolution. The Russians, however, were losing interest in this very far-off portion of their vast dominions. For one thing, Alaska's profitable fur trade had been falling off. The sea otter, gentle and inoffensive, whose only crime was the possession of a lovely pelt, had been brutally hounded into near-extinction by men of many nations, and the seal herds were shrinking, too. Each year, therefore, Alaska was becoming more of a liability to Tsar Alexander II.

Then, too, the Russians had suffered a humiliating defeat at the hands of Great Britain and France in the Crimean War of the 1850s, and she was intent on reorganization and disinclined to waste her efforts on a trackless wilderness on the other side of the world.

During the Civil War, Russia had been friendly toward the Union (partly because her most recent enemies, Great Britain and France, were friendly toward the Confederacy) and so now push and pull worked in the same direction. If Russia was to give up Alaska, the logical purchaser was Great Britain, whose dominions in Canada bordered the land on the east; but Russia did not wish to give it to the enemy. The only other possible purchaser was the United States, with whom Russia had friendly relations. So, to sell Alaska to the United States, was to oblige a friend, spite an enemy, and get rid of an unwanted burden.°

Even before the Civil War, there had been Russian feelers toward an Alaskan sale, but before anything could be done, the conflict started and Russia had to wait. After the war, they tried again.

Oddly enough, American public opinion was not enthusiastic, for Americans generally were opposed to territorial expansion. For one thing, the great expansions of the 1840s, which had involved the Mexican War (see *Our Federal Union*), were associated in their minds with the attempts to spread slavery and that had given the whole process a bad odor. Then, too, Alaska was viewed as a frozen wasteland of ice, of no conceivable value to anyone now that the fur trade was declining. After all, would Russia be willing to give it up if it had any worth?

Secretary of State William Henry Seward (see *Our Federal Union*) was, however, an expansionist, eager to add a princely domain of territory to the Union. Alaska was 586,400 square miles in area, one-fifth the size of the United States. Working through the night, immediately after the Russian minister called on him at home, Seward signed a treaty on March 30, 1867, one that agreed to exchange Alaska for $7,200,000, a sum that came to not quite two cents an acre.

Once announced, the treaty met with instant ridicule. Americans called Alaska "Seward's Folly," "Seward's Icebox," and other disparaging names. Seward, however, began a strong propaganda campaign in favor of annexation, pointing out that it was necessary to buy Alaska to keep Russia's friendship and reminding the nation of the recent time when Russia was our only friend in Europe. Senator Sumner (see *Our Federal Union*) came to Seward's aid and, on April 9, the Senate approved the treaty.

° This was the second time America profited greatly at the hands of a nation that viewed Great Britain as the enemy. In 1803, France, aware it could not hang on to the vast Louisiana Territory, sold it to the United States, rather than see it fall to Great Britain; see my book, *The Birth of the United States* (Houghton Mifflin, 1974).

It was up to the House of Representatives to appropriate the money, however, but the impeachment crisis was delaying things, and the House was more interested in getting Johnson than in getting Alaska. Here the Russian negotiator took a hand. He used well over a hundred thousand dollars on propaganda, placing some of it directly into the eager hands of a few selected congressmen. In the end, the appropriation was voted on July 23, 1868.

Long before that, however, on October 18, 1867, the actual transfer had been made and the American flag had risen over Sitka, then-capital of Alaska. A sizable piece of land had been annexed, one that, for the first time, had no land boundaries with any other piece of the nation.

It was not, however, the first piece of such land annexed. In 1859, two small islands, with a total area of two square miles, had been discovered by an American ship. They came to be called the Midway Islands because they were in the Pacific Ocean, just about midway between North America and Asia. On August 28, 1867, Seward arranged for their formal annexation by the United States. They would serve as a convenient way station for ships crossing the Pacific Ocean and they represented the first territory under the American flag outside the North American continent.

2

WEALTH AND CORRUPTION

THE END OF RECONSTRUCTION

The year 1868 was an election year. On May 20, while the impeachment trial was still on, the Republican party gathered in Chicago to nominate their next candidate. It seemed logical to the party leaders to choose a new president who would be subservient to Congress and the man was at hand—Ulysses Simpson Grant.

Grant was the war hero who had defeated the Confederacy, which meant that he gave the illusion of strength and heroism, but he was a nonpolitician, overawed by successful men in politics or in business, and safely in the Radical camp. He was nominated by acclamation.

For vice-president, the Republicans chose Schuyler Colfax of Indiana (born in New York City on March 23, 1823) on the fifth ballot. He was a popular Speaker of the House of Representatives and a safe Radical.

On July 4, the Democrats held their convention in New York. The Democratic governor of New York, Horatio Seymour (born in Pompey

Hill, New York, on May 31, 1810) presided, and it was he who won the nomination. As usual, the Democratic system of requiring a two-thirds vote for nomination meant a long wrangle and 22 ballots were required. For vice-president, Francis Preston Blair, Jr., of Missouri (born in Lexington, Kentucky, on February 19, 1821) was chosen. He had been a congressman from 1861 to 1863 and afterward a major general in the Union army.

The Republican party ran the campaign very much as they had done in 1866. They came down hard and heavy on patriotism, doing their best to rouse the anti-Confederacy passions that still slumbered close beneath the surface in the nation. This is termed "waving the bloody shirt."*

They also tried to paint Seymour as a Copperhead. He had been strongly pro-Union and as governor of New York, had suppressed the dangerous and bloody draft riots in New York City in July of 1863 (see *Our Federal Union*). In his public statements afterward, however, he had betrayed a certain sympathy for the rioters.

On November 3, 1868, the election was held, and Grant won by a lopsided electoral majority of 214 to 80, taking 26 out of 34 states. On March 4, 1869, he was inaugurated as the eighteenth President of the United States. The forty-first Congress retained the lopsided Republican majority: 56 to 11 in the Senate and 144 to 63 in the House.

As for the outgoing fortieth Congress, one of its last acts was to pass still another constitutional amendment, one that guaranteed the vote to Blacks. This finally received the votes of the necessary three fourths of the states and became part of the Constitution as the Fifteenth Amendment on March 30, 1870.

But the push for the liberalization of the ex-Confederate States and for the civil rights of the Blacks was dying. The failure to impeach Johnson had punctured the Radical balloon and only ten weeks after that failure, on August 11, 1868, Thaddeus Stevens died and with him went the soul of Radicalism.

Besides, the election itself was a sign that there had to be a change. The electoral victory had been lopsided but not so the popular vote. It

---

* The expression goes back to a massacre in Scotland in 1692, one in which the victims were knifed in their sleep. The widows were said to have waved the bloody nightshirts before sympathetic audiences to rouse passions for revenge.

was 3,000,000 for Grant to 2,700,000 for Seymour, a difference of only 300,000 despite the energy with which the bloody shirt had been waved. What is more, that majority had been obtained only through the fact that seven Southern states that had been allowed to vote were under strict carpetbagger control. Large numbers of Black voters had been herded to the polls in those states to turn in Republican ballots.

The Radical Republicans had to be aware of the fact that on the basis of White votes, Seymour had the majority. The nation as a whole had grown tired of endlessly fighting the Civil War in the halls of Congress and they were never that enamored of giving the Blacks their liberty. Radicalism inevitably began to die.

President Johnson was aware of the change in atmosphere. He remained president for five months after the election and he chose his last Christmas in office to announce an unconditional pardon for many ex-Confederates. Included on the list was Jefferson Davis (see *Our Federal Union*), who had been president of the Confederate States.

Davis had gone into hiding at the end of the war, but on May 10, 1865, he had been captured in Georgia and was imprisoned. On December 3, 1868, his trial for treason had begun, but Johnson's Christmas amnesty put an end to it. Davis lived on for twenty more years, declining to admit he had ever done anything wrong, refusing to accept American citizenship or to enter the American government again, though he could have had a senatorial seat at the mere nod of a head. He died at last in New Orleans on December 6, 1889, at the age of 81 and was given a hero's funeral.

Andrew Johnson won a kind of victory, too. After his retirement as president, Tennessee elected him senator in 1874. He was given a standing ovation when he first walked into the Senate chamber by the body that had tried to destroy him only a few years before. He died, however, on July 31, 1875, after having served only a few months.

The turn in attitude that so affected the later years of Davis and Johnson had its most marked affects on the ex-Confederate States. In each of them, one by one, the carpetbaggers were gradually driven out, the Blacks were terrorized into retreat, and the traditional White leadership reasserted itself.

By 1876, all the ex-Confederate States were under conservative leadership again, and Reconstruction was at an end. In many ways it was as though the Civil War had not happened. The Blacks were not actually slaves in the former Confederate States, but they might as well have been. The Fourteenth and Fifteenth Amendments were dead letters in those states, since the Blacks did not really have the rights of citizens and since, through one subterfuge or another, they were not allowed to vote.

The ex-Confederate States did not forget the role of the Republican party in the course of Reconstruction and for decades to come, they remained a one-party section of the nation, voting solidly Democratic on all occasions. The region became known as the "Solid South" and so they were for nearly a century after the Civil War.

As a consequence, then, of the assassination of Lincoln and of the incompetence of his successor, of the intransigence of the Whites of the ex-Confederate States and the vengefulness of the Radical Republicans, a race problem was affixed to the United States, despite the Civil War and constitutional amendments, which haunts us even today, and as a result of which the Blacks, who deserved it least, suffered the most.

THE GILDED AGE

The attention of Americans was turning from the problems of Reconstruction to the experience of a postwar continuing industrialization that was utterly transforming the one-time rural land of Jefferson and Jackson.

In 1865, the first sleeping car was made part of the railroad trains by George Mortimer Pullman (born in Brocton, New York, on March 3, 1831), and in 1868, the first air-brake for railroad trains was invented by George Westinghouse (born in Central Bridge, New York, on October 6, 1846). These greatly increased the comfort and efficiency of the railroads, something especially important in a country like the United States where long railroad journeys were becoming increasingly common.

In 1867, the railroad invaded the cities, when the first elevated railroad was opened along Ninth Avenue in New York City, which at that time had a population of three quarters of a million and had become one of the great metropolises of the world. (What is now the second largest city in the nation, Chicago, was then comparatively small and, on October 8, 1871, was temporarily wiped out in the great "Chicago fire" that blazed through the rows on rows of wooden houses.)

It was a time when fortunes could be made in railroads in every respect but in building them. Promoters could form alliances with the government, manipulate the stock market, counterfeit stocks, cook books, and, in general, perform the grandest of grand larceny. In all these ways, a few clever charlatans could get rich while many would lose their money. This period of unbridled and crooked speculation immediately after the Civil War was called "The Gilded Age" by Mark Twain (the pseudonym of Samuel Langhorne Clemens, born in Florida, Missouri, on November 30, 1835) who, in 1873, published a novel by that name, in collaboration with Charles Dudley Warner (born in Plainfield, Massachusetts, in 1829).*

Among the "robber barons" who were most notorious for their rascally financial manipulations were Daniel Drew (born in New York City on July 29, 1797), Jason "Jay" Gould (born in Roxbury, New York, on May 27, 1836), James Fisk (born in Bennington, Vermont, on April 1, 1834), and Cornelius Vanderbilt (born at Stapleton, New York, in 1794).

They were not invariably fortunate in their ventures. Drew (a very religious man on Sundays) fought Vanderbilt for control of the Erie Railroad between 1866 and 1868 and lost. Drew was ruined and was bankrupt by 1876, but Vanderbilt went on to amass a fortune of over a hundred million dollars at the time of his death in 1877.

Gould and Fisk joined with Drew in the battle but did not suffer badly in the defeat. They had a little side-venture in which they printed and sold counterfeit stock in the Erie Railroad. When exposed, they left New York State hurriedly with a net profit of six million dollars.

They are best known, however, for their attempt to corner the gold market. There were, in the years just after the Civil War, a great many

---

* Mark Twain was the most successful American writer in the last half of the 1800s, beginning with his publication of *The Celebrated Jumping Frog of Calaveras County* in 1867. By some, including myself, he is considered the best writer of his time, as well as the most successful one.

"greenbacks" in circulation—paper money issued during the war. There was a question as to whether this paper money would be called in and replaced by gold, and the price of gold went up and down according to the varying probabilities.

It occurred to Gould and Fisk to take advantage of the very unusual instability of the price of gold. If they could quietly buy gold, even perhaps all the fifteen million dollars worth then in circulation, they could force the price up and up. Then at the peak, they would suddenly sell to as many people as possible. Naturally, the price would instantly plummet, and those who bought would be ruined, but the two crooks would make an enormous profit.

In order to make this work, they had to be sure that the Grant administration wouldn't step in and sell government supplies of gold, thus driving the price down again before Gould and Fisk were ready. To insure this, Fisk entertained President Grant on his yacht.

Fisk knew that Grant, a business failure all his life, was dazzled by wealth and was completely ignorant of finance, and he did his best to smooth-talk him into keeping hands off. In addition, Fisk and Gould got round a brother-in-law of Grant, and persuaded him to keep the pressure on the president to keep government gold out of the market.

Next, the two sharpers spread the rumor that the government would *not* sell its gold supply, and the price of gold began to go up. Fisk and Gould bought and bought and by "Black Friday," September 24, 1869, the price of gold reached dizzying heights and then, just before the scheme reached its successful end, Grant announced that four million dollars of government gold would be sold. The price of gold dropped instantly from 162 to 135, ruining many speculators, and bringing considerable loss to Fisk.

Gould, however, had gotten secret information from Grant's brother-in-law about the forthcoming government sale and had quietly sold out his own holdings before Black Friday and without bothering to tell his partner. Gould cleared eleven million dollars. (Fisk was shot to death by a business associate, a little over two years later, but Gould continued to flourish.)

Grant had done nothing actually wrong in connection with Black Friday, but by allowing the speculation to go on too long, he exposed his ignorance in financial matters and contributed to the victory of evil.

If Grant was personally honest, many other politicians were not so. Politicians had an opportunity to shade the law in favor of crooked businessmen, or to make decisions, legal in themselves, which would be to the benefit of one group or another. In return, they could deal themselves into the profits with no one losing but the public. (Once, in 1882, when William Henry Vanderbilt, son and successor of Cornelius, was asked by a newspaper reporter as to the position of the public in connection with something he was doing, Vanderbilt snorted, "The public be damned!")

Many of the governments of the ex-Union States were as riddled with political theft and corruption as even the worst of the carpetbagger governments of the ex-Confederate States. It was a universal disease of the times in the United States. And just as carpetbaggers stayed in power and profited by manipulating the votes of unsophisticated Blacks, the crooked politicians in northern cities did the same by manipulating the votes of unsophisticated immigrants.

The most notorious of the crooked politicians of the day was William Marcy "Boss" Tweed (born in New York City on April 3, 1823). He was the head of Tammany Hall, an organization that controlled city politics. He held positions such as deputy street commissioner and deputy public works commissioner so that, during the 1850s and 1860s, he could order unnecessary repairs, produce fake bills and vouchers, and in many other ways divert public tax money into the pockets of himself and of the fellow politicians who helped him. All in all, he may have cost New York City as much as two hundred million dollars.

He was finally exposed by the investigations of *Harper's Weekly*. Tweed was not worried by what the journal said, for he claimed that most of those who voted for him could not read. However, they could see and *Harper's* had on its staff a cartoonist named Thomas Nast (born in Landau, Bavaria, on September 27, 1840.) He was the father of the modern political cartoon and had used them to support the war effort during the Civil War (Lincoln called him "our best recruiting sergeant.") Between 1869 and 1871, he drew one cartoon after another that vilified Tweed and Tammany. Nast destroyed Tweed in this fashion, and it was to be a full century before this feat of journalism in exposing corruption in high places was to be surpassed.

Tweed was tried, convicted, and eventually died in jail on April 12,

1878, but that didn't mean that there weren't many others like him, if not quite so brazen, throughout the country.

Corruption crept high into the federal government, too. One of the railroads that was being built across the western territories was the Union Pacific Railroad. To finance its construction, a company called Crédit Mobilier was established in 1867, and its books were manipulated in such a way that some twenty million dollars of investment money went not into construction but into the pockets of the promoters of the company.

To make sure that the government would do nothing about this thievery, the promoters shared some of the money with key figures in Congress, and even with Vice-President Colfax. Any exposure of the crooks would mean exposure of the politicians as well, so that important government figures could be relied on to fight stubbornly against any effort to investigate the company.

The railroad was almost bled to death, but in early 1872, the New York *Sun* was able to expose the whole thing and to name names. Though this was the most notorious example of corruption in the federal government in those years, it was not the only one.

Not all the knavery in the world, however, could keep the United States from advancing materially. The railroads, which were the focus of so much of the rascality, were still being built at a great rate. On May 10, 1869, the Union Pacific Railroad, which had been building westward from Omaha, Nebraska, and the Central Pacific Railroad, building eastward from Sacramento, California, met at Promontory, Utah, about sixty-five miles northwest of Salt Lake City. A golden spike was driven into place at the junction and the two ends of the nation, Atlantic and Pacific, were united by rail all the way. There was a nationwide celebration over this, and deservedly so, for the public had contributed more than they knew. The crookedness of private enterprise had been made up for by government gifts of 23 million acres of land and 64 million dollars.

In 1870, the population of the country was 38,558,371, a gain of over 22 percent compared with 1860, despite the bloodletting of the Civil War. Much of this was the result of immigration that was flooding into the United States, virtually without restriction. Between 1860 and 1870, three million immigrants had arrived, over a million of them from Great Britain and Ireland.

The United States—with its vast spaces and its cheap land, its lack of inherited status so that people who, in Europe, had to "keep their place" could move upward in America, its reputation as a land of freedom—was a powerful attraction for Europeans. As for the United States, it welcomed the immigrants, for it needed a large supply of cheap labor to carry through the vast construction projects that were to tame the wilderness.

The American attitude of this period was expressed in a poem, "The New Colossus," written by Emma Lazarus (born in New York City, on July 22, 1849). It was written in 1883 to honor the colossal statue "Liberty Enlightening the World" (popularly known as "The Statue of Liberty"), which was to be placed at the entrance to New York Harbor, into which most of the immigrants from Europe were funneled.

The best-known portion of the poem goes:

> *Give me your tired, your poor,*
> *Your huddled masses, yearning to breathe free,*
> *The wretched refuse of your teeming shore,*
> *Send these, the homeless, tempest-tossed to me:*
> *I lift my lamp beside the golden door.*

For over half a century, the United States was to hold its golden door open to the "huddled masses" of Europe.

As a result of immigration and of natural increase, the United States, in 1870, had a population higher than that of Great Britain and of France and was close behind the newly formed nation of Germany.

In coal and iron production, the basis of industrialization, the United States, in 1870, was still at but one-third the level of Great Britain, the world leader, but it was ahead of the other European nations, and it was rising rapidly.

REELECTION AND PANIC

There were plenty of reasons to be dissatisfied with Grant's presidential record. The whole country stank with corruption and while there seemed no question that Grant was personally honest, he clearly lacked the ability and sophistication to do anything about dishonesty. He was not even able to recognize clearly that it existed. He was too inclined to believe everybody and to take everything at face value; and he was hopelessly impressed by wealth.

This, of course, was fine with most of the Republican politicians and with most of the industrialists who backed the Republicans financially. They were all making money, the worst of the corruption had not yet been publicized, and there seemed to be no unduly bad political penalty. In the midterm congressional elections of 1870 for the forty-second Congress, the Democrats gained control of the House, 134 to 104, but the Republicans retained a three to one edge in the Senate, 52 to 17.

There was no question, then, but that Grant would be renominated, and on June 5, 1872, the Republican National Convention met in Philadelphia and renominated him.

Colfax, however, smelled too strongly even for the politicians. His role in the Crédit Mobilier scandal had not yet been entirely exposed, but the insiders could see that it was going to be, and that there were one or two other items in which he was involved that were almost as unsavory. He had to retire to private life.

In his place, the Republicans chose Henry Wilson (born in Farmington, New Hampshire, on February 16, 1812), an ardent antislavery politician in the days before the Civil War, and now a senator from Massachusetts.

Not all Republicans could stomach Grant, however. A number of leaders who, for one reason or another, opposed Grant's policies, gathered together to form the "Liberal Republican Party" and had met in convention at Cincinnati on May 1, 1872, a month before Grant's foregone nomination.

It was not a very cohesive group; the various members were united only in opposing Grant. On the sixth ballot, however, they chose Horace Greeley (born in Amherst, New Hampshire, on February 3, 1811). The eccentric Greeley had been the editor of the *New-York Tribune* since 1841. He had been a powerful voice against slavery in the decades before the Civil War and had been one of the founders of the Republican party. He had also been a Radical Republican who had opposed Lincoln's renomination in 1864, but his queer sense of

integrity made him stand bail for Jefferson Davis after the war—
something which cost him his popularity with the gung-ho patriots. He
is best known today for a comment he made to someone seeking
advice; that advice being, "Go west, young man, and grow up with the
country."

Greeley had always been on the trail of some political office but
could never persuade the politicians whom he supported in his
newspaper to support him in return. Now, revolted by the corruption
in Washington, and seeing a chance at running for office, he was a
leader in forming the new party and gladly accepted its nomination.

Benjamin Gratz Brown (born in Lexington, Kentucky, on May 28,
1826), an ardent antislavery orator before the war, a brigadier general
during it, and governor of Missouri after it, was nominated for vice-
president.

The Democrats, meeting in Baltimore on July 9, despaired at
beating Grant and went along with the Liberal Republicans, nominating Greeley and Brown on the first ballot.

A small fraction of the Democratic party, refusing this surrender,
met in Louisville, Kentucky, on September 3, 1872, and nominated for
president, Charles O'Conor (born in New York City, on January 22,
1804) the lawyer who had prosecuted and convicted Tweed. O'Conor,
who had been rather sympathetic to the South during the war, and
who had joined Greeley in going bail for Jefferson Davis, refused the
nomination, but his name was placed on the ballot, anyway. For vice-
president, they chose a grandson and namesake of John Quincy Adams
who had been the sixth President of the United States.

In the dreary campaign that followed, the regular Republicans
waved the bloody shirt again, leaning heavily on Grant's war record,
rather than his presidential record. They attacked Greeley without
restraint. Greeley, a most inept campaigner, said that he couldn't tell
whether he was running for the presidency or the penitentiary.

Grant did better the second time than the first, gaining nearly 56
percent of the vote; 3,600,000 against Greeley's 2,850,000. O'Conor
got a mere 30,000. It was 286 electoral votes against 63, with three
states, Arkansas, Georgia, and Louisiana still not voting.

Nor did poor Greeley get his 63 votes. Worn out by the campaign
and virtually mad with disappointment, he died on November 29, less
than four weeks after the election.

Grant and Wilson were inaugurated on March 4, 1873. Wilson, however, was in ill health and fulfilled his functions only sporadically. On November 22, 1875, he had a stroke and died in office, the fourth vice-president to do so.

One of the reasons Grant was reelected was that the United States was in the throes of a false prosperity. Everyone was speculating in railroads, and there seemed a glow of paper profits on everything. But since not all expectations could possibly be realized, especially when many of them were based on deliberate falsifications and exaggerations, there was bound to be a reckoning.

Eventually, someone would not be able to pay the money he owed, because he had incurred the debts on the expectation of speculative income that would never show up. Unpaid debts meant that someone who was counting on the payment of those debts for the payment of his own debts now could not pay them, so that the ripples would spread.

Sooner or later, something would happen to put a brake on the prosperity, some large firm overloaded with unwise investments would fail, and that would spread a sudden panic that would cause everyone to try to collect all his debts at once. That would produce more business failures and a worse panic.

The brake on prosperity came in 1872, when a vast virus epidemic affecting horses struck the United States. There was no cure, and no one at the time understood that the disease was being spread by mosquitoes. A quarter of the horses died in the United States that year and not only did this represent a loss of investment in itself, but horses in those days represented a major source of power. Many aspects of American life and industry were crippled.

Then came the matter of Jay Cooke (born in Sandusky, Ohio, on August 10, 1821.) Cooke had been a clerk of modest means who had joined a banking house in Philadelphia in 1843. His great break came with the Civil War. His brother was a close associate of Salmon Chase, then the secretary of the treasury, and Cooke got the chance of selling war bonds. He proved extraordinarily proficient at this and was widely known as the "financier of the Civil War." His usefulness to the Union cause was great, but he was well paid for it, since his commissions made him a millionaire.

He continued to be a financier after the war, transferring his efforts to private business ventures in coal, iron, and, of course, railroads. He established the specialized field of investment banking; that is, the raising and supplying of money needed for huge projects that would eventually make large profits, but only after consuming the great sums needed for construction and organization.

Cooke's most important venture was the financing of the Northern Pacific Railroad, which was being constructed from Duluth, Minnesota, to Portland, Oregon, through what is now North Dakota, Montana, Idaho, and Washington. The construction involved plenty of connivance and inefficiency, and this was made worse by the sudden shortage of horses. In the end, Cooke's obligations soared too far beyond his ability to pay and on September 18, 1873, his banking firm was forced into bankruptcy.

That was enough to start the "Panic of 1873." The New York Stock Exchange was closed for ten days, and businesses began to fail like tumbling dominoes. Some eighteen thousand failed in the next few years, wages for labor were slashed by 25 percent, unemployment rose, and railroad construction virtually stopped. It was the worst economic depression the United States had experienced in its century of existence, and nothing worse was to come along for a half-century more.

Grant's second term, then, was spent in gathering economic depression and in a step by step exposure of corruption in government. It was a deeply distressing way of celebrating the centennial of American independence, which came on July 4, 1876, in the eighth and last year of Grant's stay in office.

GREAT BRITAIN AND CANADA

While the United States was fumbling its way through domestic crises, there were, fortunately, no great foreign problems facing the nation. About the worst unpleasantness was a legacy of the Civil War. During that war the British government, which had sympathized with the Confederacy, had allowed ships to be built on its soil that later flew the Confederate flag and preyed on Union shipping. The most effective of these British-built Confederate ships had been the *Alabama*, and the United States, helpless at the time, coldly kept track of the damage done.

Once the war was over, there were many Americans who felt that Great Britain must be made to pay back every cent of that damage; not only the direct damage in terms of ships sunk and cargo taken or destroyed, but indirect damage in terms of failed businesses, and even of the cost of the prolongation of the war. Damages as high as two billion dollars were mentioned, and there was, of course, no way in which Great Britain could have paid so large a sum except in the form of the cession of Canada to the United States—and this was what many Americans really wanted.

The anti-British feeling of the time was enthusiastically supported by the Irish immigrants who had been flooding into the United States for decades.

Ireland had been under some form of domination by the larger kingdom to its east ever since the twelfth century, but it was only in Cromwell's time, in the 1650s, that the domination was made complete. Thereafter, little by little, Irish land came under British Protestant ownership, while the Irish Catholics were reduced to an impoverished and landless peasantry.

In despair, the Irish sought the help of the French revolutionaries against the British, and Great Britain responded by removing the last vestige of Ireland's (Protestant) self-rule. In 1801, Ireland was incorporated into the United Kingdom and thereafter the conquered land was ruled from London, although it could still elect a certain number of (Protestant) Members of Parliament.

As conditions in Ireland grew steadily worse, more and more Irish emigrated to the United States, which welcomed them as a source of cheap labor, although they remained suspect as Catholics and were frequently victimized. For the more desirable jobs, the catchword, all too frequently, was "No Irish need apply."

The immigration became a flood after 1845, when the potatoes growing in Europe began to wither as a result of a fungal disease called "the potato blight." In Ireland, the potatoes rotted in the ground and the Irish peasantry, which had been reduced to an all-but-exclusive dependence on the potato, proceeded to rot with it.

Out of a population of eight million, one million died (while the

British stood more or less coldly by) and one and a half million emigrated to the United States. To this day, the population of the island is only little over half what it was in 1845.

During the 1800s, all told, nearly four million Irish came through the golden door and, as unskilled laborers, helped build the vast construction works, including canals and railroads, that marked the entry of the United States into industrialization.

Despite their poverty and despite the anti-Catholic and specifically anti-Irish prejudices that greeted them, the Irish immigrants had advantages over immigrants from nations on the European continent. For one thing, they spoke English, and, for another, they were acquainted with the machinery of democratic government. In the big cities, particularly in New York and Boston, they quickly became a dominating influence in the Democratic party. Their views came to be of importance to legislators, since they controlled large sections of the vote, and those views included, very understandably, a strong antipathy to Great Britain.

Their chief spokesman was Senator Sumner of Massachusetts, for that state had gained a large share of the Irish immigrants. Throughout the agitation over the "*Alabama* claims," Sumner stood out for the maximum demands.

In the days after the Civil War, the Irish pushed hard for the annexation of Canada, and in 1866 and again in 1870, tried to organize invasions of the northern land that, however, never rose above the comic-opera level, though they did much to irritate relations between the United States on one side and Great Britain and Canada on the other.

Partly because of the menace from the United States and partly because of economic difficulties in the Canadian provinces, a reorganization now took place in British North America. The various Canadian provinces, including Ontario, Quebec, New Brunswick, and Nova Scotia, were united into a federal government that was very largely self-governing. On July 1, 1867, the Dominion of Canada came into existence. By 1871, the western provinces of Manitoba, Saskatchewan, Alberta, and British Columbia joined the Dominion, which thus took on its present shape and eventually included all of North American north of the United States and east of Alaska.

With Canada a self-governing nation, it became difficult to argue its annexation to pay a British debt. The move for the annexation of Canada collapsed and never again, in fact, was there to be serious friction between the United States and its northern neighbor. The on-again, off-again, two-century conflict first between the British and the French and then between the British and the Americans came to an end.

But then if Great Britain could not pay with Canada, it would have to pay with money, and Sumner was demanding two billion dollars, which was an impossible—but popular—sum with Congress and the American public.

Grant's secretary of state was Hamilton Fish (born in New York City, on August 3, 1808). He had served as governor of New York, and as a senator from that state in the 1850s, but had not particularly distinguished himself. With him, however, Grant had somehow blundered into the one good appointment he made, finding an honest and competent secretary of state to serve him, along with all the other corrupt and incompetent people whom he had also accepted.

Fish was above all a man of peace and he had no intention of getting into a war with Great Britain over money. Calmly and delicately, he reopened negotiations, which had broken down under Sumner's onslaughts. Fortunately, there came a good break in connection with the European situation.

In 1870, war broke out between France and Prussia. It resulted in a quick and overwhelming victory for Prussia and the end of the rule by Napoleon III over France. Prussia went on to annex other German states to form the German Empire, and Europe had a new master.

Russia took advantage of the war to strengthen the position of its fleet. Russia was, at the time, expanding its holdings in Central Asia, and Great Britain, fearing for the safety of India, felt that a war with Russia might be possible. In that case, a vengeful United States might well return the Civil War compliment by building sea-raiders for the Russians on American soil. In consequence, Great Britain became less rigid on the matter.

In early 1871, a group of ten men, including Secretary Fish and four other Americans, plus four British and one Canadian opened serious negotiations and, on May 8, a treaty was signed in Washington. By its terms, Great Britain apologized for its actions during the Civil War and agreed to a tighter definition of neutrality that would prevent such actions in the future. There were some other minor points and the whole treaty was then submitted to an international tribunal of arbitration to settle the fine points.

To settle the actual figure for damages in connection with the *Alabama* claims, a tribunal of five members, an American, a Briton, an Italian, a Swiss, and a Brazilian met in Geneva, Switzerland, on December 15, 1871. The tribunal voted against the vast sums for indirect damages that the Americans put forth and, on August 25, 1872, voted four to one (the British delegate dissenting) that Great Britain was to pay $15,500,000. Although there was no British signature on the final decision, the British government paid up a year later —in full.

The money did not matter so much. It was the principle of what happened. Here were two nations of the first rank who were in a dispute of the kind in which, usually, the decision is made on the basis of war, either actual or threatened. For the first time, "national honor" was set aside and the dispute was put before an international tribunal whose decision was accepted peacefully by both nations. It offered an alternative to war that has been accepted on numerous occasions in the century since then—though not, alas, often enough.

If American expansionism was stopped in the case of Canada, there yet remained the Caribbean, where Spain still held a foothold.

Although Spain had been driven out of the American continents a half-century before, Cuba was still Spanish. Moreover, the independent Dominican Republic on the island to the east of Cuba was ruled by a feckless dictator who, fearing invasion from Haiti on the western third of the island, turned his nation over to Spanish dominion during the American Civil War.

After the end of the Civil War, Spain, which was having trouble making its occupation stick and fearing the anger of the victorious Union, withdrew its troops. The Dominican rulers, however, still feeling the need for foreign protection, approached the United States itself.

For some reason, Grant thought it would be an excellent idea to annex the island and take over all the woes of a depressed peasantry, a corrupt ruling class, and a troubled Haitian border. He pushed hard to get a treaty of annexation through the Senate which, under the leadership of Sumner, turned it down. In revenge, Grant punctured some of Sumner's political power, but that did not change the decision. The Dominican Republic has remained an independent nation to this day.

Meanwhile, in 1868, Cuba broke out in revolt against Spain, a revolt that continued for ten years. Many Americans, including to some extent, Grant, were anxious to aid the Cubans in every way possible, but Fish again stood between the nation and war.

He pointed out that the American position was an awkward one. The United States was busy denouncing Great Britain for having aided rebels and was demanding compensation in huge sums. Could the United States, at the same time, aid other rebels without compromising its case?

Fish managed, in the end, to keep the peace, until Spain ended the war by promises of reform. The island subsided, but only temporarily. It was to flare up again and set off a still greater crisis.

3

REPUBLICANS TRIUMPHANT

THE INDIAN WARS

Despite eager eyes across borders and oceans, the chief area of expansion of the United States during the Civil War and for the generation following was within its own boundaries, into the area west of the Mississippi River. It is called the "winning of the West" and is celebrated as the heroic taming of a wilderness, the conversion of unused land for herding and agriculture, the settling of millions, and the growth of empire.

But it was done, alas, over the bodies of unoffending Indians with whom the United States, from first to last, never kept faith. In colonial times, the Indians had been driven out of the Atlantic coastal regions. By the time of Andrew Jackson, they had been driven beyond the Mississippi. Always they were told that thereafter their remaining lands would be inviolate; always the promise was broken. Now their final strongholds were in jeopardy, and 200,000 Indians rallied for the last stand.

Unfortunately for themselves, they were not united, as they never had been. They depended on their enemies for arms, as always, and never developed their own industrial base. Nor did they ever develop the art of warfare beyond the surprise raid.

The Sioux family of Indian tribes, who controlled the northern half of the Great Plains, was most resolute in resistance. On July 23, 1851, the United States had signed a treaty at Fort Laramie (in what is now southeastern Wyoming) in which the various tribes of the northwest were assigned specific areas that were reserved for them (hence "reservations") and supposedly immune from White encroachment. The tribes were also granted annual subsidies. In return, they signed away their lands in Iowa and Minnesota and promised to allow certain roads and forts to be built by Whites, who were to be immune from attack.

The trouble with this, as with all such treaties, was that invariably the incoming settlers encroached on Indian lands and treated the Indians themselves with hatred and contempt. And, as invariably, most government officials could not worry about the sanctity of treaties and the requirements of abstract justice, when multiplying settlers with the vote were on one side, and voteless "savages" were on the other.

Thus, when in January 1869, a Comanche chief introduced himself to General William Tecumseh Sherman at Fort Cobb (in what is now Oklahoma) as "Me good Indian," meaning he felt friendly toward Whites, Sherman replied, with incredible callousness, "The only good Indians I have seen were dead." This statement, usually stated as "The only good Indian is a dead Indian," is a fair representation of American feeling in the matter through almost all our history.

When the Indians, hounded to desperation by encroachment, struck back, it was in the only way they knew how to fight—sudden raids—with settlers massacred and mutilated, regardless of age and sex. The Whites then struck back in far greater strength and outdid the Indians in massacre and mutilation. It was, of course, the Indian villainies that roused anger among the Whites, while the White methods of retaliation were shrugged off, if mentioned at all. Indeed, right down into recent decades, the very popular Westerns, both in print and in the movies, treated Indians as villains who were forever threatening innocent settlers and being killed off. "Another redskin bit the dust," was the cliché.

The first serious Sioux uprising came on August 18, 1862, when the Civil War was preoccupying American energies. The eastern Sioux raided their old lands in Minnesota, killing hundreds of settlers in surprise attacks. The Union might be busy but it had plenty of soldiers. Contingents were rushed northwestward under John Pope, fresh from his defeat at the hands of the Confederate team of Robert E. Lee and "Stonewall" Jackson. The Indians were less redoubtable foes, and Pope crushed them.

As usual, the Indian attacks served as excuses for violent and sometimes indiscriminate reaction. In the course of battles in what is now Colorado, some two hundred Indian warriors, along with five hundred Indian women and children, all of whom had surrendered, were ordered to Sand Creek in southwestern Colorado, and then on November 29, 1864, simply killed to the last child.

What was worst for the Indians was the spread of any report of gold. Ever since the discovery of gold in California in 1848, there was particular sensitivity to the report of gold finds anywhere in the west. Any report of gold on an Indian reservation meant the instant arrival of hordes of prospectors regardless of treaties.

The report of gold in southwest Montana, led to the establishment of the Bozeman Trail (charted from 1863 to 1865 by John M. Bozeman, born in Georgia in 1835). The government attempted to establish army posts along the trail to make it a military route, and this time it was the western Sioux who went on the warpath.

Under the Indian chief Mahpiua Luta (better known as Red Cloud), some 16,000 Sioux and Cheyenne warriors attacked and, over the next three years, managed to create enough trouble for the Americans to force a second treaty of Fort Laramie in 1868, in which the Bozeman Trail was abandoned (only temporarily, as it turned out).

The most memorable incident of the war was the "Fetterman massacre," the trapping and killing of eighty soldiers under Lieutenant Colonel William Judd Fetterman on December 21, 1866. Bozeman himself was killed by Indians in 1867. Red Cloud lived on to die on a South Dakota reservation on December 10, 1909.

In the southwest, at this time, the leading Indian tribe was the Apache. The Apaches were under the capable leadership of Cochise (born about 1815), who did his best to keep the peace with the Whites, foreseeing that war could bring only disaster.

He was forced into war, however, by brutal mistreatment and throughout the Civil War, the Apaches made the southwest a no man's land for Whites. It was not till after the war that George Crook (born near Dayton, Ohio, on September 23, 1829) was sent into Apache country. He was one of the best "Indian fighters" and an honest man besides, who actually won over some of the Indians by decent treatment. By 1872, he had brought peace to the southwest.

Then, in the middle 1870s came a new report of gold, this time in the Black Hills section of South Dakota. Again would-be prospectors rushed in, and again the Sioux rose. This time they were under the leadership of Tashunca-Uitco ("Crazy Horse"), born about 1849, and Tatanka Yotanka ("Sitting Bull"), born in what is now South Dakota in 1834.

In February 1876, George Crook led the American forces into the Big Horn mountains in order to attack the Sioux in their winter hideout. For half a year, it was a drawn fight, and then Crook was forced to retreat.

The overall commander of the campaign, Alfred Howe Terry (born in Hartford, Connecticut on November 10, 1827), then sent a column of men under George Armstrong Custer (born in New Rumley, Ohio, on December 5, 1839) to pursue the Indians and keep them pinned down till converging columns could meet and finish them.

Custer had been last in his class at West Point, but he had fought with great success throughout the Civil War, was a brigadier general by the time he was twenty-three, had successfully hounded Lee's fading army in the last weeks of the war, and helped force the surrender. He had also fought successfully against the Indians after the war. He was, however, a glory-hound, who could not be relied on to cooperate with others if that meant shining less brightly himself.

On June 25, 1876, Custer came upon the Sioux forces, under Sitting Bull, at the Little Big Horn River, at a point about sixty miles southeast of the present city of Billings, Montana. Custer was unaware of the size of the Sioux forces, some of which were hidden by a rise in the ground.

Forgetting his proper task of keeping them pinned, pending the arrival of the main forces under Terry, Custer could not resist the temptation of doing the job himself with his own small group. Dividing that small group into three still smaller ones, he sent two on flanking movements, while he himself with no more than 266 men plunged into a frontal attack against 4000 Indians. The entire contingent, including Custer himself was wiped out. Only one horse survived.

This encounter, the Battle of the Little Big Horn, more popularly known as "Custer's Last Stand" was the most famous Indian victory of the western wars and cast a pall over the forthcoming centennial celebration, but it came to nothing in the long run.

For a while, the rattled American army could not find the Indians but, by fall, Crook was on their trail again, along with a new commander, Nelson Appleton Miles (born in Westminster, Massachusetts, on August 8, 1839). Miles, who had fought successfully through most of the great eastern battles of the Civil War, tracked down Crazy Horse to his home village in January 1877 and forced his surrender on May 6. He was not trusted to keep his surrender, however, so he was arrested on September 5, 1877, and shot. The official report said he was attempting to escape.

After that, further Indian wars were mere sputterings. The end was certain. Even as Crazy Horse gave in, the Nez Perce tribe, living in the state of Indiana, rose in resistance to the steady encroachment of the Whites upon their land. They were under the very capable leadership of Hinmaton-Yalakit ("Joseph") born in Wallowa Valley, Oregon, about 1840, and the son of a Christian convert.

Joseph showed remarkable military qualities and had his Indian soldiers fighting with the discipline of regulars. He managed to hold his own against the army, but realized that he could not do so forever. With no more than seven hundred warriors, he managed to make his way across Wyoming and Montana, keeping discipline and trying to deal decently with all the White civilians he encountered.

Finally, at a point only thirty miles from the Canadian border he was trapped at last by Miles. For four days, Joseph fought off an army that outnumbered his band by four to one and then on October 5, 1877, he was forced to surrender, saying "Hear me, my chiefs; my heart is sick and sad. From where the Sun now stands, I will fight no more forever." He lived on till September 21, 1904, trying to the end to reconcile his tribe to the new way of life on huddled, barren reservations.

In the southwest, after the death of Cochise, an Apache chieftain, Goyathlay ("Geronimo"), born in southern Arizona, in June 1829, kept up a bloody patter of raids against the settlers of New Mexico and Arizona, retiring for safety, now and then, into Mexico. Twice, in 1882 and again in 1886, he was captured by Crook. His final submission came on September 4, 1886, to Miles. He was settled on a reservation in Oklahoma and there became a farmer and a member of the Dutch Reformed Church, which eventually expelled him for gambling. He died in 1909.

In 1890, Sitting Bull was stirring again. He had survived the defeat of Crazy Horse, escaped to Canada, and after having been pardoned, he returned to the United States. He even stooped to entertaining the gapers as part of a Wild West show. But now he was accused of dreaming of revenge. On December 15, 1890, near Fort Yates in North Dakota, he was killed. Again, the story was that he was attempting to escape.

The Sioux were reduced to a despairing mysticism, to the hope that somehow the Whites would disappear as the result of a "ghost dance." The army, fearing that the excitement of the ghost dance might result in Indian raids, attacked the Sioux at Wounded Knee, in southern South Dakota on December 20, 1890. The so-called Battle of Wounded Knee was a simple massacre and it was the last of the more than a thousand skirmishes that marked the quarter-century long Indian Wars in the west.

The year 1890 is often said to mark the "end of the frontier." That is a gentler way of saying that it marked the end of the Indians as anything more than broken wards of the government, hidden on out of the way reservations.

Among the casualties of the Indian wars of the west was the magnificent herd of bison (popularly, but inaccurately, called "buffalo") that roamed the western plains. Fifty million strong, they were the most numerous large mammalian species in the world (except for man and his protected herds), and were the chief food supply and general resource of the plains Indians.

To the Whites they were largely a nuisance, getting in the way of the railroads. They were killed to supply meat for the railroad workers. In 1871, a process was developed for tanning bison hides and producing leather, so they were killed for the hides. They were killed out of some sort of perverted pleasure in the act. Also, they were killed out of a deliberate policy of destroying the basis of the Indian way of life. It was a kind of economic warfare and under the protection of a patriotic cloak, the deliberate and horrible extermination of inoffensive animals was carried on. A million bison a year were killed; many more than could be used, so that large numbers were simply left to rot.

By the time the frontier was gone and the Indians were broken, the mighty herds of bison had dwindled to nearly nothing. Out of 50 million, only five hundred were left. This remnant, fortunately, received protection. They have multiplied and there are now 30,000 bison in the United States and Canada.

Associated with the disgrace of this indiscriminate slaughter was the last of the great American frontier scouts, William Frederick Cody (born in Scott Country, Iowa, on February 26, 1846). He served in the Indian wars, carrying dispatches and spying out the enemy. On July 17, 1876, he killed an Indian chieftain, Yellow Hair, in hand-to-hand combat and coming, as this did, soon after Custer's Last Stand, he won fame by it.

Somehow, though, what has rung through the ages was his ability to kill bison from horseback. As a bison-butcher supplying meat to railroad construction workers, he killed a record 4862 bison in one season, managing 69 in one day, and for such microheroism (the only danger lay in being caught by a possible stampede, though this was by no means an insignificant risk) he was named "Buffalo Bill" and was semideified in the popular literature of the day.

When the Indians and the bison were on the decline, Buffalo Bill Cody conceived the idea of putting the remnants on exhibition and established his Wild West show in 1883. It even included Sitting Bull at one time. The show made him rich for a while, though in the end he lost his fortune through mismanagement.

Cattle filled the ecological vacuum left by the destruction of the bison. The west became a cattle kingdom and for a quarter of a century, large cattle herds roamed over unfenced territory of indefinite extent, herded by cowboys on horseback.

The Civil War increased the demand for meat and, after the war was over, great profits were at hand for the Texan herders (anxious to recover from the war) if only their cattle could be brought to the railroad, which would carry them to the east.

As a result, the long cattle trails were established, the first being the Chisholm Trail, named for Jesse Chisholm (born in Tennessee, about 1806) who scouted a route from Kansas down to southern Texas. The legendary task of the cowboys began; the arduous roundup of cattle spread out over square miles, and then driving them up the long trails.

Along the Chisholm Trail alone, about a million and a half head of cattle were driven to the railroads between 1867 and 1871. Other trails were established, the herds grew and herders multiplied. Some 300,000 cattle a year were driven north and by 1880 about 4,500,000 cattle roamed the plains.

The end was not far off, however. For one thing, increasing numbers of settlers who intended to farm led to the inexorable fencing off of lands; the overstocking of the plains led to a depletion of the grass and to a vulnerability for mass death of cattle in bad winters; the multiplication of the railroads made the long cattle-drives unnecessary.

By 1890 the short age of the cowboy had come to an end, along with the Indians and the frontier—but the cowboy lived on in endless and repetitive tales in books, movies, radio and television, stylized and idealized into as little relationship to reality as have been any of the hero tales of any culture.

THE DISPUTED ELECTION

The year 1876 saw the Centennial, the hundredth anniversary of the signing of the Declaration of Independence. At the thoroughly successful Centennial Exposition, opened in Philadelphia by President Grant on May 10, 1876, the typewriter and the telephone were put on display; each an invention that has bulked larger and larger in American (and world) life ever since.

The typewriter had been patented on June 23, 1868, by Christopher Latham Sholes (born near Morresburg, Pennsylvania on February 14, 1819), and the telephone was patented on February 14, 1876, by Alexander Graham Bell (born in Edinburgh, Scotland, on March 3, 1847, and not yet an American citizen, although he was living in Boston).

The Brazilian Emperor, Pedro II (a descendant of the Portuguese kings), was visiting the United States at the time of the Centennial—

the first crowned monarch ever to visit the nation. He tried the telephone at the Exposition and dropped it with the surprised exclamation, "It talks!" And so it did, and there could have been no more effective advertisement of the fact.

For all the technological splendor of the Centennial Exposition, however, 1876 was not a prideful year for the United States. It was the year of another presidential election, and the dominant political fact of the time was that Grant's two-term administration had reeked with corruption. The Republican party was sunk in disgrace, and it didn't look as though even the memory of the Civil War and of Democratic defeatism could save it now. Grant's reelection in 1872 had made both Houses of the forty-third Congress Republican again, but the 1874 midterm elections for the forty-fourth Congress had given the House of Representatives back to the Democrats, 169 to 109, and left the Republican majority in the Senate, 45 to 29, at its lowest since the Civil War.

The Republicans met in convention in Cincinnati, Ohio, on June 14, 1876. The front-runner at the time was James Gillespie Blaine (born in West Brownsville, Pennsylvania, on January 31, 1830). In 1854, he had moved to Maine, with which state he was afterward identified. There, he became an influential newspaper editor and a Republican early in the history of that party.

In 1863, he entered Congress, where he proved to be an eloquent speaker with a magnetic personality. He was a born politician and by 1869 he had become Speaker of the House. He was a radical Republican during the Reconstruction era and won a devoted band of followers, who found him brilliant.

At the convention, Blaine's name was placed in nomination by Robert Green Ingersoll (born in Dresden, New York, on August 11, 1833) whose real fame in history has been as the most outspoken and famous atheist of the nineteenth century. At a time when religion had a deep hold on the people and when those who were dubious of its worth were too cautious to say so publicly, Ingersoll shouted his opinions from the lecture stage and in books.

Yet perhaps his most famous words had nothing to do with religion but came from his nominating speech. He said, "Like an armed warrior, like a plumed knight, James G. Blaine marched down the halls of the American Congress and threw his shining lance full and fair against the brazen forehead of every traitor to his country and every maligner of his fair reputation." Ever after, Blaine was known as the "Plumed Knight"; his enemies using the phrase in sarcasm.

For Blaine was no plumed knight really. Whatever his abilities, he was a badly tarnished man, for he shared in the corruption of the times. He used his political influence to benefit railroads in which he had a financial interest, for instance, and in the process, wrote injudicious letters to a railroad official. These letters came into the hands of the official's accountant, James Mulligan.

Mulligan appeared before a congressional committee on May 31, 1876, and revealed his possession of these letters. Blaine managed to get hold of the letters himself but refused to reveal them. Instead, on June 5, 1976, he read selected excerpts from them to the House of Representatives, interrupting himself to explain. (It was rather a preview of the even more famous case of President Nixon and his tapes, a century in the future.)

The congressmen, who were perhaps not too anxious to be too hard on such things as profiting from political office since so many of them had hands that were none too clean, seemed to be convinced that Blaine had cleared himself—but the public remained doubtful. If he were innocent, why did he not reveal the letters as they were and let the people judge? This he continued to refuse to do, and Ingersoll's comment, ten days after Blaine's reading-show, did not in the least convince many a "maligner of his fair reputation."

Though Republican politicians would have loved to have him as president, there was enough doubt as to his ability to carry the election, thanks to the Mulligan letters, to cause a number of them to look about for some other Republican—an honest one, if possible.

They found their man in Rutherford Birchard Hayes (born in Delaware, Ohio, on October 4, 1822). Hayes had fought in the Civil War, volunteering for service and displaying remarkable bravery. Having been wounded five times, he ended as a major general. In 1864, he was nominated for representative and though he remained in the army and refused to campaign, he was elected. Later on he served two terms as governor of Ohio. He was a Radical Republican but was so notoriously honest, that he was called "Old Granny" by politicians who felt that honesty was a trait better left to old women than to men like themselves.

In 1871, he retired from politics, but in 1875, Republicans who feared the loss of the state to the Democrats, urged him to run again and he won a third term very handily. This ability of an honest man to win marked him as presidential material. After six ballots at the national convention in which Blaine held the plurality without managing to gain the majority, the delegates gave in and voted for Hayes on the seventh ballot.

For vice-president, the nomination went to William Almon Wheeler (born in Malone, New York, on June 30, 1819), a congressman who, like Hayes, had a reputation for rigid integrity. In 1873, he was one of the few who opposed an act by which Congress voted itself a higher salary, and when the salary increase passed, he returned the excess to the government.

On June 27, 1876, the Democratic Convention met in St. Louis. In view of the Republican nominations, they needed a standard-bearer equally renowned for integrity, and one who had at least a respectable record in the difficult war years when so many Democrats were defeatist. That meant Samuel Jones Tilden (born in New Lebanon, New York, on February 9, 1814) who, at the time, was governor of New York.

Although a Democrat, he had been strongly antislavery in his youth, though he grew conservative and cautious with age, and had supported the Union cause only lukewarmly during the war. In the years after the war, he had participated in the drive to clean out corruption, but did so rather belatedly and carried on the fight against the Tweed Ring only after it had been exposed. After he became governor in 1873, he made a rather effective name for himself as a graft-smasher, and it took only two ballots for the Democrats to reach the necessary two-thirds vote to nominate him.

For vice-president, the Democrats nominated the governor of Indiana, Thomas Andrews Hendricks (who was born near Zanesville, Ohio, on September 7, 1819). His record as a Democrat was rather like Tilden's.

The election should have gone to the Democrats. Between the strench of corruption and the misery of the Panic of 1873, it would have seemed the Republicans didn't have a chance. What made the election close, however, was, for one thing, the unimpeachable personal character of the Republican nominees, and the ability of the

Republicans to continue to label all Democrats as traitors to the Union. (Ingersoll led this part of the attack, and did so very dirtily.)

Then, too, Tilden was a very weak campaigner. He had an unimpressive voice, nervous mannerisms, and delicate health. He had no personal charisma at all.

Even so, Tilden won a majority of the vote, leading with 4,300,000 to 4,000,000 for Hayes. It is, however, the electoral college that counts and not the popular vote.

At the time there were thirty-eight states in the Union; Colorado, the thirty-eighth, having just entered the Union on August 1, 1876—so that it is called the "Centennial State." There was no question about the electoral vote of thirty-four states. These thirty-four states gave Tilden 184 electoral votes and Hayes 165. In order to gain the majority, 185 votes were needed so that Tilden was one short.

The remaining four states, Oregon, Florida, Louisiana, and South Carolina were disputed. They possessed twenty electoral votes and if Hayes got all four of them, he would win 185 to 184.

In each of the disputed states, there were two election counts; one upheld by the Republican party and one by the Democratic party. The question was, which votes should be counted. In Oregon, the Republicans had really won, and the Democratic governor had illegally disqualified a Republican elector.

In the three southern states, Florida, Louisiana, and South Carolina, carpetbaggers were in their last days of control and they had simply thrown out Democratic votes wholesale in order to give the Republicans a phony majority. But who was to decide, legally, that these abuses had really taken place. The Constitution gave no guidance.

Congress had to improvise and do something before Inauguration Day. On January 29, 1877, it set up an Electoral Commission that would do the deciding. It was to contain five senators, five congressmen, and five Supreme Court justices. This would mean an odd number of members so there couldn't be a tie vote.

The senators and congressmen were so chosen that there were five loyal Republicans and five loyal Democrats. Of the Supreme Court justices, two were loyal Republicans and two loyal Democrats. Of those 14, it was certain that the vote would be 7 to 7, regardless of the evidence. The fifth Supreme Court justice was to be David Davis of Illinois (born in Cecil County, Maryland, on March 9, 1815). He was an independent Republican who had fought Grant in 1872, and it was supposed that he would vote the evidence and decide the case while the remaining fourteen were simply window-dressing.

Davis, however, was elected to the Senate by the Illinois state legislature and he decided to take the post. This meant he wasn't a justice and didn't qualify for a place on the commission. In his place, Justice Joseph P. Bradley (born near Albany, New York, on March 14, 1813) was appointed. He was supposed to be independent, too, but he voted right down the line with the Republicans, who received every one of the 20 disputed electoral votes, so that Hayes won, 185 to 184. It was a stolen election for the triumphant Republicans. (However, the House remained Democratic, 153 to 140, and the Republican majority in the Senate was reduced still further to 39 to 36. The forty-fifth Congress was a clear sign of the waning of Republican fortunes.)

HAYES

The 1876 election marked a low point in the history of American politics. It was the only time in American history that the legally elected president of the United States was denied his seat by open and unashamed crooked dealing.

Hayes was not quite honest enough to refuse a post to which he had not been elected, and he underwent the humiliation of having to take his inaugural oath of office in private and of being forced to omit the inaugural parade and ball.

Things might have been more serious still, if Tilden had not called on his angry supporters across the nation to accept the decision rather than resort to violence. (It may be that Tilden was secretly relieved at not having to take over the burden of the presidency.)

With Hayes as president, the rule of the carpetbaggers came to a final end in the south. One of the ways in which the Republicans persuaded southern states to accept the theft of the election quietly was to promise that carpetbagging, having made possible that one last climax of corruption, would be wiped out. Federal troops were withdrawn and by April 24, 1877, all the states that had once belonged to the Confederacy were under home control. All gained conservative governments that devoted themselves to keeping the Blacks in their place of strictly enforced inferiority.

Hayes was a religious man who held prayer-meetings in the morning and hymn-singings at other times. His wife, Lucy, was an ardent Methodist and a devout prohibitionist. She refused to serve alcohol at presidential functions and was called "Lemonade Lucy" behind her back. (She also originated the custom of the annual Easter egg-rolling contest on the White House lawn.)

His religion did not make Hayes particularly sympathetic, however, with those Americans who were on the lower rungs of the economic ladder. He believed, for instance, in a rigid "sound money" policy.

This caused hardship because in the aftermath of the Panic of 1873, the debt load was high. The law required that debts be paid off in gold (which was the "sound money" referred to). Those who owed the debts, however (farmers, laborers, the poor generally) wanted to pay them off in paper money, called greenbacks, which was less valuable than gold. This would be a way of reducing the debt.

The Greenback Labor party was founded, which not only called for cheap money with which to pay off debts (something that required inflation, of course, since the cheaper the money, the higher prices would go), but also for a limit to the hours workmen would be required to work, and a limitation on the immigration of Chinese, who were willing to work at low wages. The Greenbackers had run candidates for president and vice-president in the 1876 election, and had collected 83,000 votes.

Failing an absolute reliance on paper money, there was the prospect of using silver in addition to gold. Silver had been discovered in great quantities in Nevada, Colorado, and Utah in the early 1870s, and if it could be used to pay off debts on a scale that would make it cheaper than gold, that would be good, too, for the debtors.

The business interest of the nation, however, backed by Hayes, wanted a complete reliance of gold as the only legal standard by which the payment of debts was to be measured. This "gold standard" would insure minimum loss to the creditors, maximum hardship for the debtors. It meant making it easier for the already prosperous to remain prosperous, and more difficult for the already impoverished to cease being impoverished.

In 1873 the gold standard had been put through, and as the years of depression passed there was an increasing outcry against what Congressman Richard Parks Bland of Missouri (born near Hartford, Kentucky, on August 19, 1835) called the "Crime of '73."

The Democratic House, responding to the cry against the solidly Republican business interests, pushed for a law that would establish bimetallism (silver, as well as gold, would become legal as a standard for payment of debts). Under the leadership of Bland and of Senator William Boyd Allison of Iowa (born in Petry Township, Ohio, on March 2, 1829), the Bland-Allison Act was passed. Hayes vetoed it, but it was passed over his veto. By the act the government was required to coin silver dollars for use in paying debts.

The Republican secretary of the treasury, John Sherman (born in Lancaster, Ohio, on May 10, 1823), complied with the law only to the very minimum, so that it did not have much effect either for good or for evil. Since, by 1879, the nation was recovering from the panic, the "free silver" agitation subsided, but it was, however, to remain a problem for the rest of the century.

As for labor, it was at the total mercy of the employers. When a panic, such as that of 1873, struck, it was routine for laborers to be fired, or, failing that, to have their wages reduced. There was no one and nothing to prevent this, and no governmental provisions existed that would save men who were fired from starving, together with their families. Nor was there any way in which laborers could oppose such action by the employers through united resistance, since if they tried to do so and to strike, the government would intervene—invariably on the side of the employers.

Thus, in 1877 the Baltimore and Ohio Railroad announced a 10 percent wage cut, the second in eight months. The railroad workers struck, and the action spread until it was the worst such strike thus far in American history. The employers for their part had the support first of the local police, then of the state militia, and finally President Hayes found it consistent with his religion to force the workers into line by sending in the army. The strike was broken, but some wage concessions were won.

Despite the fact that Hayes stood for sound money and for total control of the economy by the employers, he did not get along with his party. He was, after all, an honest man who felt that those in power could get quite enough legally and ought not to labor to increase their wealth by corruption.

One of the worst sources of corruption was the ability of men in office to hold at their disposal many well-paid, low-labor political plums with which to reward the faithful—and which they could take away if the recipients did not remain faithful. With this "patronage," men in office could retain themselves in power indefinitely by what amounted to a legalized form of bribery. Moreover, they could indulge in all kinds of graft without fear of reprisal, since political officeholders in a position to fight corruption would scarcely do so if their own jobs were also on the line.

What Hayes was hoping to do would be to separate government work from politics. Ideally, it seemed to him (and to other rational people) that a man who was qualified to do a job would get it because he was qualified and for no other reason. Nor should he lose it except for failure to do his job well. His politics should have nothing to do with it.

Standing against Hayes were, of course, those party leaders who had loyally supported Grant because he had been too unsophisticated to get in their way and who wanted the Grant system of corruption for all and all for corruption to continue.

Foremost among the Republican politicians who were determined to keep patronage going was Senator Roscoe Conkling of New York (born in Albany, New York, on October 30, 1829). He had been a Radical Republican and now he took to calling his branch of the party the "Stalwarts," presumably because they stood stalwart for corruption. Hayes and those who supported him, he called "Half-Breeds," implying that they were half Democratic. Conkling had tried for the nomination in 1876 and he didn't like Hayes any the better for having won it.

The immediate point at issue was Chester Alan Arthur (born in Fairfield, Vermont, on October 5, 1829). Arthur was a tall, handsome, and very capable man who was utterly loyal to Grant and to Conkling. He had been appointed to the post of collector of customs at the Port of New York, which meant he controlled a thousand jobs. And while he did his job well, he also used it skillfully for political purposes. He did not, however, use the post for personal profit.

Hayes tried to fire Arthur together with some other friends of

Conkling and that meant open war. In those days, the odds in such a fight were with the senator, for since the Civil War the presidency had been weak. And of all the senators, Conkling was the least likely to brook interference from a mere president. Conkling was described as having a "turkey-gobbler strut" and on this occasion he managed to make the rest of the Senate back him. After all, senators, as a general rule, refused to approve any appointment that lacked the approval of the senators from that state (each senator wanted the same courtesy extended to himself), and Conkling took to opposing all appointments.

In the end, Hayes won out by obtaining Democratic support—which meant he became a Half-Breed in truth and a virtual outcast in the eyes of the Stalwarts.

Hayes, however, did not care. He did not intend serving more than one term. He did not enjoy the presidency and, besides, the Republicans had suffered further in the congressional elections of 1878 and that made the renomination seem less attractive in any case. In the forty-sixth Congress, the Democrats held both houses for the first time since the Civil War, the Senate by 42 to 33 and the House by 149 to 130. (The Greenback Labor party elected 14 representatives, and that was the high point of its political success.)

THE STALWARTS

The year 1880 saw the United States returning to prosperity. The census counted a national population of 50,155,783, nearly twice that of Great Britain and higher than that of any European nation but Russia. New York City, with its streets beginning to be lighted by electricity, had passed the million mark and was ahead of Berlin and Vienna. It was still behind Paris, however, and far behind London's record-holding 3.3 million. The United States remained second to Great Britain in the production of coal and iron, but it had more miles of railroad than all of Europe.

It was clear, what is more, that the United States was now becoming what it has remained ever since, the technological leader of the world. In 1878, the phonograph was patented by Thomas Alva Edison (born in Milan, Ohio, on February 11, 1847). Edison, the most ingenious inventor in recorded history, went on to patent the electric light in 1879. By 1880, there were 50,000 telephones in use in the United States, and in 1879, the first telephone link between two cities (Boston and Lowell, in Massachusetts) had been set up. On a lesser scale, 1878 saw the first two-wheeled contraption that could be called a bicycle appear on the city streets of America.

And, of course, 1880 was also a year for a new presidential election. With Hayes absolutely refusing to run for reelection (the first one-term president to do so since James K. Polk, thirty-two years earlier), the field was wide open for the Republicans. The natural choice would have been Blaine, who had lost it four years before only because of the Mulligan letters. Four years of Hayes had quieted the corruption issue and Blaine might have had a chance.

Against him, however, was an embittered Conkling, who considered Blaine the leading Half-Breed and who would have nothing to do with him. Conkling, in fact, longed for the easy days of Grant and decided he would have no one else. It would mean a third term for Grant, which was against nearly a century of tradition, but Conkling did not care, and poor Grant, driven by his wife's longing to live in the White House again, agreed to let himself be used.

If Blaine and Grant were the only two in the field, one or the other would have ended with a majority on the first ballot. There was, however, a third candidate, the secretary of the treasury, John Sherman. He was a most careful politician who, once, when about to return to his home town on political business, refused to admit the motivation and said he merely had to "mend some fences" on his property. Ever since "fence-mending" has meant, in politics, a trip home to strengthen the political organization there.

Sherman was one of the many men in American history whose heart was set on the presidency and who would not give up striving after it. He stayed in the race under the shrewd management of his fellow Ohioan James Abram Garfield (born in Cuyahoga County, Ohio, on November 19, 1831). Garfield, who had fought well in the Civil War, rising to the rank of major general, had been in the House of Representatives for seventeen years and had just been elected to the Senate.

The Republican National Convention met in Chicago on June 2,

1880, and the fight was bitter from the start as ballot after ballot was cast. Neither Sherman nor Blaine would give in to each other, and preventing either from winning was Conkling, who held just over 300 votes for Grant and delivered them without fail at every ballot.

Conkling might have become a king-maker by delivering his votes to either one of the others, but he would not do so. It was his hope that when the convention saw that he was prepared to keep it in session forever, they would give in out of sheer desperation and let it be Grant.

That was not how it happened. After thirty-five useless ballots, the convention turned to a "dark horse" candidate (one who had not figured in the preconvention calculations). Garfield's politicking on behalf of Sherman had been skillful enough to stop both Blaine and Grant, who were each much more formidable candidates, and that had won the admiration of the delegates. On the thirty-fifth ballot, he got a scattering of votes, and then on the thirty-sixth, there was a flood of them, almost all but Conkling's faithful 300, and Garfield was the Republican nominee to everyone's surprise, including Garfield's own.

The delegates realized that Conkling would willingly cut the throat of the party if he didn't get *something*, so they voted in that most loyal of all the Conkling stooges, Chester Alan Arthur, as the vice-presidential nominee.

On June 22, 1880, the Democrats met in Cincinnati. Tilden could have been renominated and then, probably, elected since there would have been many who would have voted for him out of indignation at the raw deal he had received. Tilden, however, still lacking that edge of determination, played it coy. He may have been serious in not wanting the nomination, but if he was waiting to be begged hard enough, he waited too long, and the Democrats turned elsewhere.

The corruption issue had largely vanished, thanks to Hayes, so they tried to wipe out the stigma of defeatism that had destroyed their chances ever since the Civil War by nominating someone who, like Garfield, had been a Union general during the war.

Their nominee for president was the portly (his weight was 250 pounds) Winfield Scott Hancock (born in Montgomery Square, Pennsylvania, on February 14, 1824). His military record was unimpeachable; it was the men under his command who had turned back Pickett's Charge at the Battle of Gettysburg. During Reconstruction, he had been in military control of Louisiana and Texas, where he openly opposed the Radical Republicans and supported the policies of Andrew Johnson. It was that which had won him high regard among the Democrats. For the vice-presidency, they nominated Congressman William H. English of Indiana.

It was a dull campaign, since there were scarcely any issues. The two party platforms were almost identical except that the Democrats wanted a low tariff and the Republicans a high one. Garfield campaigned in person which, at that time, was unusual. He delivered some seventy speeches, which novelty alone made effective. Hancock, on the other hand, was without political experience and conducted a campaign of no consequence whatever.

The returning prosperity and the old bloody-shirt sentiments favored the Republicans, and Garfield won by 214 electoral votes to 155. The popular vote, however, was much closer: 4,450,000 for Garfield versus 4,410,000 for Hancock.

Garfield didn't actually have a majority of the popular vote for some 300,000 votes were cast for James Baird Weaver (born in Dayton, Ohio, on June 12, 1833), a Civil War colonel who ran as the candidate of the Greenback Labor party. (There was also a Prohibition candidate who gained 10,000 votes, indicating the increasing importance some people were placing on the legal prohibition of the sale of alcoholic beverages.)

Garfield was inaugurated on March 4, 1881 as the twentieth president of the United States. The forty-seventh Congress also began its new term, with the Senate tied at 37 to 37 and the Republicans having narrow control of the House, 147 to 135.

One interesting point about the election was that with the end of the Reconstruction era, there were no carpetbaggers in control in any southern state so that for the first time since the Civil War, all the ex-Confederate states, plus three of the four border states, voted Democratic. This was the actual beginning of the "Solid South" and that term was first used in a speech by a senator from Alabama on December 17, 1878.

Although once again, and for the sixth presidential election in a row, the Republicans were triumphant, the election victory did not heal the split in the party. Though Conkling's henchman, Arthur, was vice-president, Conkling was not satisfied. Garfield had selected Blaine as his secretary of state and Conkling, hating Blaine to death, was sunk in bitter brooding.

As for Garfield, he was determined to challenge Conkling. The presidency had shown some signs of life under Hayes—after its eclipse under Johnson and its supine surrender under Grant—and Garfield intended to carry on the offensive. Quite deliberately, on March 23, 1881, he appointed a political enemy of Conkling as collector of the Port of New York, Arthur's old job.

Conkling reacted predictably. He threw himself across the path of the appointment and for six weeks managed to stall the confirmation. Garfield held firm, however, and by mid-May it was clear that the Senate would vote to confirm his appointment.

Now Conkling, in his blind wrath, and driven by enormous vanity and self-assurance, decided to teach the president a lesson. On May 16, 1881, two days before the confirmation vote, he resigned and, what is more, forced the reluctant junior senator from New York, Thomas Collier Platt (born in Oswego, New York, on July 15, 1833) to resign as well. The idea was to have the New York state legislature° reelect them as senators to the tune of a great popular outpouring of support that would teach Garfield where the power lay.

Rarely had any skillful politician miscalculated more grossly. The state legislature refused to reelect the senators, and Conkling's power was suddenly, unexpectedly and permanently broken. He remained a successful lawyer, however, till his death in New York City on April 18, 1888. Platt had better luck. After a few years of retirement, he made his way back into politics and, in time, became the Republican boss of New York State.

Garfield's victory over Conkling was not a matter of mere political in-fighting. It showed that the power of the presidency was on the way up again (though it was to be half a century yet before it became the clearly dominant power in the nation.)

It was an expensive victory, however, for Garfield; a fatal one, in fact. Among the followers of the Stalwarts was Charles Julius Guiteau, born about 1840, who greatly desired a post as consul in Marseille,

---

° Until 1917, senators were elected by the state legislatures and not by popular vote.

France. Apparently, he was sufficiently unbalanced, mentally, to brood himself into taking criminal action over his failure to get the post—which he blamed on Garfield.

He lay in wait for Garfield at a railroad station in Washington and shot him on July 2, 1881, screaming, "I am a Stalwart of the Stalwarts, and now Chet Arthur is president."

Garfield was not killed outright, but lingered on in pain. Bell, the inventor of the telephone, devised a metal-locating instrument to find the bullet in the president's body. The device was a workable one but was frustrated on this occasion because no one thought of removing the steel-springed mattress, the metal of which interfered with the search.

On September 19, Garfield died, having been president for six and a half months. Only William Henry Harrison, forty years earlier, had held the post more briefly. The next day, Chester Alan Arthur was sworn in as the twenty-first President of the United States.° Guiteau was tried for his crime, found guilty, and hanged on June 30, 1882.

The assassination of Garfield ruined the respectability of the patronage system forever. To be killed over a consulship! Was that all a president had to do, worry about two-bit jobs for two-bit political workers? There was a loud public outcry and in the 1882 congressional elections, the Democrats won a decisive majority in the House of Representatives of the forty-eighth Congress, 197 to 118, though the Senate remained with the Republicans 38 to 36.

Before it left office, the forty-seventh Congress, on January 16, 1883, passed the Pendleton Act (sponsored by Senator George Hunt Pendleton of Ohio, born in Cincinnati on July 29, 1823, and once a Democratic candidate for vice-president in 1864). By the terms of this act a three-man Civil Service Commission was set up to devise examinations to be given to those applying for certain positions in order that their qualifications might be judged on grounds of ability

---

° To those interested in meaningless coincidences, the name of the first of the Hebrew patriarchs, Abram or Abraham, has been fatal for presidents. Only two of them bore the name, Abraham Lincoln and James Abram Garfield, and both were assassinated. Garfield was the third president in a row to have been elected in a year divisible by 20 and to die in office. Before him were William Henry Harrison, elected in 1840, and Abraham Lincoln, elected in 1860.

rather than of political loyalty. Civil servants could no longer be assessed for political contributions or be fired if they did not pay.

At first these rules applied to only about one tenth of the federal employees, and only to those who were to be appointed in the future. It was a weak act to begin with, but it was to grow and be extended and while patronage never stopped, it was never to be so all-encompassing a political weapon as it was before Conkling resigned and Guiteau fired his gun.

4

GROVER CLEVELAND

IMMIGRANTS AND LABOR

In the ten years that followed 1880, the stream of immigrants flowing through the Golden Door passed the five million mark, but a change had come over the character of that immigration.

Prior to 1880, the great majority of immigrants had come from northern and western Europe, from Great Britain, Ireland, Germany, and Scandinavia. They were either Anglo-Saxons or possessed cultures that could fit into the Anglo-Saxon one without too much trouble.

But then, on March 13, 1881, the comparatively liberal Tsar of Russia, Alexander II, was assassinated by a terrorist, and in the reaction that followed, the heavy hand of the police and of the Cossack cavalry fell upon all dissidents and particularly upon the Jewish population. A flood of Russian Jewish emigration to the United States began that was to continue for forty years (and in the last stages of which my parents and I were to arrive in New York). In addition, immigrants began to arrive in increasing numbers from southern Europe, from Italy, in particular.

On the other hand, increasing prosperity in northern Europe, and particularly in the newly founded German Empire, dried up that portion of the flow. Thus, the large American cities began to include large blocs of Europeans existing in cultural islands that tended to resist absorption into the general American culture.

Those Americans whose parents or grandparents, but not themselves, had been immigrants, and who therefore considered themselves native to the soil, looked with increasing scorn and dismay at these newcomers, and the feeling began to grow that the Golden Door ought not to be quite so wide open.

Naturally, where the cultural and physical differences were greatest, the suspicions and resentment were greatest, too. However unassimilative Jews, Italians, Greeks, and Czechs might be, they were at least white Europeans. On the West Coast, however, the Chinese were entering the nation in increasing numbers and that was quite another thing.

The Chinese were a quiet and humble people, frugal and hardworking. What made them particularly desirable to employers was that they were willing to work for less money than non-Chinese laborers would, and the employers were enthusiastically willing to pay them less. This meant losses of jobs for the Whites, who reacted not so much against the employers who paid less (and who were entrenched behind the power of the law) but against the Chinese who were exposed and helpless.

In 1871 and in 1877, there were anti-Chinese riots in California, not very different in spirit from the anti-Jewish pogroms in Russia, and pressure grew for a bar to further Chinese immigration. As the number of Chinese immigrants grew to nearly 40,000 in 1882, so did the pressure grow for exclusion.

Hayes had vetoed a Chinese-Exclusion bill in 1879, but in 1882 a bill to exclude Chinese laborers for ten years was signed by Arthur on May 6 (after he had vetoed a stronger version), and Chinese immigration instantly dropped to 8,000 in 1883.

An act restricting general immigration passed on August 3, 1883. It excluded paupers, convicts, and mental defectives. Surely it was hard to quarrel with this, but it, along with the Chinese-Exclusion Act, was an indication that the Golden Door was beginning, however slightly, to close.

Increasing pressure against those of different races who were already citizens also grew. The southern states, under their new conservative regimes began passing laws that would enforce the segregation of Blacks into a life of inferiority from which they could not legally emerge. The first of these "Jim Crow" laws° was passed in Tennessee in 1881, and it forbade Whites and Blacks to ride in the same railways coaches. There had to be special coaches for Blacks, in theory equal to those of the Whites, but never so in practice. In every phase of life, segregation grew—even in prisons. In 1884, Alabama passed a law making it illegal to confine Whites and Blacks in the same cell. (While Blacks were segregated and oppressed outside the South as well, such acts did not have legal sanction—and that made a difference.)

Nor did the poorer Whites find life a matter of unrestrained joy. Though the labor movement continued to grow stronger, the government continued to side with the business interests, so that strikes were almost invariably broken by military force if nothing else sufficed. The government's attitude was that it was being neutral—merely seeing to it that order was preserved. However, since order was always preserved by breaking strikes, the neutrality was entirely on the side of the employers.

Even reform politicians were usually reformers only in the sense that they wanted government money handled honestly and government offices run efficiently. They were not at all sympathetic with the plight of the poor, nor with the pleas of the poor for better housing, higher wages, and shorter hours.

It was clear to increasing numbers of laborers that the only way they could improve their situation was to combine into organizations that could speak for the workman with a united voice. The employers were quite able to see the danger in this for themselves and so they routinely fired any employee suspected of joining such a "labor union."

° The origin of "Jim Crow" is uncertain. Some minstrel shows (in blackface and in Black dialect) featured a popular song with a refrain that included the phrase "Every time I wheel about I jump Jim Crow" and there was also the obvious allusion to the Black in the crow's ebony plumage.

The government, moreover, was inclined to view union activity as conspiracy, while turning a blind eye to combinations of employers. (This is not surprising, since the employers had money to contribute to political campaigns or to donate as outright graft, while labor at that time had not.)

The result was that the first labor unions had to be secret organizations, and their actions had to be terrorist, since no legal recourse was left to them. Thus, in 1854, the Irish miners of the Pennsylvania coal mines organized into a secret organization called the "Molly Maguires." The membership was finally exposed by a spy hired by the coal companies to infiltrate the organization. Men like Jay Gould could steal millions and remain respected members of the society they bilked; but not so the Molly Maguires who sent crude threatening letters to mineowners. Nineteen of them were tried, convicted, and hanged in 1875, and the organization was destroyed.

The first important national labor organization was the Knights of Labor founded in 1869, also a secret order, originally to avoid reprisals. By 1886, it has a national membership of 730,000 and in that year it called 1600 strikes, the aims of which for the most part were to establish an eight-hour day, so that laboring men could have an hour or two of daylight leisure each day. For this they had to withstand a constant stream of vilification by the newspapers (almost all antilabor) and violence by the employers' hired toughs, or by the police, which was almost the same thing. Jay Gould boasted that he could always hire half the laboring class to kill the other half, but the Knights of Labor won a strike against Jay Gould's railroad just the same.

The peak of the struggle came during a strike in Chicago against the McCormick Harvesting Machine Company. It was called on May 1, 1886 and on May 3, the police took a hand, killing six strikers. Union leaders called a protest meeting in Haymarket Square on May 4, a meeting that remained peaceful until the police charged in, unprovoked. Someone (no one every found out who) threw a bomb, and seven policemen were killed, together with many others who were hurt.

Eight anarchists who had joined the protest meeting and who had made violent speeches were arrested. There was no evidence that any of them had thrown the bomb, but the nation was whipped into hysteria by the newspapers and the police and, after a more or less

farcical trial, they were convicted on August 20, 1886. Four were
hanged and one committed suicide. The remaining three were imprisoned.

The Knights of Labor did not survive that fatal year but shriveled
rapidly. In its place came the more political American Federation of
Labor. It was headed by Samuel Gompers (born in London, on January
27, 1850). In 1886, he led his cigar-makers union out of the Knights of
Labor and became president of the new organization, which, with the
exception of one year, he continued to head for the rest of his life.

Gompers led unionism into conservative paths. He confined the
federation to the skilled workers, who weren't as badly off in the first
place, and labored to prevent strikes and to work slowly within the
framework of the social order. In the long run, his penchant for
avoiding politics and social theory, and just sticking to the nuts-and-
bolts, day-by-day striving to improve the economic lot of labor, won
out—particularly since he made labor seem more respectable and
defused the hysteria with which its every move was met. In the short
run, however, it meant that millions of laborers were left without
voice and were abandoned to misery.

And yet if things were not altogether idyllic in the United States,
Americans were better off than people elsewhere in the world. There
was precious little liberty in the world then, and precious little now,
for that matter, but then and now, the United States had considerably
more than its share.

It was entirely fitting therefore that the Statue of Liberty was
dedicated on Bedloe's Island (now called Liberty Island) in New York
Harbor on October 28, 1886. The statue was a gift of the French
people who, since the fall of Napoleon III, had been living under a
republic of their own. It was constructed by the French sculptor,
Frédéric Auguste Bartholdi.

What is more, the United States continued to take on more and more
the aspect of the technological giant it was to become. In 1882, Edison
opened his first commercial electric lighting plant in New York City.
The first of the great suspension bridges, the Brooklyn Bridge, was put
into use on May 24, 1883. Long distance telephone service opened
between New York and Boston in 1884 and, in that same year, the first
"skyscraper"—a building constructed around a steel framework—was
built in Chicago. It was ten stories high.

The Northern Pacific completed a second transcontinental rail link on September 8, 1883, and over the next decade three more railroads were to connect the two coasts. A grimmer development was the invention of the automatic machine gun in 1883 by Hiram Stevens Maxim (born in Brockway's Mill, Maine, on February 5, 1840). In later years Maxim moved to England, became a British subject, and was knighted.

BLAINE GETS HIS CHANCE

On the whole, Chester Arthur was not the kind of president the reformers feared he might be. A tall, impressive-looking widower (his wife having died of pneumonia in 1880), Arthur brought class and culture to the White House. Although he had been loyal to Conkling and had supported him vigorously in the senator's last fight against Garfield, the assassination changed everything.

Thanks to Guiteau's proud cry, the Stalwarts were temporarily wiped out as a political force, and Arthur dared not be associated with them. He broke off relations with his erstwhile cronies, promised to avoid factionalism, and kept that promise. He was a good and capable president, to the surprise of everyone—and to the anger of the Republican politicians.

It meant that he could not be nominated again. Although Arthur, unlike Hayes, was willing to run again, the fact was that he was an ill man (something he kept secret) and had not long to live. He died in New York City on November 18, 1886.

Earlier, a more important symbol of the Civil War and of the evil days that followed passed from the scene. Ulysses Grant, the great general and inadequate president, had a difficult life in retirement. Ex-presidents were not cared for by the nation in those days and in 1884, naive to the last, he was bilked of his savings by crooked promoters. He was suffering from cancer of the throat and, fearing he might leave his family penniless, he began to work on his memoirs with the encouragement of Mark Twain, who planned to publish them. Grimly, with a resolution that was a throwback to the general, not the president, Grant held on to life until he had completed the last word of what turned out to be an excellent work. He died almost immediately after its completion, on July 23, 1885, was buried in what is now called Grant's Tomb in upper Manhattan, and was mourned by millions. His memoirs were a huge financial success, and his family was secure.

On June 3, 1884, the Republican National Convention met in Chicago. With Arthur out of the picture, the politicians finally did what they had wanted to do in 1876 and in 1880. They nominated James G. Blaine on the fourth ballot and rejoiced in the hope that the happy days of Grant might return at last.

For vice-president, they nominated one of the losers in the presidential nomination ballot, the eloquent Senator John Alexander Logan of Illinois (born in Jackson County, Illinois, on February 9, 1826). He was still another Union general of the Civil war, and had been one of the leaders in the attempt to impeach and convict Andrew Johnson.

Blaine ran under a handicap. The Mulligan letters, some might have thought, were a thing of the past, but the Democrats promptly brought them up again. What was worse, a new letter was discovered and publicized; one that was quite incriminating and, worst of all, had, at the end, "P.S. Burn this letter."

Unfortunately for Blaine, it wasn't burned, and at Democratic rallies the chant would be taken up (with some justice):

> Blaine! Blaine! James G. Blaine!
> Continental liar from the State of Maine!
> P.S. Burn this letter.

Reform-minded Republicans were horrified at this nomination of an all-too-probably corrupt politician. Leading the rebellious "Independents" was the German-American reformer Carl Schurz (born near Cologne, Germany, on March 2, 1829). He had been a Union general in the Civil War, a senator from Missouri from 1869 to 1875, secretary of interior under Hayes, and was an influence for reform and against corruption within the Republican party. He had deserted the organization Republicans in 1872 because he could not support Grant for a second term, and now he deserted them again because he could not support Blaine. He, and others with him, supported the Democratic candidate.

The regular Republicans, affecting to find the Independents a group of elitist holier-than-thou individuals, called them, in contempt, "mugwumps" from an Indian word for "chief." The name was accepted and has been used ever since for Independents who could not be trusted to vote the party line blindly.

On July 8, 1884, the Democratic National Convention met in Chicago. They already had a mugwump promise to support the Democratic candidate if he were a clear reformer—and the candidate was at hand.

The governor of New York was Stephen Grover Cleveland (born in Caldwell, New Jersey, on March 18, 1837). Cleveland had been a reform mayor of Buffalo and had become governor on the strength of that ("A public office is a public trust," he said, and this was widely quoted).

As governor, his financial honesty had been impeccable, and he was good enough for the mugwumps. Cleveland succeeded on the second ballot. He was bitterly opposed by the politicians who ran Tammany and other big city machines, but that redounded to his benefit. One of the delegates who nominated Cleveland said, "They love him most for the enemies he has made."

For vice-president, the Democrats nominated Hendricks who, in 1876, had been nominated for the same office under Tilden.

The campaign was a dirty one indeed. Cleveland, although a model of public and financial rectitude was self-indulgent in private life. Between good food and good beer, he had grown fat (260 pounds) and, although a bachelor, he indulged in female company. To expect anything else would have been ridiculous, but it turned out that one such indulgence had resulted in an illegitimate child whom he was supporting. When the story broke during the campaign, his followers asked him what to do. "Tell the truth!" he said, and there was no attempt at a denial.

The result was the derisive Republican chant:

> *Ma, Ma, where's my Pa?*
> *Gone to the White House, ha, ha, ha!*

Running on the Greenback Labor ticket was Benjamin Franklin Butler (see *Our Federal Union*). Known as one of the most incompetent commanders of the Civil War, and as a twister and turner in politics, he apparently did have some feeling for labor and for immigrants. As nominee for president, however, he accepted secret campaign contributions from the Republican party, which hoped that he would draw votes away from Cleveland.

It was a close race. For everyone who was repelled by Blaine's inability to keep his fingers off the public dollar, there was another who was repelled by Cleveland's illegitimate child.

It was clear that New York might be the swing state; that whichever candidate carried New York would take the election, and the race in that state seemed to be nearly a dead heat.

Blaine pushed hard for the Irish vote, which was prominent in New York City, by making a number of speeches in which he denounced Great Britain. (This sort of thing was called "twisting the lion's tail," and was indulged in by American politicians down into the 1930s. It was a practice that often did the politician a lot of good and never did Great Britain, as far as anyone could tell, any harm.)

Then, on October 29, 1884, in the last week of the campaign, when Blaine was in New York, a group of several hundred Protestant clergymen called on him. At the head was a Presbyterian minister, Samuel Dickinson Burchard (born in Steuben, New York, on September 6, 1812). He was an ardent Prohibitionist and he made a little speech in which he denounced the traitorous mugwumps, saying, "We are Republicans and don't propose to leave our party and identify ourselves with the party whose antecedents have been Rum, Romanism, and Rebellion."

The Rum and Rebellion were all right, but in searching for the third R, Burchard had let his Protestant zeal run away with him. The Irish were zealous Roman Catholics and when the report of that speech was gleefully spread far and wide by New York's Democrats, over went enough Irish votes from Republican to Democrat to carry New York State for Cleveland on November 4, by 1047 votes. (Another factor, perhaps, was that President Arthur, a New Yorker who was not fond of Blaine and who was annoyed at being snubbed by the party, did not campaign. He might have swung enough votes to count if he had done so.)

The vote in the 1884 election was the reverse of that of 1880. This time it was the Democrats who won by a tiny popular margin: 4,880,000 to 4,850,000. The Democratic vote was not an actual majority because of Butler's 175,000 votes and another 150,000 for the Prohibitionist candidate. The vote in the electoral college, however, was 219 for Cleveland to 182 for Blaine, with New York making the difference.

THE DEMOCRATIC PRESIDENT

Beginning with Lincoln's election in 1860, the Republicans had won six presidential races in a row. They had lost the seventh, however, and now Cleveland was moving into the White House as the first Democrat to be elected president in twenty-eight years, the first Democratic president since the Civil War.

He was inaugurated as the twenty-second President of the United States on March 4, 1885. With him came the forty-ninth Congress in which, despite the Democratic victory, the Republicans had gained strength in both houses. The Democrats still controlled the House 183 to 140, but the Republicans led in the Senate, 43 to 34.

The new vice-president, Hendricks, did not long survive the inauguration, however. He died on November 25, 1885.

Cleveland was the second bachelor to enter the White House, the first having been James Buchanan in 1856. Unlike Buchanan, however, Cleveland did not stay a bachelor.

Back in 1875, Cleveland's law partner, Oscar Folsom, had died in a buggy accident, leaving behind an eleven-year-old daughter, Frances. Cleveland took over responsibility for her and when he became president, she was a college student, tall, attractive, and just half her guardian's weight. By then, Cleveland felt more than a guardian to her and, despite the difference in ages (he was forty-eight to her twenty-one years), they were married on June 2, 1886.

Cleveland was not the first incumbent president to marry. In 1844, President John Tyler had married a second time after the death of his wife, and with an even greater age disparity (fifty-four to twenty-four). Tyler, however, had married in New York City, while Cleveland's wedding took place in the White House itself, with every church bell in Washington pealing.

Frances Cleveland proved to be a delightful and popular First Lady and gave her presidential husband five legitimate children. There were rumors, assiduously spread, that the president beat his wife, but the chances are very high that this was merely malicious scandal mongering.

As president, Cleveland's sense of rigid honesty consisted of doing his best to keep expenditures low, and of keeping the government out of private endeavors. His reforming zeal, however, did not go beyond that. There was no sensitivity at all to the plight of the hungry and miserable.

There was, for instance, a drought in Texas, and Congress passed a bill permitting the expenditure of $10,000 in seed grain for distribution to the drought-stricken farmers. Cleveland vetoed it on the ground that this would develop bad habits in people, who would begin to expect government to help them out of every trouble and would thus find their sense of self-reliance weakening. (Maybe so, but this sort of hard-hearted piety would have come with better grace from someone who had had some recent experience of hunger, and who was not portly and gaining weight steadily throughout his stay in the White House.)

Moreover, the rich and powerful were frequently helped out by government action without anyone ever worrying about their self-reliance suffering. The railroads, particularly, were riding high. They were absolutely vital to the nation, since in those years there was no alternative way of transporting goods, and this gave them an almost dictatorial ability to charge whatever fees they wished, favoring one group over another, as it suited their pocketbooks. They had obtained enormous quantities of public land through connivance with a lenient government and they held up virtually the entire nation for ransom. Nor could the states do anything much about it since the important railroads were interstate in nature and beyond their control for that reason.

The conventional wisdom of the time was that the federal government was merely an umpire and should not take part on one side or the other, but such neutrality in any quarrel between the powerful and the powerless was equivalent to siding with the powerful.

A rising tide of public discontent among the farmers of the south and west against discriminatory rates by railroads began to make itself felt. There were even businesses in the north and east who felt short-changed and who joined in the clamor. Something had to be done, and the government could not remain impartial.

On February 4, 1887, the Interstate Commerce Act was passed. The act ordered railroads engaged in interstate commerce to establish reasonable charges that did not unfairly favor some groups over others; that these charges be made public and not be changed without notice. A number of other abuses and unfair practices were banned.

The act also set up the Interstate Commerce Commission, the first regulatory commission in the history of the United States. It had the power to investigate the management of railroads, to look through their books and papers, to call witnesses, and so on.

The railroad companies were clever enough to find all sorts of loopholes in the law, and rich enough to bribe officials. The government itself was not enthusiastic about engaging in any actions that would annoy the well-to-do, and the Supreme Court consistently forced a narrow interpretation of the law.

Still, even though the Interstate Commerce Act failed to accomplish its immediate purpose, it did remove some abuses. More important, it established the principle that the federal government was not an impassive witness of events, dedicated to seeing to it that the poor suffered their misery just as cheerfully and quietly as the rich enjoyed their wealth. It substituted the principle that the government must place its influence on the side of those without power in order that there might be a more even-handed justice among the American people. What is more, it was also the beginning of the notion that economic problems had grown in complexity to the point where they could not be solved by private actions or even by local government, but only by the federal government itself.

Cleveland's refusal to spend money meant that there was a continuing and growing surplus in the Treasury, most of it derived from tariff revenues. (Those were the days before any real income tax.) Having lots of money in the Treasury sounds good, but it has its bad points. The money, withdrawn from circulation, contracts the ability to borrow and invest on the part of the public generally, and, therefore, limits prosperity.

Cleveland would not get rid of the surplus by spending it on such unworthy projects as supplying hard-pressed farmers with seed, but pushed instead for reducing the tariff. This annoyed businessmen who would then find it more difficult to compete with imported goods and who would thus lose some of their profits.

Cleveland also annoyed Democratic politicians by refusing to make a clean sweep of all the Republican officeholders who had accumulated in the decades of the Republican domination of the presidency.

On the whole, Cleveland won high marks for integrity, but it was a miserly, close-fisted variety that did not do anything to win hearts. In the 1886 congressional elections, the Democrats failed to capture the Senate of the fiftieth Congress, and lost some of their margin in the House.

Still, when the Democratic National Convention met in St. Louis, Missouri, on June 5, 1888, there was no way in which the first Democratic president since the Civil War could fail to be renominated. Cleveland was renominated by acclamation, but, somehow, without real enthusiasm. For vice-president, Senator Allen Granberry Thurman of Ohio (born in Lynchburg, Virginia, on November 13, 1813) was nominated.

On June 19, the Republican National Convention met in Chicago. It took them eight ballots to settle on Benjamin Harrison (born in North Bend, Ohio, on August 20, 1833). Harrison was a grandson of William Henry Harrison who had served as the ninth President of the United States, for the final month of his life, and a great-grandson of Benjamin Harrison who had been a signer of the Declaration of Independence for Virginia. Harrison had fought well in the Civil War and was promoted to brigadier general by the war's end. He had just completed a term as senator for Ohio.

Harrison's chief competitor for the nomination was the New York banker, Levi Parsons Morton (born at Shoreham, Vermont, on May 16, 1824). Having failed, he was consoled with the nomination for vice-president.

The campaign was a vigorous one, and it gave every sign of being every bit as close as those of 1880 and 1884. Cleveland had the advantage of being an incumbent president, but there were factors against him, too. His refusal to spend money disappointed many who were ready for a handout. In particular, Cleveland had set his face hard against any bills designed to hand out pensions to veterans of the Civil War—and there were a great many veterans who were annoyed with that. Harrison promised those veterans their pensions.

Then, too, while Cleveland pushed for a low tariff, Harrison promised a high tariff, and this was the key issue of the campaign.

Perhaps what hurt Cleveland most was something he had nothing to do with, something that was another's foolish error.

A private citizen of California, George Osgoodby, who happened to be a Republican, sent a letter to the British minister to the United States, Sir Lionel Sackville-West. Osgoodby, pretending to be an English-born citizen of the United States, said he would vote for Cleveland if that would be to Great Britain's interest, and asked for advice.

Sackville-West had no business answering such an inquiry since that would be interference with the domestic affairs of the nation to which he was accredited. In a fit of idiocy, however, Sackville-West replied and advised Osgoodby to vote for Cleveland. Osgoodby passed it on to the Republican National Committee, and it was published just before the election.

It was a terrible blow to Cleveland for it threatened the Irish vote. Cleveland promptly demanded the recall of Sackville-West, but the damage was done. Yet he could scarcely complain; he had profited by Burchard's similar bonehead play on the Republican side in 1884.

When all was done, however, Cleveland's incumbency and his reputation for fiscal prudence overcame the Sackville-West letter, and he finished with a larger plurality than he had had in 1884. In the 1888 election, Cleveland had 5,500,000 votes to 5,410,000 for Harrison, a plurality of 90,000 compared to the 30,000 he had piled up four years before.

Nevertheless, the plurality didn't count. It was electoral votes that decided the election. Cleveland's votes were too heavily concentrated in the south. He won some states with more than enough votes and lost others narrowly—winning the plurality but losing the states. In particular, the Sackville-West letter lost him New York, which the Burchard speech had given him in 1884.

Harrison received 233 electoral votes to Cleveland's 168, and it was Harrison who was elected. It was the first time in forty-eight years that an incumbent president was defeated for reelection. (The previous case had been Martin Van Buren in 1840.)

For the second time in twelve years, the Democrats got more votes than the opposition, yet lost the presidency. This time, at least, the vote was reasonably honest, and the result was owing to the workings of the electoral college, which considers not only the total vote but also the general acceptability. (There is something to be said for this. Overwhelming support in a few states should not necessarily outweigh lack of interest in many states.)

For the third time in a row, neither major candidate got over 50 percent of the vote, thanks to the presence of minor parties. In 1888, the Prohibition party garnered 250,000 votes, and the Union Labor party (an attempted combination of farmers and laborers pushing for their common goals) got 150,000.

BENJAMIN HARRISON

On March 4, 1889, Benjamin Harrison was inaugurated as the twenty-third President of the United States.

His face reminds us of the role played by fashion in the development of facial hair. Mankind has always wobbled between much and little facial hair and, at the time of the birth of the United States, the cleanshaven countenance was in style. The first fifteen presidents were all cleanshaven, though John Quincy Adams and Martin Van Buren, the sixth and eighth presidents respectively, had sideburns.

Lincoln, the sixteenth president, was cleanshaven when elected, but grew a beard (though not a mustache) immediately thereafter, and the Civil War era saw a great flourishing of beards that continued for several decades thereafter.

Andrew Johnson was old-fashioned enough to be cleanshaven, but Grant was the first President to wear a full mustache and beard. Hayes and Garfield, who followed, were also fully haired on lips, cheeks, and chin. Arthur had only a mustache and sideburns and Cleveland only a mustache, but Benjamin Harrison was again bearded. He was the last bearded president, so that there were four altogether.

The first consequence of Harrison's election was the entry of a group of new states into the Union. The west was rapidly increasing in population thanks to the railroads, and the various territories in the northwest each had a considerably higher population than Nevada, which had been a state for thirty years. Nevertheless, since the entry of Colorado in 1876, no new states had joined the Union. For one thing, the territories were all Republican in politics, and the Democrats were reluctant to let them in.

Benjamin Harrison was chairman of the Committee on Territories while he was in the Senate and he had demanded the formation of new states. He was unsuccessful as long as Cleveland was in the White House, but when he himself was installed, that was another matter, especially since he brought in with him a Republican fifty-first Congress, with a lead of 39 to 37 in the Senate and of 166 to 159 in the House.

On November 2, 1889, North Dakota and South Dakota entered the Union. It had been a single territory but by dividing it in two, there would be four new Republican senators rather than only two. The two bills were signed without notice being taken of which was first so that neither state could claim seniority over the other. Whatever the order might be, the Dakotas became the thirty-ninth and fortieth states of the Union.

On November 8, 1889, Montana became the forty-first state and on November 11, Washington became the forty-second state. A little over a half a year later, two more states joined: Idaho on July 3, 1890, became the forty-third state, and Wyoming on July 10 became the forty-fourth state.

In less than nine months, six new states had joined the Union and almost all the continental area was divided. There was room for only a few additional states, all in the southwest.

The new House of Representatives, under narrow Republican control, had Thomas Brackett Reed of Maine (born in Portland, Maine, on October 18, 1839) as Speaker. Because the Republican margin was small, the Democrats were quite capable of using all sorts of delaying tactics—as for instance, by refusing to vote so that no quorum (minimum number of legislators required to be present for official action) would exist. Reed therefore interpreted rules with new strictness and introduced innovations such as counting nonvoting Representatives as present if they were physically present. He was called Czar Reed and made the Speakership very important. The Democrats denounced him, but when it was the Democratic turn to control the House, the new Speaker retained the power Reed had introduced.

Under Reed's guidance, the fifty-first Congress passed several controversial laws.

One of them took up the question of the so-called trusts. These consisted of combinations of corporations with dealings that involved some particular product. Such combinations were so powerful economically, and dominated the market so completely, that they could force out any attempt at competition. If a group of corporations controlled 90 percent of iron production, for instance, they formed an iron trust that could lower the price of iron and take a temporary loss until smaller groups outside the trust, who lacked the great reserves of the giant, were crushed. Then the trust could raise its prices to any level it desired, and the consumers, unable to get what they wanted anywhere else, had to pay.

The American economy has always paid lip service to "free enterprise" and to "healthy competition," and it was clear that the trusts subverted this and instituted monopolies. These were no less powerful and no less destructive of the people's rights because they were controlled by private individuals than if they had been controlled by the government. In fact, the relationship between the powerful businessmen of the trusts and the powerful politicians of the government was often close enough to make it difficult to see where one began and the other ended.

Nor could local governments, even up to the state level, do anything about trusts, since they invariably had interstate ramifications. If one state grew hostile, a trust could establish itself in another state that was more accommodating.

There had to be federal action, therefore, and the rising popular clamor made certain there would be some.

A law against the trusts was passed on July 2, 1890, one that made it illegal for organizations to combine in such a way as to exercise

unreasonable restraint of trade (preventing someone else from engaging in business) or from monopolizing or attempting to monopolize.
The act received its name from Senator John Sherman, who had
struggled so hard for the Republican nomination in 1880 and who had
introduced it to Congress. It was therefore called the "Sherman
Antitrust Act."

The Sherman Antitrust Act sounded good, but it was empty. For one
thing, it was so vaguely written that a great deal depended on its
interpretation. What was *unreasonable* restraint of trade? Exactly at
what point would a combination become a monopoly? Then, too, was a
labor union the kind of organization that exercised unreasonable
restraint of trade? One of the formulators of the act, Senator George
Franklin Edmunds of Vermont (born in Richmond, Vermont, on
February 1, 1828), was convinced that labor unions were the real
dangers and he worked on the act with that in mind.

In fact, the first time the Sherman Antitrust Act was used it was
indeed turned against a labor union and as time passed it proved
almost useless as a way of combating the economic power of trusts and
of other industrial combinations. Yet, along with the Interstate Commerce Act passed three years before, it represented the toe of the
federal foot being placed in the regulatory ocean. As time went on
(too much time for those who suffered, of course) the role of the
government against economic tyranny strengthened.

By 1890, there was a depression on, one which particularly affected
the mineowners of the west and the farmers everywhere. The price of
silver was falling, and the debts of the farmers were increasing. What
was needed, in the view of those suffering, was cheaper money with
which to pay off the debts. If the government bought all the silver
being produced at some figure profitable to the mineowners and then
used it to manufacture coins that, by increasing the money in circulation, would produce a cheapening of the money, then all might be
well. Prices, particularly farm prices, would go up, too, and the net
effect would be that wealth would tend to shift, at least to some
extent, from creditor to debtor. To the sufferers it seemed that the
creditors would merely be giving up some of their superfluity, while
the debtors would be gaining what they needed direly.

On July 14, 1890, the Sherman Silver Purchase Act, with this in
mind, superseded the Bland-Allison Act of twelve years before and

further extended the requirements of government purchase. (Grover Cleveland, now in retirement as an ex-president, publicly objected to this policy as dangerously inflationary and favored a strict adherence to the gold standard—which meant dear money, a prosperous business, and no mercy for those who got into debt.)

Another inflationary act was Harrison's policy of increasing the extent to which pensions were being paid off to Civil War veterans and their dependents—in line with his campaign promises. During the four years of his administration, the number of those receiving pensions rose from 670,000 to 970,000 and the annual disbursement from 80 million dollars to 135 million.

Clearly, if the government was going to pay out pensions and purchase silver, the treasury surplus left behind by Cleveland would soon be exhausted. This was a good thing in the eyes of those who wanted money in circulation, but a bad thing to the more conservative groups.

The one way to restore the surplus was to increase the rate of inflow of money into the treasury and, in the days before income taxes, this meant a rise in the tariff rates. By increasing the price of imported goods in this way, it would make it easier for American manufactured goods to sell, and this, too, pleased businessmen.

The tariff had been raised high at the start of the Civil War, and had gone higher still as the war progressed, because of the government's desperate need for revenue then. By 1864, the average level of import duties had reached 47 percent of the base value of goods imported. After the Civil War, there were moves to bring down the duties to the level that prevailed before the war, but those who profited from high duties and who were influential in the councils of the Republican party resisted. The duties did go down after the war, but only slowly and erratically.

Now, under Harrison, who had promised a high tariff, duties were due to be pushed up. A bill to that effect was sponsored by Congressman William McKinley of Ohio (born in Niles, Ohio, on January 29, 1843). He had served in the Civil War and had reached the rank of major by the war's end. He was one of the most eloquent proponents of a high tariff in Congress and, as a result of his labors, the bill finally became law on October 1, 1890, as the McKinley Tariff Act.

The McKinley Tariff was the highest yet seen in the United States, with the average duty standing at 49 percent. Some agricultural items were included that would benefit the farmers by cutting down foreign competition, but for the most part it was business that would benefit. Included, to be sure, was a reciprocity feature whereby duties on goods imported from a certain country could be lowered if that country would lower duties on goods it imported from the United States.

The McKinley Tariff Act came at a particularly bad time for the west. With the Sioux Indians beaten and the bison herds melting away, homesteaders and herdsman had been flooding into the west, encouraged by the expanding railroads. For ten years, the weather had been good and a kind of euphoria had seized the region. The cattle herds and the farms both multiplied, land prices went sky-high, and everyone was speculating in land, buying chiefly in order to sell at a profit.

Bad years were, however, bound to come. At the start of 1887, blizzards destroyed cattle by the million, and the following summer saw a severe drought that was to open a ten-year cycle of deficient rainfall. Those farmers and ranchers who survived went into debt, and the McKinley tariff raised prices on almost everything they needed to buy without increasing the prices of grain and meat, out of which they hoped to gather the money for their debts and current needs.

Industrially, the nation as a whole was increasing its strength, to be sure. The population stood at 62,622,250 in 1890, just about twice that of Great Britain. In coal production the United States was still second to Great Britain (143 million tons to 184 million tons per year) but in steel it had outstripped Great Britain and was producing more than half as much as all of Europe put together.°

Yet the growing wealth of the northeast did not help the depressed farmers, ranchers, and miners of the west, and this was reflected in the congressional election held on November 4, 1890, just five weeks after the McKinley Tariff became law.

Expecting the worst from it, the voters turned massively against the Republican party and the result was a Democratic landslide in the

---

° In 1888, another facet of ordinary life that we now take very much for granted began. That was the year in which George Eastman (born in Waterville, New York, on July 12, 1854) produced the first self-contained cameras that would snap pictures at the press of a button for later development. It brought photography to the general public.

House of Representatives. Of the 166 Republican seats of the fifty-first Congress, only 88 survived in the fifty-second, while the Democrats held 253.

The Senate, however, elected only one third of its seats and those were voted by the state legislatures that were generally in conservative hands. It remained Republican therefore and, indeed, increased the Republican lead from 2 in 1888 to 8 (47 to 39) in 1890, thanks to the senators from the new Republican states in the northwest.

McKinley remained the hero of the conservatives and in 1891 he was elected governor of Ohio.

THE POPULISTS

The farmers were desperate. They were battling (without quite knowing it) two fundamental changes that technology had brought about. First, the growing mechanization of agriculture had increased farm productivity, so that fewer farmers were required to produce the food of the nation; and the larger, more efficiently mechanized farms did better than the smaller ones. Second, the increasing efficiency of transportation meant that farmers in the United States were competing with farmers all over the world, and the American farmer could no longer count on the national market at any price.

Even granting all that, however, the situation was made worse by sharp railroad practices, by high interest rates on debts, by dear money, and by the manner in which the government leaned in the direction of protecting those actions profitable to manufacturing and commerce.

To the farmers, indignant over their plight, the factors that favored their impoverishment seemed even worse than they were. It became easy to persuade them that there was some conspiracy against them on the part of the financial institutions. "Wall Street" became a villainous phrase to much of the country and stayed so for decades.

In 1866, Oliver Hudson Kelley (born in Boston, Massachusetts, on January 7, 1826), an employee of the Department of Agriculture, while inspecting farming areas for the government, was increasingly impressed by the isolation and helplessness of the individual farmers. He conceived the idea of organizing them into an association that could present a united front to the legislators and force some readjustment of the laws in their favor.

On December 4, 1866, he and six others founded "The Order of the Patrons of Husbandry," which was popularly known as the "Grange" (a word for a farm and the buildings on it, from the same root as the word "grain").

The Grange began as a secret organization, and it spread rapidly through the nation, particularly in the South and the Middle West. Its chief targets were the railroads and the warehouses, the charges of which they felt to be exorbitant. The Grange was able, by 1875, to get several of the western states to pass laws regulating these charges, and the Supreme Court upheld the constitutionality of these laws.

The movement tightened into a pair of "Farmers' Alliances," one in the north and the other in the south. In the southern states, which were strongly rural, the Democratic party was virtually taken over by the Farmers' Alliance. In the Democratic landslide of the 1890 congressional elections, over 50 Congressmen who had been elected by Farmers' Alliance influence were sent to Washington.

To many farmers, however, that was not enough. They wanted a party dedicated to their interests from the start. In 1889, therefore, a new party, supported largely by farmers, was formed in various states and it absorbed the older Greenback party.

On May 19, 1891, it held its first large convention in Cincinnati, Ohio, and called itself the "People's party." It is more commonly known, however, as the "Populist party," which is the Latin version of the name.

On July 2, 1892, it held its first national convention, in Omaha, Nebraska, for the purpose of nominating a candidate for president. The platform of the new party was drawn up by Ignatius Donnelly (born in Philadelphia, Pennsylvania, on November 3, 1831.) He had served as a congressman from Minnesota during the war and was a Republican. When the Republicans turned conservative after the war, Donnelly did not. He joined the Greenback party and then the Populists. (Donnelly is far better known today for the odd books he wrote. He first wrote several volumes tending to show that Atlantis had really existed as an island in the Atlantic and had been violently submerged and that it was the source of Western civilization. Then, in 1888, he went on to compose a particularly elaborate book entitled *The Great Cryptogram* in which he tried to demonstrate that Shakespeare's plays had really been written by Francis Bacon. Both of these theories, as he advanced them, were utterly worthless, but both drew large groups of followers and still do so. Donnelly also wrote several science fiction novels, one of which, *Caesar's Column*, about a futuristic New York City, in which the hero helps lead a revolution against a banking aristocracy, was very popular in its time.)

The Populist party's platform, as written by Donnelly, must have seemed as wild to conservatives as any of the man's books. The platform favored a graduated income tax, for instance, one which took larger and larger percentages as income went up, as a way of reshuffling the money that otherwise tended to accumulate with the wealthy. It also favored the direct election of senators; that is, by popular vote rather than by the vote of state legislatures, as a way of making the Senate more responsive to the public will. It also favored postal savings banks, an eight-hour day for laborers, secret ballot, machinery for recalling corrupt officials and initiating legislative action by direct popular vote, public ownership of the railroads, and so on. Almost all of this has since come to pass, but in 1892, it all seemed as unbearably wild-eyed radicalism to most respectable people.

The Populists also favored unlimited coinage of silver ("free silver"), as a way of expanding the money in circulation and thus favoring debtors. This plank eventually swallowed up everything elso so that free silver came to seem an economic cure-all, which, in actual fact, it was not and could not be.

For president, the Populists nominated James Baird Weaver (born in Dayton, Ohio, on June 12, 1833). He was a Civil War veteran who had ended the war as a colonel. Like Donnelly, he had left the Republican party for the Greenback party, and had served as a Greenback congressman from Iowa for six years. He ran for president under the Greenback label in 1880 and obtained 300,000 votes, the most the party ever gained in a presidential year. Now he would try again as a Populist.

James G. Field of Virginia was nominated for vice-president. He had been a Confederate general in the Civil War, but it was now twenty-seven years since the end of the war, and passions were cooling.

In the previous month, the Republicans and Democrats had also held nominating conventions.

The Republicans met in Minneapolis, Minnesota, on June 7. There was no real question as to whom they would nominate. Harrison was popular with the Republicans and wished to continue in office so he was renominated on the first ballot, though there were some votes for that old warhorse, Blaine, and a few, also, for McKinley.

Vice-President Morton was not renominated, however.* The vice-presidential nomination went instead to Whitelaw Reid of New York (born in Xenia, Ohio, on October 27, 1837). He was the editor-in-chief of the *New York Tribune*, which Greeley had once run, and which was then the most influential newspaper in the United States.

The Democratic National Convention met in Chicago on June 21, 1892, and for the third time in a row nominated Grover Cleveland—and on the first ballot, too. Each time Cleveland ran, however, it was with a different vice-presidential nominee. This time it was with Adlai Ewing Stevenson (born in Christian County, Kentucky, on October 23, 1835). He had served two terms in the House of Representatives in the 1870s and had been assistant postmaster-general in Cleveland's cabinet.

Again, the tariff was the chief issue between the major parties. In 1888, the tariff had been relatively low and the Republicans had offered an increase. Now, in 1892, it was high and the Democrats offered a decrease.

Meanwhile, the Populists thumped the tub for their social reforms and, among the western farmers particularly, they were heard. The Populist party worked against the Republicans for they drew off crucial votes in the west. Indeed, the Populist party polled a little over a million votes, getting 8.6 percent of the whole, a greater vote and a larger percentage than any third party had gained since the Civil War. The Populists won four western states with a total of 22 electoral votes, votes that would surely have gone to the Republicans had the Populists not been in the field.

The Democrats under Cleveland, carried the Solid South and some of the northern states, too, including the big electoral blocs in New

* He survived the disappointment for a long time, dying only on May 16, 1920, on his ninety-sixth birthday.

York and Illinois—since Cleveland's firm stand in favor of the gold standard and fiscal conservatism attracted a number of votes in the commercial centers, votes that might ordinarily have gone Republican.

As a result, Cleveland won handily, with 277 electoral votes to 145 for Harrison. It was the first (and so far, the only) time in American history when two men contested the presidency in each of two successive elections, with victory favoring one man the first time and the other man the second. It was the first time a candidate unseated a sitting president who had earlier unseated *him* as a sitting president.

Cleveland's popular vote was 100,000 above the figure that had lost him the 1888 election, but his percentage of the total vote failed once again to reach an absolute majority, thanks to the Populist vote and to more than a quarter million votes gained by the Prohibitionists.

On March 4, 1893, Grover Cleveland was inaugurated president for the second time. For the first time in the history of the United States, someone was president for two *discontinuous* terms; nor has it happened again since. Cleveland was the twenty-second president in 1885, and then Harrison had become the twenty-third president in 1889. It seemed odd to go backward in the numbering, so Cleveland was considered as the twenty-fourth president in 1893. He is both the twenty-second and the twenty-fourth, the only president to get two numbers.°

Cleveland carried in with him a comfortable Democratic majority in both houses of the fifty-third Congress; 44 to 38 in the Senate and 218 to 127 in the House. There were, in addition, two Populist senators and eleven Populist representatives. Four of the western states had elected Populist governors and there were 354 Populist representatives in the various state legislatures.

° Thus, it is that the present occupant of the White House is the thirty-ninth president even though he is only the thirty-eighth person to have served in the office.

5

CLEVELAND'S SECOND TERM

DEPRESSION AGAIN

Cleveland's victory and reinauguration were the only good news for him, however. The Republican policies of the previous four years were producing their results, and it was Cleveland who had to deal with them. The Republican generosity with pensions depleted the Treasury surplus, and the McKinley Tariff, which was supposed to restore that surplus, had placed its duties so high that imports fell off and total revenue decreased.

As the Treasury surplus sank, at a time when the financial community was convinced that only gold was a safe repository of wealth, everyone tried to trade in what they had for gold. An important financial house in Great Britain failed, and British investors also unloaded their American securities in favor of gold, in order to be safe.

With everyone screaming for gold and with not enough gold in existence to go around, what could one expect? The result was the "Panic of 1893." The stock market crashed on June 27 of that year and by the end of 1893 nearly 500 banks and over 15,000 other businesses had failed.

(Even while this was happening, personal tragedy struck Cleveland. He developed cancer of the mouth, and much of the left side of his upper jaw had to be removed and replaced with an artificial structure of hard rubber. This was kept secret from the American public, for Cleveland felt it would further shake public confidence if it were known and make the panic worse. The truth did not come to light till 1917, years after Cleveland's death. On the lighter side, Cleveland's second legitimate child, a daughter, was born on September 9, 1893, the only presidential child to be born in the White House.)

To Cleveland, to whom gold was almost a fetish as a symbol of financial stability, it seemed that the great villain of the Panic was the Sherman Silver Purchase Act, passed in Harrison's administration, which compelled the government to trade gold for silver each month. Reasoning that repeal of this law would allow the Treasury to conserve gold and rebuild its surplus, and that only thus could prosperity return, Cleveland called Congress into special session.

Congress was Democratic but a good many of the Democratic senators and congressmen were from the rural and mining states and they wanted free silver. They were not on the president's side in this issue, and Cleveland had to fight a grim arm-twisting battle before he finally managed to get the act repealed on November 1, 1893.

This resulted in two things: First, it did *not* restore prosperity, and the American economy remained depressed throughout Cleveland's second term. He therefore received no benefits whatever from his action. Instead, the "Silver-Democrats" blamed him and treated him with the hostility they would naturally accord a traitor.

Second, the Democratic party was split just as it had made good its recovery from the trough of the Civil War and Reconstruction. It was thrown back into a new trough from which it was not fully to recover for forty years.

The split Democratic party, rebelling against Cleveland, would not pass a tariff of the kind he desired and, in 1894, benefiting from the continuing depression, the Republicans regained control of both Houses of the fifty-fourth Congress—45 to 39 in the Senate (with 6 Populists) and 244 to 105 in the House (with 7 Populists.)

When the repeal of the Sherman Silver Act did not result in a rise in the Treasury's gold surplus, the government had to offer to sell interest-bearing bonds for gold, thus building up its gold supply at the expense of having to pay back more than it borrowed—hoping that when the time for repayment would come, returning prosperity would have given it plenty of money with which to carry the load.

The bonds did not sell, however, and, in the end, Cleveland had to turn the job over to private bankers, notably to John Pierpont Morgan (born in Hartford, Connecticut, on April 17, 1837) who, at this time, was the very personification of high finance to the American people. Morgan succeeded in getting the bonds sold and in securing 65 million dollars in gold for the Treasury, but he collected a profit of a million and a half dollars for himself and other bankers in doing so. All this convinced many Democrats (who by now scarcely needed convincing) that Cleveland had sold out to Wall Street.

Those who suffer most in any depression are those who lose their jobs and are fated to either steal, beg, or starve. In the nineteenth century, the government did not feel responsible for these unfortunate citizens. It was left to private charity to take care of them, and private charity is notorious for its inadequate practical donations and its superadequate moral preaching.

In the winter of 1893–1894, the jobless huddled together in pathetic "armies." One of them became famous under the leadership of a "general," Jacob Sechler Coxey (born in Selinsgrove, Pennsylvania, on April 16, 1854). At the time of the depression, he was living in Massillon, Ohio, where he operated a sandstone quarry. It was his idea to gather a large group of unemployed and to march on Washington, where he would petition Congress for help. Congress, he hoped, would then issue $50,000,000 in paper money and establish public works for the unemployed. On May 1, 1894, about 20,000 people, termed "Coxey's Army," were converging on Washington from different directions.

Although the march struck terror into the hearts of the conservatives, who visualized a massive rebellion by the scum of the earth, it was a fiasco. Only some 600 men persisted through the length of the march to reach Washington and march down Pennsylvania Avenue. Then, when Coxey tried to make a speech from the steps of the Capitol, he was arrested for trespassing and that was about all it came to.* Coxey lived on for more than a half-century, dying in Massillon, Ohio, on May 18, 1951, at the age of ninety-seven.

A more serious weapon on the part of those laborers who still had their jobs (but at rock-bottom wages and under the constant threat of dismissal) was the strike. In the year 1894, some 750,000 workers went on strike and, in almost every case, the government, in the name of law and order, interfered as a strike-breaking instrument.

The most serious strike began in Chicago, where George Pullman had built an empire on the basis of his sleeping-cars. Pullman and the stockholders reaped huge profits from the business, but the laborers did not and, in 1894, Pullman preserved the profits of his stockholders by cutting the wages of his workers. He housed them in a "model village" for which he charged rent, and the rent was *not* decreased. The result was that the cut wages just barely covered the rent with virtually nothing left over for such nonessentials as food. When the laborers protested, Pullman refused to discuss the matter.

The strike began on May 10, 1894, and it was supported by the American Railway Union under the leadership of Eugene Victor Debs (born in Terre Haute, Indiana, on November 5, 1855). Eventually a quarter of a million railroad employees in twenty-seven states and territories participated, and rail transportation was paralyzed throughout the north.

Pullman remained intransigent and it was clearly necessary for the government to do something. Cleveland might have intervened on the side of arbitration or he might have pushed the idea of encouraging the two parties to discuss the issues — but that was unthinkable in those days. On the pretext of guarding the delivery of the mails, Cleveland prepared to send a regiment of army troops into Chicago after the federal courts had issued injunctions against the strike, thus making its continuance illegal.

The governor of Illinois at the time was John Peter Altgeld, who had been born in Germany in 1847. He had been brought to the United States when he was one year old by parents fleeing the repressions that followed the abortive revolution of 1848. He was an honest man

* Even as late as the 1920s, I remember hearing the phrase, "the whole Coxey army" to refer to a huge mob of people. Neither I, nor the boy using the phrase, had any idea who or what "Coxey" was.

who, on June 26, 1893, convinced that the Haymarket anarchists were innocent and had not received a fair trial, pardoned the three survivors. But honesty is not often a marketable commodity in politics, and the reaction to this deed was such that it was clear he would never be elected to public office again—and he wasn't.

But he was still governor in the summer of 1894 and he protested to Cleveland against the use of the army troops, insisting that Illinois state troopers were sufficient for the purpose of maintaining law and order. Cleveland did not listen but followed, instead, the advice of his attorney-general, Richard Olney (born in Oxford, Massachusetts, on September 15, 1835), who had been a railroad lawyer and who was on the board of directors of one of the railroads that had been struck so that he was scarcely impartial in the matter. Cleveland sent 14,000 troops into Chicago on July 3, 1894, and more troops to other places.

The strike that, until then, had been reasonably peaceful, now turned violent and in the days that followed, thirty-four strikers were killed. But the strike was broken, the Railway Union shattered, the workers sent back to their jobs on a bare subsistence basis and, on December 14, 1894, Debs went to jail for half a year.

Debs, who had been quite conservative to begin with, turned to socialism. Socialism, as a political force, had originated in February, 1848, when two Germans, Karl Marx and Friedrich Engels, published the goals of such a movement for the public and common ownership of the means of production and distribution in *The Communist Manifesto.*

Socialism had established itself in Germany in the 1860s, in France and Great Britain in the 1870s. In the United States, it was looked upon by the capitalists (those who favored the private ownership of the means of production and distribution) as a kind of foreign aberration, and it was only after the the great strikes of the 1890s that it took some hold on this side of the ocean.

Socialism was never to become very powerful in the United States in terms of the numbers of people won over to its tenets. Its ideas, however, were always to hound those who were in control of the American government and economy and, in time, many of them were adopted.

One bright spot of the period was the addition of yet another state to the Union. Utah had been the home of the Mormons who had fled there in 1847, when it was still Spanish territory, to escape religious persecution in Illinois. The United States took over the region in 1848, after the Mexican War, and in 1850, it was constituted as the Utah Territory (from the Ute tribe of Indians).

Since then, it had qualified as a state in terms of population and development but statehood was steadily denied because the Mormon Church permitted polygamy (marriage of a man to more than one woman), and this horrified Americans generally.

In 1890, after many less qualified territories had become states, the Mormon Church disavowed polygamy, and the wheels of statehood finally began to turn. On January 4, 1896, Utah entered the Union as the forty-fifth State.

And the United States continued to advance technologically. In April 1893, Henry Ford (born in Greenfield, Michigan, on July 30, 1863) built his first automobile. Others had built automobiles before him but it was Ford who, over the next fifteen years, was to work out the concept of the assembly line and mass production. With that, the United States and, eventually, the world, would enter the automobile age.

On a lesser scale, the first use of an electric chair for execution took place in Auburn, New York, on August 6, 1890. Technology reached into even that corner of social activity.

THE PACIFIC ISLANDS

During the turmoil of the 1890s, the United States was beginning to look outward again.

Since the Civil War, the United States had been preoccupied with filling its internal spaces, with defeating the Indians, with developing its technology. Even as the nineteenth century approached its end, the territory of the United States was still confined entirely to the North American continent, except for the central Pacific flyspeck of the Midway Islands.

In those same decades, however, the European nations were expanding overseas in Asia, Africa, and the Pacific, and it was somehow taken for granted that it was right for them to do this because the European white man was inherently superior to people of darker skins and should take over as a matter of course. (When one nation extended its rule over alien peoples it formed an "empire," from the Latin, "imperium," and those who believed in the rightness of doing so are called "imperialists.")

This view seemed to be made "scientific" by the works of the English sociologist Herbert Spencer, who applied the views of evolution, first elaborated by the English naturalist Charles Robert Darwin, in 1859, to society. Where Darwin had talked about the changes in living species, changes that took place slowly over millions of years, and where Darwin produced enormous quantities of evidence in favor of his views, Spencer talked about changes in society that supposedly took place over mere centuries and presented very little real evidence for his theories.

Spencer coined the phrase "survival of the fittest" and in 1884 argued, for instance, that people who were unemployable or burdens on society should be allowed to die rather than be made objects of help and charity. To do this, apparently, would weed out unfit individuals and strengthen the race.

It was a horrible philosophy that could be used to justify the worst impulses of human beings. A conquering nation could destroy its enemy (as the Americans destroyed the Indians) because it was "more fit," and it could prove it was "more fit" because it destroyed its enemy.

Indeed, the exploitation of the rest of humanity by white Europeans could be made to seem a noble gesture—as the superior Whites reached out to help the inferiors on other continents by employing them as servants and allowing them to live on scraps. In 1899, the English poet, Rudyard Kipling, was to refer to it as "the white man's burden."

There were many in the United States who were affected by the Spenserian philosophy and who ached to have the United States help spread the blessings of imperialism, especially since the "end of the frontier" in 1890 seemed to leave American expansive energies with little to do at home.

The United States, however, had allowed its military forces to deteriorate since the Civil War (safe as it was behind the ramparts of two oceans, defended by a reasonably friendly British fleet), so that it could barely defeat the disorganized Indians and could not interfere effectively in the third-class squabbles in Latin America. It could scarcely compete, therefore, with Great Britain and France on the Old World continents.

There was the broad Pacific Ocean, however, littered with thousands of islands, which, at this time, were being swept up by the European powers. The United States, building up its fleet again, realized that some of them would, like the Midway Islands, come in handy as coaling stations and harbors for its ships. What is more, there was the desire to achieve status on a par with the European "great powers," and this meant, for one thing, the acquisition of colonies in order to show how "fit for survival" the United States was.

And even in the 1890s, not all the islands were clearly occupied. There was Samoa, for instance, a group of fourteen islands about 8200 kilometers southwest of Los Angeles. The total area of the islands is about 3000 square kilometers, or just a bit more than that of Rhode Island. Most of this area is included in the two large islands of what is now called Western Samoa. The small islands of Eastern Samoa include, as their largest, Tutuila, which is about 135 square kilometers, or some two and a half times as large as Manhattan Island (to which it is rather similar in shape). In the middle of this small island is a magnificent harbor on the shores of which the village of Pago Pago existed.

The first European to visit Samoa was the Dutch explorer, Jacob Roggeveen, in 1722. The first American was the explorer Charles Wilkes in 1839, who reported on the harbor. After Wilkes's visit, British and Germans both moved in, with the Germans in the lead. By 1870, most of the Samoan land was owned by Germans. In 1872, however, the United States signed a treaty with the native ruler of Pago Pago that gave the Americans exclusive control of the harbor as a coaling station.

Naturally, both the British and Germans took over other parts of the Samoan coastline for coaling stations for their own ships and, for a few years, Samoa was run by the three nations working together. It was not a smooth relationship, however, as the representatives of each of the nations intrigued against the other two, and all tried to use the Samoans themselves as pawns.

Germany was united as the German Empire under King Wilhelm I of Prussia, who became the German Emperor, but this happened only in 1871. Through this union, Germany became the most powerful military nation in the world—at least on land—but it had arrived too late for the imperial banquet overseas. When the time came for it to demonstrate that it, too, was "fit" enough to have colonies, most of the exploitable areas of the world had been parceled out by Great Britain and France, with minor regions to Portugal, the Netherlands, Italy, and even Belgium. There seemed little room for Germany and she was all the more aggressive in those areas that still remained open to her.

One of the open areas was Samoa and it was clear that Germany intended to take over the entire group of islands. Great Britain, rich in colonial areas, was ready to agree to that in return for concessions elsewhere among the Pacific Islands. The United States, however, equally a latecomer and hungry, was *not* ready to make concessions.

The Germans, moving aggressively, deported the Samoan king in 1888 and placed a puppet ruler over the islanders, one subservient to themselves. Some of the Samoans rebelled and were supported by the United States. Tempers grew high and in Apia, a port on the northern coast of one of the large islands, seven hostile warships gathered in early 1889, three German, three American, and one British.

There might have been a full-fledged naval battle had not nature taken a hand. On March 16, 1889, a hurricane struck the island and only the British ship escaped. The German and American ships were all sunk or beached with much loss of life. That rather cooled the combatants and on June 14, all agreed to a return to the three-nation control, and the old king was restored to the throne. On the whole, it was a victory for the United States.

In the course of this dispute it was the Republicans, for the most part, who took up a bellicose, imperialist stance, favoring the establishment of an American colonial empire. The Democrats, for the most part, feared the expense and the danger of entanglements and war. They preferred dealing with the nation's own ample continental territory and were "anti-imperialists."

The issue of imperialism versus anti-imperialism showed up even more sharply in connection with the Hawaiian Islands in the mid-Pacific some 3400 kilometers southwest of Los Angeles, and the same distance north of Samoa. Eight of the Hawaiian Islands are sizable, the largest being Hawaii itself with an area of 10,500 square kilometers, about twice the size of the state of Delaware. All eight islands together have an area of 16,500 square kilometers, and are a little larger, all told, than the state of Connecticut.

On the third largest island, Oahu, which is 1550 square kilometers in area (about twice the size of the five boroughs of New York City), there is a magnificent harbor, on the shores of which is the city of Honolulu.

The first human beings to reach Hawaii were Polynesians who in the first millennium A.D. had paddled across the wide Pacific in their canoes, completing the most remarkable voyages ever made without benefit of a magnetic compass. They reached the Hawaiian islands about A.D. 400 and there, for thirteen centuries, they lived in their balmy climate untouched by the outside world except for occasional contacts with other Pacific islanders.

This came to an end on January 18, 1778, when the English explorer, Captain James Cook, landed on the islands. He named them the Sandwich Islands after the Earl of Sandwich who happened at that time to be First Lord of the Admiralty. Captain Cook returned the next year and, in the course of a squabble between the sailors and the Hawaiians, Cook was killed on February 14, 1779 and, presumably, eaten.

The islands were, at that time, divided under a number of chiefs, but one of them, only twenty years old at the time of Cook's arrival, gradually beat all the rest and, by 1809, had united all the islands under his rule as Kamehameha I. Through the rest of the nineteenth century, the Hawaiian Islands remained a kingdom under the descendants of Kamehameha.

Various nations were interested early in the Hawaiian Islands as a stopping place on trading journeys to the Far East, and the United States was not behindhand. American missionaries arrived in the islands in 1820 and converted large numbers of the Hawaiians to the Protestant version of Christianity.

France and Great Britain were interested in the Hawaiian Islands, and the United States labored to keep either from annexing the land. As early as the 1850s, at a time when the United States had just expanded its control to the Pacific Ocean, there were already strong pressures for American annexation of the islands. This was firmly resisted by the Hawaiian king, Kamehameha IV, and then came the American Civil War and American attention turned elsewhere for a time.

After the Civil War, the pressure began to increase again and on January 30, 1875, a reciprocity treaty with the United States was signed in which Hawaiian sugar was allowed to enter the United States without duty and the Hawaiians agreed to cede no land to a third power. In 1887, the treaty was extended, and the United States gained the right to use Honolulu's harbor as a naval station. (The harbor was called Pearl Harbor because of the pearl oysters found there.)

The dominance of the Americans grew steadily more marked in the Hawaiian Islands and, among the Hawaiians, there were many who resented this. In 1891, Lydia Liliuokalani (born in Honolulu on September 2, 1838) came to the throne and initiated a strong Hawaiian reaction against the Americans. On January 14, 1893, she attempted to replace the constitution that had been devised by the American settlers for their own protection with one that would give her autocratic powers and make the Hawaiians a dominant force in what were, after all, their islands.

The Americans were ready. Under the leadership of Sanford Ballard Dole (born in Honolulu on April 23, 1844) they demanded American protection against what they described as a threat to their lives and property. The American minister in Honolulu, John Leavitt Stevens (born in 1820) was an ardent imperialist, and he acted at once, having over 150 armed men from the cruiser *Boston* land in Honolulu.

Liliuokalani, realizing she could not resist the United States in a clash of arms, at once retreated from her position, but it was too late. Dole declared her deposed and set up a Republic of Hawaii under his own leadership. Stevens promptly recognized the Republic as the legal government of the islands.

At once, a move started for the annexation of the islands by the United States. Had Harrison won the election of 1892, that would undoubtedly have come to pass. As it was, the treaty of annexation was ready, but it had not yet been acted on when Cleveland was inaugurated for his second term.

Cleveland, an anti-imperialist, withdrew the treaty, fired Stevens, and tried to restore Liliuokalani. Dole, however, refused to allow the restoration, and Cleveland was not in a position to use force against an American on behalf of a non-American, when much of the nation, if not most of it, sympathized strongly with Dole.

Hawaii remained a republic, its government being established officially on July 4, 1894. The United States recognized it on August 8, and Dole then settled down to wait until the political shuffles in the United States would allow annexation.*

VENEZUELA AND CUBA

The flexing of American muscles in the Pacific fed American belligerency in the American continents.

In 1823, the United States had set forth the Monroe Doctrine in which she stated that European nations would no longer be permitted to interfere with the internal affairs of nations on the American continent. For many years afterward, the United States had not been in a position to enforce that policy but there had been few occasions when really important violations had taken place. The European nations were busy elsewhere and they were content (Great Britain, particularly) with establishing economic domination of the region — something the doctrine did not prohibit.

The grossest violation of the Monroe Doctrine had been France's occupation of Mexico during the years when the United States was occupied with the Civil War. When, after the war was over, the United States forced France out, that triumph made the Monroe Doctrine virtually holy to Americans. In some ways, the United States began to act as though Latin America were part of an American Empire, something the Latin Americans tended to resent bitterly.

The only portion of South America that was under the control of European powers in the latter part of the nineteenth century was Guiana, on the north-central coast of the continent. It was originally

*Liliuokalani withdrew from public life and died on November 11, 1917, at the age of 79. She is best known today as the composer, in 1898, of the song "Aloha Oe."

Dutch, but had come to be divided into three portions. The westernmost part was controlled by the British since 1814, and the eastern by the French. Only the central portion remained Dutch.

The western portion, British Guiana, was the largest, with an area of 215,000 square kilometers (about the size of Utah). The Monroe Doctrine promised no interference on the part of the United States as far as European areas at the time were concerned, so British Guiana remained British.[*]

West of British Guiana was the nation of Venezuela that had gained its independence from Spain in 1811. The boundary between the two had never been settled. In 1841, a British geographer had marked off a boundary line that placed the northwesternmost point of British Guiana at the mouth of the Orinoco River, Venezuela's major waterway. Venezuela protested, but since the area was jungle country inhabited only by native tribes, it didn't seem worth making a fuss over.

As the years passed, however, settlers infiltrated the area, and in 1877, there came rumors of gold finds there. Venezuela grew restless over the possibility that Great Britain might hold the mouth of the Orinoco and dominate the nation in that fashion. Venezuela therefore laid claims to most of the British Guiana territory, hoping to settle for less and still have a good deal, while Great Britain countered with equally inflated claims.

In 1887, Venezuela and Great Britain broke off diplomatic relations and Venezuela, realizing it could do nothing on its own, carried the plea to the United States, pointing out that Great Britain was violating the Monroe Doctrine by trying to extend its rule over an independent Latin American nation. The United States therefore tried to act as arbitrator in the dispute, but Great Britain steadily refused the American offer—something that irritated Americans.

By the time Cleveland became president the second time, in 1893, the situation was beginning to heat up. Wildly anti-British pamphlets were appearing in the United States, and both houses of Congress passed unanimous resolutions urging Great Britain to submit to arbitration. Cleveland kept cool, however, and when Great Britain landed armed men in a Nicaraguan city to collect compensation for

[*] It did so until 1966, when it was granted its independence under the name of Guyana.

action against British nationals the year before, Cleveland did nothing about that either, on the ground that the occupation was temporary.

Cleveland began to be assaulted by the press on all sides as being pusillanimous and being afraid to react to British arrogance. The Democratic party began to fear disaster and Cleveland was urged from all sides to do something about Venezuela. Reluctantly, he asked his secretary of state, Walter Quintin Gresham (born in Harrison County, Indiana, on May 17, 1832), to prepare a note on the subject. What Gresham might have done, no one knows, for he died almost immediately afterward, on May 28, 1895. In his place, Cleveland appointed Richard Olney, the attorney-general who had been instrumental in using the courts and the army to break the Pullman strike. Now he had a chance to use similar overbearing tactics in the field of foreign affairs.

Olney prepared a note which, on July 20, 1895, he sent to the American ambassador in London for forwarding to the British government. In it, he accused Great Britain of violating the Monroe Doctrine, which he declared part of "American public law." That violation, he said, justified American intervention and he added, "Today the United States is practically sovereign on this continent, and its fiat is law upon the subjects to which it confines its interposition." Moreover, he made it clear that the United States did not fear war because "its infinite resources combined with its isolated position render it master of the situation and practically invulnerable as against all other powers." He virtually ordered the British to reply before Congress opened its next session in December.

The language was violent and pleased American imperialists no end, but Great Britain could scarcely accept it without humiliation. The British deliberately did not answer till after Congress met, and when they did so, they did not retreat an inch. In fact, they specifically maintained that the Monroe Doctrine had no validity in international law and was merely a one-sided American statement.

Cleveland and Olney were infuriated, and Cleveland asked for authority to establish an independent boundary commission that would settle the dispute and for power to enforce the decisions of that commission. Congress granted Cleveland the authority and, by and large, the public applauded. It began to look very much like war.

But then events took an unexpected turn. In South Africa there was increasing friction between the British and the Boer Republics north of the British holdings at the southern tip of the continent. On December 29, 1895, an over-enthusiastic Britisher led a raid into Boer territory. It was defeated, and the new German Kaiser, the young and bellicose Wilhelm II, sent a telegram of congratulations to the Boers.

Quite suddenly, Great Britain realized that it was Germany that was the great danger. A war with the United States, however it ended, over a bit of jungle territory on the other side of the world, would represent a chance for Germany and the United States to combine against Great Britain. Without warning, British intransigence vanished into thin air, and she began smiling and talking about arbitration.

An arbitration tribunal was set up, and British wisdom in the new course of action was soon evident. The arbitration decision handed the British about 90 percent of the territory that was in dispute. It followed almost exactly the line marked off in 1841, but made a minor correction in favor of Venezuela in the south, and (quite important) drew the line back from the Orinoco River in the north. Venezuela was forced to be content.

Both Great Britain and the United States had won. Great Britain had most of the territory, and the United States had forced the recognition of the Monroe Doctrine. In addition, the precedent of the *Alabama* claims was upheld. In any dispute between Great Britain and the United States, the answer was arbitration, not war.

As a matter of fact, the Venezuela boundary dispute was important in a way neither nation could foresee. It was the last dispute between them that carried with it the threat of war. A century and a quarter of periodic alarms (including two actual wars) came to an end, and in the twentieth century, the United States was to join with Great Britain against mutual enemies on a number of occasions.

But if the Venezuelan affair ended happily, that was not to say that the United States did not have other foreign problems, and closer to home, too. As the century drew to a close, Spain was still master of Cuba. Now, however, a new Cuban rebellion broke out on February 24, 1895, just as the Venezuelan boundary dispute was heating up, and it was worse than the one that had taken place in Grant's administration.

The cause of the new rebellion was twofold. In the first place, the corrupt and inefficient rule of Spain rested heavily on the Cubans. In the second place, the United States controlled Cuba economically, buying almost all its sugar and owning almost all its important properties—and this meant that the American depression of the 1890s destroyed Cuban prosperity as well.

Both the Spaniards and the Cubans fought with abandon. The Spaniards sent in some 200,000 troops under General Valeriano Weyler who was intent on crushing the rebellion by brutal action. He established concentration camps for people of both sexes and all ages, gathering them together almost indiscriminately and treating them with heartless cruelty.

As for the Cuban rebels, their only hope in the long run was American intervention and with that in mind, they deliberately set about destroying sugar plantations and mills in which Americans had invested heavily. They felt the Americans would come in to save their property.

Many Americans were willing. Anti-Spanish feeling ran high, and this was encouraged by a new development in journalism.

The man behind it was William Randolph Hearst (born in San Francisco, California, on April 29, 1863), who was the son of a gold mineowner who had served a term as a senator from California. The younger Hearst grew interested in journalism and cut his teeth on a paper his father had bought for him in 1880, the *San Francisco Examiner*. In 1895, Hearst bought the *New York Morning Journal* and began to compete with the older established *New York World* of Joseph Pulitzer (born in Hungary on April 10, 1847).

The fight between the newspapers was wild and relentless. The price of each paper was reduced to one cent and each competed for the reader's attention in every possible way. Hearst used sensational articles, illustrations, magazine sections, huge headlines, and strong attention to crime and pseudoscience to gain readers. Color printing was coming in, and in 1896 colored comic strips were just being established. Yellow was prominent in the first such comic strip, "The Yellow Kid," so that the new way in which Hearst ran his paper came to be called "yellow journalism."

Hearst was extreme in foreign policy and was a reckless imperialist. He called for war against Great Britain in connection with Venezuela, and he called for war against Spain in connection with Cuba. General Weyler's actions were made to order for the kind of trashy material

Hearst would publish — cheerfully adding fiction if the truth didn't suit him well enough.

Cleveland, however, held back and refused to allow the United States to become involved, so that the Cuban question, like the Hawaiian question, had to wait for a new election.

WILLIAM JENNINGS BRYAN

That election seemed to be in the bag for the Republicans. The continuing hard times would certainly have put the Democrats out of business, since the party in power is always blamed for any downtrend in the economy. If that wasn't enough of a handicap for the Democrats, the party had split into "Gold" and "Silver" factions that were at violent war with each other. In fact, there was some speculation that the Democratic party was disintegrating and that the Populist party would become the major party in opposition to the Republicans.

Under those circumstances, the Republicans could afford to nominate someone who was absolutely safe, who would go right down the line for the gold standard, and who could be counted on to do what was right for business. Cleveland hadn't been bad, from the Republican viewpoint, in those respects, but the party wanted someone who could be counted upon to be imperialist as well.

The Ohio politician Marcus Alonzo Hanna (born in New Lisbon, Ohio, on September 24, 1837) thought he knew exactly the man. Since 1890, he had been working with William McKinley of tariff fame, a fellow Ohioan he had been carefully grooming for the presidency. There were stronger men the Republican party, but a certain weakness was desirable in the president who might in that way be counted upon to be swayed in the direction of doing what was right for commercial profits.

When the Republican National Convention met in St. Louis, Missouri, on June 16, 1896, Hanna did such clever wheeling and dealing with the delegates that McKinley was chosen on the first ballot. For vice-president, a close friend of McKinley, Garret Augustus Hobart (born in Long Branch, New Jersey, on June 3, 1844), was nominated.

On July 7, the Democrats met in turmoil. The Silver Democrats were clearly in charge, and Cleveland the Gold Democrat was an outcast in his own party. The convention would not even accept a routine resolution commending him for his accomplishments.

Instead, the majority of the delegates began to rally round "free silver" as the battlecry (the coining of silver in unlimited amounts), and loud were the speeches against the money-powers of the northeast—against Wall Street and the big cities, against the wealthy, the merchants, the traders.

Bland of the Bland-Allison Act was the admitted leader of the Silver Democrats, and it was expected he would be nominated. However, there was a new young face on the political scene, William Jennings Bryan of Nebraska (born in Salem, Illinois, on March 19, 1860). He had served as a congressman from 1890 to 1894 and since then he had edited the *Omaha World-Herald*.

On July 8, William Jennings Bryan delivered a speech that concluded the debate on the platform. It was a carefully worked-out speech that Bryan had rehearsed until it was absolutely perfect for the occasion. It was given in a voice that, seemingly without effort, could be heard booming out in glorious organ tones through the large auditorium (and these were the days before public address systems). No one had heard such a voice since the great days of Daniel Webster, a half-century before.

Carefully, Bryan played his audience as he boosted silver and agrarianism till he reached the crescendo of his final sentence of warning to the gold-standard businessmen: "You shall not press down upon the brow of labor this crown of thorns, you shall not crucify mankind upon a cross of gold." And the audience simply went mad.

This "cross-of-gold speech" was easily the most effective speech ever given at any nominating convention before or since. Before the speech, no one, no one at all (except perhaps Bryan, who knew what he was planning) considered Bryan for the nomination. For one reason he was too young—only 36—and no one that age, only one year above the minimum for a president, had ever been nominated by a major party before.

Suddenly, however, he was the "Boy Orator of the Platte" (the Platte River runs across Nebraska into the Missouri), and sentiment for him grew wildly. By the fifth ballot, he had passed beyond the necessary two thirds of the delegate votes and was nominated. Bland never knew what hit him.

To balance the ticket, the Democrats nominated an eastern banker for vice-president, one who managed to support silver. He was Arthur Sewall (born in Bath, Maine, November 25, 1835).

The Gold Democrats who supported Cleveland could not stomach Bryan. They seceded and nominated candidates of their own, but this, as it turned out, had no influence on the race.

As for the Populists, who had been hopefully expecting to take over the role of the major party, the nomination of Bryan and the complete conversion of the Democrats to the cause of silver had utterly changed the situation. With their thunder stolen, the Populists found themselves without a cause. They met in St. Louis on July 22 and dispiritedly accepted Bryan as their candidate also, but nominated Thomas Edward Watson (born in Columbia County, Georgia, on September 5, 1856) for vice-president, for they wouldn't have a banker, however silvery his views might be.

But it didn't help. The Populists, after their promising run in 1892, were dying. They continued to nominate candidates over the next dozen years but with a continually dwindling pull on the electorate. Nevertheless, the Populist party had accomplished its purpose, since one reason for its death was that its issues were gradually taken over by the major parties and eventually became an accepted part of the American scene.

The campaign of 1896 was a study in contrasts. Bryan was the first presidential candidate in the nation's history to take full advantage of the advance of technology in conducting his campaign. He used the railroads to take his case to all parts of the nation—something that has since become standard. He traveled 13,000 miles, making hundreds of speeches, and rousing great enthusiasm everywhere.

The Republicans were taken aback. They had expected no trouble in winning, but the Bryan phenomenon frightened them. Hanna knew better than to try to pitch his colorless man against the orator-prodigy of the age, so he worked in other ways. He kept McKinley at home and arranged to have people brought to him in a "front-porch campaign." The railroads, sympathetic to McKinley, set up tours to his home at prices so low that someone quipped that it was cheaper to visit McKinley than to stay at home.

Furthermore, Hanna initiated the modern hard-sell method of collecting enormous campaign contributions from frightened businessmen. He used part of these contributions to finance the Gold-Democrat campaign, which he hoped would siphon votes away from Bryan.

Republican propaganda pictured Bryan as a wild anarchist with every vice imaginable (which was ludicrous really, because except for his views on silver, Bryan was as proper and conservative a churchgoer as anyone could imagine). There were also scare tactics, as when businessmen told their employees that the factory would be shut down and all of them would be fired if Bryan won.

So on November 3, 1896, when the election was held, Bryan's travels came to naught and stay-at-home McKinley won. Bryan got the Solid South and ten of the states west of the Mississippi, but did not carry a single industrial state. McKinley carried the Northeast and the Midwest with their heavy electoral blocs and won by the handy electoral majority of 271 to 176.

In the popular vote, McKinley won with 7,100,000 votes compared to Bryan's 6,500,000. McKinley gained 51 percent of the total vote, the first presidential candidate to get an actual majority since Tilden in 1876, and the first winning candidate to do so since Grant in 1872.

Both houses of the fifty-fifth Congress were safely Republican, by 47 to 34 in the Senate and by 204 to 113 in the House, with a small number of third-party members in each body.

6

IMPERIALISM TRIUMPHANT

THE TURN OF THE CENTURY

McKinley was inaugurated the twenty-fifth president of the United States on March 4, 1897, and at once set about fulfilling the Republican program. He called Congress into special session to consider the tariff, which had declined slightly during Cleveland's second administration.

Under the sponsorship of Representative Nelson Dingley of Maine (born in Durham, Maine, on February 15, 1832), the Dingley Tariff became law on July 24, 1897. The duties were raised beyond that of the McKinley Tariff to a record high average of 57 percent. It did continue to provide for reciprocal lowering of tariffs for any nation that would lower tariffs on American goods.

In addition, McKinley labored to end the question of free silver once and for all by placing the United States, legally and unquestionably, on the gold standard. Gold would then be the only basic method of measuring values, and all currency of any other kind must be redeemable, at request, in gold. This would sharply limit the amount of money it was safe to have in circulation and that would prevent inflation. These measures would be at the expense of the debtors and the poor, generally, but under the fashionable Spenserian philosophy of those days, one did not worry about these unfit sections of society.

The United States went on the gold standard officially on March 14, 1900, but by that time the question of free silver had, in any case, died forever. (When the time came for the United States to go off the gold standard again, a third of a century later, the whole concept of finance had changed and questions of gold and silver had become irrelevant.)

What happened to change matters was that the gold supply of the world suddenly, and unexpectedly, increased sharply. In 1886, gold had been discovered in South Africa and it turned out to be the richest source of that metal the world had ever seen. To this day, two thirds of all the gold produced in the world is produced in South Africa.

In 1896, gold was discovered closer to home, along the Klondike River, a tributary of the Yukon. The strike was in northwestern Canada near the Alaskan frontier, and the gold fever struck the United States as it had not done since the discoveries in California a half-century earlier. Within three years, some thirty to sixty thousand people flocked into that forbidding Arctic area, and several tens of thousands of others died on the way. The Canadian town of Dawson, which had contained a few houses at the time of the discovery, became a city of 20,000 in almost no time.

The strike focussed attention on Alaska, where some gold had been found even before the rich strike in the Klondike, which, for the first time, came to be looked on as something more than a frigid, icy waste. It was at this time that an American explorer, William A. Dickey, found a particular mountain peak in southcentral Alaska to be higher than any other then known in North America—nor has any higher mountain been discovered since. It is 6194 meters high, and Dickey named it Mount McKinley, for the Republican nominee.

The gold supply in the Klondike didn't last long. Most of it was taken out of the earth in about ten years, so that it could in no way compare with the more durable discovery in South Africa. Still, something like a hundred million dollars worth of gold was extracted in a decade and, in the peak year of 1900, $22 million in gold was added to the world supply by the Klondike mines.

When it was all over the area subsided, and Dawson now has a population of but a few hundred. Yet the Klondike is not utterly dry. It still produces a couple of million dollars worth of gold a year, extracted by methods more sophisticated than those available to the miners who worked there at the turn of the century.

The short, glamorous life of the Klondike strike was pinned down on the printed page forever by the stories of Jack London (born in San Francisco, California, on January 12, 1876). He had been one of the unemployed in the depression of the 1890s, and the experience had turned him into a militant socialist.

He had gone to the Klondike in 1897, but had gained no wealth in the process. His own particular gold mine came (and went, as fast as it came) with the books he wrote about the gold rush after he returned. His first book, *Son of the Wolf*, was published in 1900 and his best received, *The Call of the Wild*, in 1903. In 1907, he published *The Iron Heel*, a picture of governmental tyranny closely anticipating the type of fascism that arose, in Germany, in particular, a quarter-century later. Success was as painful to him as failure had been, and he died of an overdose of drugs, possibly a suicide, on November 22, 1916.

The Klondike also lives on in the popular verses of the Anglo-Canadian poet, Robert William Service (born in England, on January 16, 1874). He had been stationed in the Yukon for eight years as an employee of a Canadian bank, and his poems, such as "The Shooting of Dan McGrew" and "The Cremation of Sam McGee," might not be great poetry, but they had a swing to them that caught the public fancy.

The steep increase in world gold production meant that gold flooded into the American Treasury, which no longer had any problem in maintaining the kind of reserve required to back the currency. Farm prices rose, prosperity returned, radicalism declined, and everyone lost interest in the Wall Street ogre except for a few idealists, who found themselves isolated.

Thus, when the midterm congressional elections of 1898 came, the usual swing to the opposition in the House did not take place. The Republicans lost a few seats but the fifty-sixth Congress saw the

House of Representatives still firmly Republican, 185 to 163. In the Senate, the Republicans actually gained and stood 53 to 36.

The world of finance flourished as never before. On February 25, 1901, J. Pierpont Morgan launched United States Steel, the first corporation to do business in excess of a billion dollars a year. In general, the world of business was concentrated into fewer and larger concerns. At no time were businessmen as rich, happy, contented, and powerful as in the golden times of President McKinley.

As an added sign of bigness, New York City, which had been confined to the island of Manhattan since its founding nearly three centuries before, now absorbed nearby sections in Long Island, Staten Island, and the continental area to the north. On January 1, 1898, it became "Greater New York" with five boroughs and a population of 3,500,000. It was far and away the largest city in the United States at the time (and although its boundaries haven't changed since, its population has doubled). Indeed, next to London, New York was now the largest city in the world.

By 1900, the population of the United States had reached 75,994,-575, and, thanks to the operation of the Golden Door, over 10,000,000 of them were immigrants (nearly 3,700,000 had entered between 1890 and 1900) and many millions more were the sons and daughters of immigrants. In fact, the order of the most populous nations became China, India, Russia, and the United States, and that order has remained ever since.

There were nearly 14,000 automobiles on American roads in 1900 and, in coal, steel, and oil production the United States now led the world. There was no question but that by the turn of the century the United States had become the most technologically advanced, and therefore potentially the strongest, nation in the world.

The potential supremacy of the United States was not generally recognized in Europe for the following reasons: In the first place, it was hard to shake myth. Europe had long thought of the United States as large, but as heterogeneous, disorganized, and essentially barba- rous—a kind of white man's China that could make a brave show but could not stand before the smaller and more efficient European powers.

Second, the United States was seen as militarily weak. As far as its army was concerned, this was so, but the American fleet had been building up since the early 1870s. That fleet was still far behind Great Britain and France and was only on a par with the now-beginning-to-grow naval strength of Germany, but it was capable of astonishing feats. That this was so, and that the United States was a world power, became evident before the century turned.

"REMEMBER THE *MAINE!*"

McKinley, unlike Cleveland and Bryan, was an imperialist and as such had the support of the Republican party in general. The jobs that Cleveland had left unfinished, McKinley now mopped up.

Samoa, which had been placed under an uneasy three-nation control in 1889, fell apart again after the death of its king in 1898. Once again, the Germans tried to set up a puppet king, but by now Great Britain was so much at enmity with Germany that it did not try to keep the peace. Instead, it joined the United States in opposing Germany and on November 14, 1899, signed a treaty with Germany that divided Samoa into two parts. Only the two large western islands of West Samoa were to become German outright. America joined the treaty on December 2, and the numerous small islands to the east, including the harbor of Pago Pago, became an American colony on February 16, 1900.° Great Britain reserved nothing to herself, content to leave the United States and Germany as neighbors, and possibly enemies.

As for Hawaii, soon after McKinley's inauguration, a treaty of annexation was signed with the United States and, on August 12, 1898, it, too, became American territory. The century that had begun with the United States confined to the land east of the Mississippi River ended with the nation's flag firmly planted on distant Pacific Islands.

That left only the problem of insurrection in Cuba. It was clear that

---

° In 1962, Western Samoa became the first independent nation among the Polynesian islands, but American Samoa has remained American to this moment.

McKinley would take a firmer role than Cleveland had, and with that in mind Spain began to backtrack. A new, more liberal ministry came to power in Madrid in October, 1897, and it promptly recalled General Weyler, against whom most of the American animus was directed. The new ministry eased the concentration-camp policy, offered Cubans greater control over their own affairs, and, in other ways, sought peace.

For a while, it seemed that the Cuban affair might blow over, but that did not suit the more extreme imperialists of the Republican party, who pushed for immediate independence for Cuba, hoping that Spain would fight rather than permit that.

One of these Republicans was Senator Henry Cabot Lodge of Massachusetts (born in Boston on May 12, 1850). He had started as a rather liberal independent, but his political ambitions were high and his principles low, so he became a loyal follower of Blaine. Lodge was a cold, unlikable intellectual (the first congressman with a Ph.D.) of an aristocratic family, who had taught history at Harvard, and who probably looked at war as a historical process rather than as something that killed and maimed.

Another was the assistant secretary of the navy, Theodore Roosevelt of New York (born in New York City on October 27, 1858, of an aristocratic family of Dutch origin, dating back to New York's days as a Dutch colony). Roosevelt was a physical weakling when young and he overcompensated for that all his life. He overcame his weakness by a strenuous self-imposed devotion to exercise and hard life (which may, in the end, have shortened his years). He became a man of action who longed for war, which he thought of as a scene against which he could perform glamorous acts of heroism. He was a reformer within the Republican party structure and, unlike Lodge, with whom he had close friendly relations, he remained a reformer. He had made himself well known in New York politics and was very much mistrusted by the party regulars.

McKinley, who dreaded being personally responsible for a war that might go wrong, and who, as a Civil War veteran, knew that war was not glamorous, was not a strong-willed man, and it was difficult for him to withstand the pressures of those who, like Lodge and Roosevelt, equated mindless bellicosity with "strength" and "manliness."

For that matter, there were intransigents in Cuba, too. There were loyalists who favored the Spanish government against their fellow-Cuban rebels (as there had once been loyalists in the American colonies who favored, and had fought for, the British government). These loyalists objected to the manner in which the Spanish government was turning soft under American pressure and, on January 12, 1898, they held a violent demonstration in Havana.

This was naturally viewed as a bit of Spanish governmental manipulation by the expansionists in the United States. The yellow press notched their howls an octave higher, and McKinley was forced to put on a show of strength by sending the American battleship, *Maine*, to Havana on the usual pretext of protecting American lives and property.°

The situation grew still worse when the Spanish minister to the United States wrote a private letter to someone, in which he called McKinley "weak, and a bidder for the admiration of the crowd" and further accused him of being a trimmer who tried to please both sides. Unfortunately for Spain, the letter somehow fell into the hands of the Cuban rebels. They turned it over to a representative of the Hearst press, and it was promptly published on February 9, 1898.

The minister just as promptly resigned, but the damage was done. The fact that the minister's judgment was pretty accurate made it even worse. Since McKinley really was weak, he became desperately afraid of the appearance of weakness. And, of course, to the super-patriots the fact that a Spanish official had dared criticize an American president seemed, in itself, to be grounds for war.

Then came the worst. On February 15, 1898, at 9:40 P.M., the *Maine*, while in Havana's harbor, blew up, with a loss of 260 officers and men out of the 355 on board. No one has ever determined what caused the explosion. Considering that the warship, like any warship, carried explosives, it could have been an accident brought on by the carelessness of an American crewmember. If it was the deliberate action of an

---

° This is always done by a strong power to a weak power. In 1891, a mob in New Orleans had lynched eleven men who were either Italian nationals or Italian-born naturalized citizens. Italy protested and, in the end, the United States, very reluctantly, paid out some compensation. Can you imagine the reaction in the United States if Italy had sent a warship to New Orleans to protect Italian lives and property?

outsider, it might have been that of a Cuban rebel anxious to produce a cause for American intervention. The least likely explanation is that it was the deliberate action of the Spaniards since there was nothing they wanted less than a war with the United States, and since the explosion could bring them nothing but such a war.

The Navy Department at once appointed a court of inquiry, and the government asked the nation to suspend judgment, but there was no chance of that at all. Many jumped to the immediate conclusion that Spain had deliberately sunk the vessel without ever stopping to figure out what possible rational motive that nation could have for such an action. The yellow press, with Hearst in the lead, assumed Spanish guilt in the largest headlines and coined the slogan, "Remember the *Maine*, to hell with Spain!"

On March 28, the court of inquiry announced that the explosion was external and that an underwater mine had blown up the *Maine*. It is generally believed these days that that conclusion was wrong and that the explosion was internal. However, even if it were an underwater mine, who had planted it there? There was nothing to show that it was the Spanish loyalists rather than rebels and, if one argued from motive, it would have to be the rebels.

That same day, McKinley sent Spain an ultimatum that demanded an immediate armistice in Cuba, an immediate end to the concentration-camp policy, and an acceptance of American mediation of the revolution. This undoubtedly meant independence for Cuba, since American mediation could end with nothing less.

Spain was caught in an unbearable dilemma. It did not want war, but to give in completely would destroy the Spanish government, which had its supply of jingoes at home, too—Spaniards who remembered the great days three centuries before when Spain was the most powerful nation in the world. The only way out that the Spanish government could see was to consult the Vatican. The strongly Catholic Spanish people might permit their pride to be humbled at the request of the man they accepted as the representative of the Church and of God.

Spain therefore turned to the Pope and by April 9, had received enough Vatican backing to grant all American conditions except that of having the United States mediate the Cuban rebellion. A little more pressure short of war and a little willingness to find a face-saving formula and Spain would surely have yielded on that point, too. She was in no position to fight, and all the European powers she had approached had refused to intervene on her behalf with the United States. There were gathering rivalries in Europe itself, and none of the Great Powers wanted to offend the United States on behalf of so weak a nation as Spain.

McKinley, however, lacked the guts to achieve the professed aims of the United States without war. There was too much mindless yelling for war and too many "Young Republicans" telling him that unless he went to war, he would prove himself a weakling, and destroy the Republican party's chances in the upcoming congressional elections. And McKinley proved himself a weakling by yielding.

On April 11, he sent a war message to Congress and, after an acrimonious debate, Spain was sent a three-day ultimatum on April 21, one that insisted on the immediate independence of Cuba. Spain, driven to the wall, and seeing that the United States was determined on war no matter what, stood on the pride that was the only thing it had, and declared war. The United States in its turn declared war on April 24 and made it retroactive to April 21, the day of the ultimatum since it would look more heroic to declare war first.

About the only thing the anti-imperialists could salvage out of the mess of an unnecessary war was an amendment to the congressional war resolution that specifically denied any intention on the part of the United States to annex Cuba. This "Teller Amendment" was advanced by Colorado Senator, Henry Moore Teller (born in Granger, New York, on May 23, 1830), a free-silverite of Populist tendencies.

THE SPANISH-AMERICAN WAR

Since the war was fought by two nations nearly five thousand kilometers apart, with an ocean between and an island at stake, it was clear that it was going to be a naval war, essentially.

Spain had a respectable navy, if one were to sit down and count the ships. Most of those ships, however, were small and obsolete. The morale of the Spanish naval leaders was virtually nonexistent, as they contemplated fighting thousands of kilometers from home, with a home base of a poor and backward nation possessing nothing more than a proud and ancient tradition.

Not only that, but Spain could not even concentrate her fleet near Cuba, for there was an additional insurrection in progress against her in other islands—another remnant of her one-time world-girdling empire—in the Philippines, on the other side of the world from Cuba.

The Philippine Islands are a collection of some 7100 islands (most of them very small) about 800 kilometers southeast of China. The total land area of the island group is 300,000 square kilometers, about that of Arizona.

The first Europeans to reach the Philippines were Spaniards under the Portuguese captain, Ferdinand Magellan, who was engaged in what proved to be the first circumnavigation of the world. They reached the Philippines in 1521, and Magellan died there. The Spaniards did not begin to colonize the islands till 1565 and they then named the islands for their king, Philip II. Manila was founded in 1571.

The Philippines remained under Spanish political and religious rule of an almost medieval nature until well into the 1800s. By the 1880s, however, some of the Filipinos were able to send their children to Europe for an education and with that came the birth of nationalism. It was at a very modest level at first, being expressed largely in terms of a literary output. As is so often the case, however, those in power believed that a strong fist at the outset would crush rebellion in the bud. As almost always happens, the dreamy nationalists were radicalized as a result, so that the poets gave way to the guerrillas.

The most dangerous of these fighters was Emilio Aguinaldo, born in Cavite Province, Philippines, on March 22, 1869. In 1895, he was elected municipal chief of his hometown, succeeding to a position his father had once held. He had become a revolutionary, however, in response to Spanish repression and, on August 30, 1896, had led a group into open revolt. Within months, he was defeating detachments of Spanish regulars.

Spain poured reinforcements into the Philippines, and Aguinaldo was forced to retreat into the mountains. There he held out precariously and finally accepted a bribe from the Spaniards to leave the country. He kept the money intact (he said) for use in a future insurrection under more favorable conditions, and waited. As it turned out, he was waiting for the American fleet.

The Americans had fewer ships than Spain had, but those ships were new and beautifully designed. For once, the United States was ready for war, at least on the seas.

This was partly because of the work of the American naval officer, Alfred Thayer Mahan (born in West Point, New York, on September 27, 1840). The son of a professor at West Point, he himself went to the Naval Academy at Annapolis. He served on blockade duty during the Civil War and remained in the Navy till his retirement as a rear admiral in 1896.

He was a great military theoretician, writing *The Influence of Sea Power upon History, 1660–1783* in 1890, *The Influence of Sea Power upon the French Revolution and Empire, 1793–1812* in 1892, and *The Interest of America in Sea Power, Present and Future*, in 1897.

The thesis was this: The ocean is continuous and worldwide; the land discontinuous and consisting of isolated portions. A landlocked military power can occupy regions adjacent to the homebase, but must stop at the coast, if it lacks a navy. A naval power if separated from the military power by the ocean, can isolate itself and, by means of its navy, attack the enemy at every coastal point, could safeguard its trade, could blockade its enemy. A sea power would have the world as its supply-source and would, in the end, defeat a continental power. It was in this way, Mahan pointed out, that Great Britain had finally defeated all its enemies, including Napoleon, and had gained her world empire.

No nation could grow strong any longer without a navy, Mahan said. As for the United States, which had no powerful nations sharing land boundaries with it, and which had two wide oceans on either side, it could be particularly strong, even invulnerable, if it had an effective navy. Mahan pointed out the necessity of a base in Hawaii, and of coaling stations on smaller islands since the Pacific Ocean was so much wider than the Atlantic. He also advocated the building of a canal across the isthmus of Panama, so that the United States could, at need, quickly concentrate its navy in either ocean.

Following Mahan, the Americans worked hard at developing an

efficient navy and though, at the time the war with Spain came, there was no canal across the isthmus, there were American ships in each ocean.

The Pacific Fleet was particularly well placed through a historical accident. The secretary of the navy, John Davis Long (born in Buckfield, Maine, October 27, 1838) was away from his desk, and his assistant secretary served briefly in his place as acting secretary. That assistant secretary was Theodore Roosevelt, who was a great admirer of Mahan's° and very keen on using the navy properly. He ordered six warships in the Pacific to proceed to Hong Kong in order to be ready to act against the Philippines the moment war was declared. Secretary Long, when he returned, was furious, but he did not countermand the order.

If the United States had a serviceable navy, it had virtually no army at all. Spain had 155,000 soldiers in Cuba at the time, while the United States had a total of 28,000 soldiers altogether, and these had fought no one but Indians for a generation.

Volunteers were called up but they were not stiffened by scattering veterans through new enlarged army units. Instead, the veterans were kept intact and the rookies were left to themselves. Furthermore, the supply organization, both food and medical care, was abysmally poor—the last war in which the United States permitted itself this disgrace.°°

As soon as news of the declaration of war was received in Hong Kong, the American squadron, under Commodore George Dewey

° Another admirer of Mahan was Kaiser Wilhelm II of Germany. A month before the Spanish-American War started, Germany, aware of Mahan's theories began the building of a modern navy designed, eventually, to surpass that of Great Britain. Great Britain was already suspicious of German ambitions and this hit at the very heart of its strength. Great Britain and Germany became deadly enemies and sixteen years later they were on the opposite sides of a great war.

°°It was also the last important war fought with gunpowder, which had been the mainstay of battle for five centuries, and which had fouled the guns, choked the gunners, and hidden the battlefield with its endless smoke. In 1891, the British chemists James Dewar and Frederick Augustus Abel had invented Cordite, the first of the smokeless powders, and a substance more powerful and shattering than gunpowder. Future wars would be fought with such smokeless powders.

(born in Montpelier, Vermont, on December 26, 1837), a veteran of the Civil War, had to leave, as otherwise Hong Kong's status as a neutral port would be in question. That suited Dewey. His orders were to go to Manila, 1050 kilometers to the southeast.

Dewey had six ships under his command, four cruisers and two gunboats, and on April 27, 1898, after having put all his ships in complete battle readiness, he sailed for Manila. Waiting for him were ten Spanish ships together with Spanish shore batteries. The Europeans in Hong Kong, imagining the Spaniards to be what they once had been, it seemed certain that Dewey was steaming to his destruction; but there was really no chance of that. Dewey's ships were of the latest design and in tiptop shape. The Spanish ships were little more than hulks, and the Spanish admiral was expecting defeat.

The Spanish admiral lined up seven of his ships just off Manila in order to protect the city, but there was nothing to protect the ships. Dewey reached Manila Bay, saw nothing to prevent his entering, did so, and reached the neighborhood of Manila itself on the night of April 30.

When daybreak of May 1, 1898, revealed the two opposing fleets to each other, the Spaniards fired high and did no damage. At 5:40 A.M. Dewey said quietly to Captain Charles Vernon Gridley (born in Logansport, Indiana, on November 24, 1844), captain of the flagship, *Olympia*, "You may fire when ready, Gridley."

The American ships paraded back and forth before the Spanish fleet, firing steadily. They pulled off briefly at 7:30 so that the men could have a quiet breakfast, then returned to work. By 11 A.M. the Spanish fleet was destroyed. Every ship had been sunk or beached and 381 Spaniards had been killed. In the process, Dewey lost not a man. Eight sailors had received minor wounds, that was all. And when the American ships moved in to bombard Manila itself, the Spaniards agreed to silence the shore batteries.

Despite the total victory at sea, Dewey could not take Manila. For that he needed a land force, and he had none. On May 19, he brought in Aguinaldo from Hong Kong so that he might lead his Filipino insurgents against the Spaniards on land and keep them occupied and incapable of taking any agressive action against the ships. Even that didn't give Dewey the wherewithal to take the city, and he had to wait for the arrival of American soldiers.

The wait wasn't particularly comfortable. He was isolated and far from any friendly port and by June 12, British, French, and German ships had arrived. They were there, ostensibly, to guard the lives and properties of *their* nationals, but were clearly hoping to pick up some pieces if the fall of Spanish power in the Philippines created a vacuum there. The Germans were especially aggressive in their provocations and at one point the desperate Dewey was forced to tell a German officer, "Tell your Admiral if he wants war I am ready."

But the Germans didn't actually want war; they just wanted whatever they could get without war. With Dewey ready (and the worth of his ships having been dramatically exhibited) and with the United States finally making it clear that whatever happened to the Philippines, no other nations would be allowed a look-in, the German ships sailed off. Dewey settled down to maintain his blockade, and wait for his soldiers.

Meanwhile, in the Atlantic, Spain's fleet had reached the West Indies and by that time they were completely out of fuel. They could not possibly fight before getting into some Cuban port in order to load coal. The American navy knew this, and it was only a matter of finding the fleet while it was in port and keeping it there. (From their Florida base, the American ships had to go only a few hundred kilometers to reach any part of the Cuban coast, so they had no fuel problem.)

On May 19, the Spanish fleet reached Santiago on Cuba's southeastern coast and entered. On May 29, the American fleet, under Rear Admiral William Thomas Sampson (born in Palmyra, New York, on February 9, 1840)—who had been head of the board of inquiry in connection with the sinking of the *Maine*—located the Spanish fleet there and instantly blockaded the harbor.

If the American fleet could have entered the harbor, as Dewey had entered Manila Bay, they would surely have destroyed the Spanish ships. However, the channel entrance was narrow and was littered with mines, and the United States did not wish to lose any of its modern and expensive ships if that could be avoided. Yet something had to be done, for as long as the Spanish ships were intact, there was always the possibility that they might do some damage.

It was decided to leave the American fleet outside the harbor and to invade Cuba with a land force that could attack Santiago from the rear. On June 10, marines landed in Guantánamo Bay, 65 kilometers east of Santiago, to establish a first foothold. (During some preliminary skirmishes, one American commander—a Confederate veteran—forgot who the enemy was and shouted, "Come on, boys, we've got the damn Yankees on the run.")

More than that was needed though, and the main American army, gathering in Tampa, Florida, had been ordered to Cuba on May 30. It was under General William Rufus Shafter (born in Galesburg, Michigan, on October 16, 1835). He was a veteran of the Civil War and had fought bravely and well, but he now weighed 310 pounds and did not know how to organize a large command.

It took eleven days before embarkation could get started, and four days to complete the embarkation; everything being done in complete chaos, with Shafter doing virtually nothing. By June 20, the transports reached the neighborhood of Santiago. Shafter decided not to attempt a direct attack on the city but to land at a point 30 kilometers east of Santiago. In this, he followed the advice of General Calixto Garcia° who commanded the Cuban rebels in this area.

The disembarkment was even more ragged and disorganized than the embarking had been, and had the Americans faced an efficient and well-commanded enemy, that would probably have been the end of most of them. As it was, the Spanish command was bad enough to make even Shafter look good, and the Americans were placed on Cuban soil without opposition and without casualties resulting from enemy action.

By June 30, the Americans were ready to march on Santiago. On July 1, two battles were fought, one at El Coney, 8 kilometers northeast of Santiago and the other at San Juan Hill about 1.5 kilometers east of Santiago. Both were American victories, and it was in the latter that Theodore Roosevelt distinguished himself.

° In the course of the war, an American officer, Lieutenant Andrew Summers Rowan, had made contact with Garcia in order to coordinate action. In 1899, the American journalist, Elbert Green Hubbard (born in Bloomington, Illinois, on June 19, 1856) wrote a moralistic essay entitled "A Message to Garcia" exalting this action, and using it as a lesson to "get things done" through what seems suspiciously like mindless obedience. The essay gained tremendous popularity and was read and memorized by uncounted hordes of schoolchildren—including the author of this book who, even as a child, disagreed with its simplistic philosophy, but thought it the better part of valor not to say so.

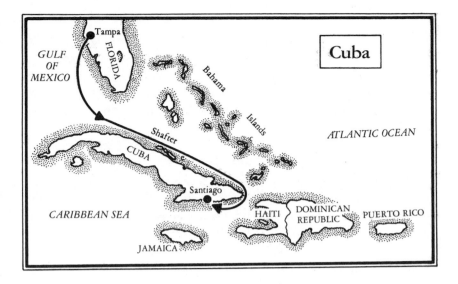

At the outbreak of the war Roosevelt resigned and joined the First
Volunteer Cavalry unit, as a lieutenant colonel. He wasn't its commander, but he was always spectacularly visible, and in the popular
mind, the unit was "Roosevelt's Rough Riders." At San Juan Hill, the
Americans were pinned by fire from Spaniards holding the heights and
the Rough Riders weren't riding, roughly or otherwise, for they were
dismounted. Fighting on foot, they led the charge under enemy fire,
though it wasn't actually much of a charge, since they moved up the
heights slowly and with difficulty. But they moved, and drove the
Spaniards off.

It was Roosevelt's only chance at the military glory he longed for.
(As he said, "It wasn't much of a war, but it was all we had.") And it
was better than nothing, for he made the most of it in after years. The
American satirist, Finley Peter Dunne (born in Chicago on July 10,
1867) had his famous Irish-dialect hero, Mr. Dooley, remark that
when Roosevelt wrote up his Spanish-American experiences he should
have entitled it "Alone in Cuba."

Once on the heights, the Americans were in a position to bombard
the city of Santiago and the Spanish fleet from land. The Spanish
Admiral, whose orders forbade surrender, had no choice but to try to
break out of the harbor. On July 3, he made the attempt and the
American ships pounced at once. In four hours, every Spanish ship was

destroyed with the loss of 474 Spaniards killed and wounded and 1750 taken prisoner. The American loss was 1 killed and 1 wounded.

On July 17, Santiago itself, after a week's bombardment, surrendered, and on July 25, an American army occupied another Spanish colony, Puerto Rico, against virtually no resistance. That just about ended the war in the Atlantic.

In the Pacific, the Spanish island colony of Guam, 1800 kilometers east of the Philippines, had not even heard that a state of war existed until American ships arrived. Since the Spanish governor lacked ammunition, he surrendered at once, on June 20. Wake island, 2500 kilometers northeast of Guam, which was unclaimed by any power, was occupied by Americans on July 4.

Only Manila was still holding out but on July 1, the first army contingents had begun to arrive. By the end of July, 11,000 American soldiers were under Dewey's command and on August 13, Americans, together with Aguinaldo's Filipino insurgents took Manila and the war was over. In fact, it had ended the day before with a formal agreement between Spain and the United States to end hostilities.

The fighting had lasted less than four months, and the total number of American battle deaths was 385 — but over 2000 American soldiers died of disease.

Final peace negotiations began in Paris on October 1. Spain, without even the pretense of a navy, had to give in to all American demands and dismantle almost all of what was left of her once enormous empire. She had to give up Cuba and Puerto Rico in the Atlantic. (Puerto Rico had been in her hands for 505 years.) In the Pacific she had to give up Guam and the Philippines, receiving, in exchange, $20,100,000 from the United States to cover damage to Spanish property. Of all Spain's empire, only some bits of the African coast were left to her.

THE PHILIPPINES

By the terms of the Treaty of Paris, signed on December 10, 1898,

Cuba received her independence as the United States had promised she would.

Guam and Puerto Rico, on the other hand, were taken over by the United States. The United States had never promised them independence and they had not been in rebellion. It was argued further that Guam would make a useful naval base of the United States fleet, and that if the United States did not take it over some other nation would. As for Puerto Rico, that was only 1600 kilometers southeast of Florida and would serve as an important site from which to control the Caribbean Sea.

That left the question of the Philippines. The Philippines were 11,200 kilometers west of San Francisco, and not far from the coast of Asia. They were in a part of the world in which we had never taken any particular military interest. The Philippines, like Cuba, had been in rebellion against Spain, and the Filipino insurgents had helped us take Manila. Since Cuba was being given its independence, ought not the Philippines to get it also?

Many Americans thought so, but the imperialists in the United States thought otherwise. Cuba's independence had been promised (something they regretted), but the independence of the Philippines had *not* been promised, and the demand for its annexation arose. It would look nice to have it in the same color on the map as the United States; it would mean that the United States would have a colony, too, and could hold up its head in the society of European powers.

McKinley gave in. He decided that we couldn't give it back to Spain and that we couldn't allow any other European nation to have it. Once he persuaded himself that in addition its people were unfit for independence, the United States could have no choice but to take it over.

The Treaty of Paris was finally approved by the Senate (after strenuous objections from anti-imperialists) on February 6, 1899. The vote on Philippine independence was a tie, and it was then the duty of the presiding officer of the Senate to vote and break the tie. The presiding officer was Vice-President Morton and he voted for the Philippine takeover. (On November 21, 1899, Morton died in office at Paterson, New Jersey.)

And indeed, with the Treaty of Paris, the United States joined the band of "great powers" and, to this day, has never left it. The proud European nations, accustomed to dismissing the United States, as a loud-mouthed, big-bodied disorganization, who fought inefficiently and could only defeat Indians and Mexicans, were astonished at the manner in which she had utterly crushed Spain in a matter of months. The United States, fighting in both oceans simultaneously, had wiped out the Spanish fleet and lost only one man and no ships in the process. It had won the few land battles it had fought and had forced its will on the loser.

On February 4, 1899, this new view of the United States was put into literature by the poet, Rudyard Kipling, apostle of European imperialism. He welcomed the United States into the imperial club with a poem entitled "An Address to the United States." It was in this poem that he invented the phrase "the white man's burden" and indeed it is by that phrase that the poem is usually entitled. The first stanza goes:

> Take up the White Man's burden—
> Send forth the best ye breed—
> Go bind your sons to exile
> To serve your captives' need;
> To wait in heavy harness
> On fluttered folk and wild—
> Your new-caught, sullen peoples,
> Half devil and half child.

Kipling made it sound as though Americans were going to be sent to the Philippines to pull the rickshaws for Filipino riders and polish the shoes on Filipino feet. It was the other way around and Kipling knew it, of course.

And so did the Filipinos, who did not see the glory in the American victory at their expense. They had fought side by side with the Americans in the belief that they would get independence as Cuba did. Nor would they settle for less. When Aguinaldo saw that the war had only been, for the Filipinos, fought for the sake of changing masters, he renewed his rebellion—against the United States, this time.

The Filipinos did not want to be a burden to the white man. They did not want to be waited on by American sons in exile and in heavy

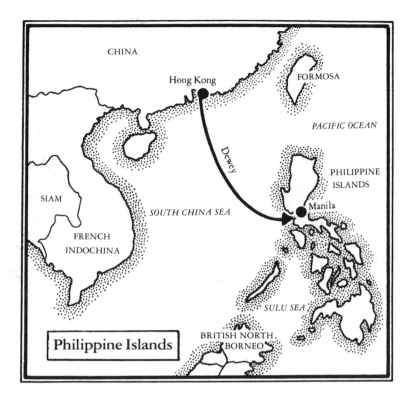

Philippine Islands

harness. The Filipinos wanted to run themselves—whether poorly or well was no one else's concern.

At first, Aguinaldo attempted a pitched battle. He sent his men against Manila on the same day that Kipling's poem was published, and he failed. His men were numerous, but ill-armed, and many of them were without rifles. In addition, they were accustomed to the Spaniards who tended to wait for the cool of the evening before bothering to fight. The Americans, well-armed, and quite willing to fight in the heat of the day, smashed the oncoming Filipinos and it looked as though their defeat was final.

It wasn't. Aguinaldo had been taught the valuable lesson of not fighting on the enemy's terms. If the enemy has weapons and organization, then you must fight the sort of war in which weapons and organization are not very important. You must fight an endless guerrilla war—and for the first time the United States learned how difficult it was to fight ill-fed, ill-clad, ill-armed natives, fighting on their homeground for a cause they valued. It was not to be the last time.

The Philippine Insurrection (as it was called—for it was not dignified by the term "war") went on in a fashion that to Americans of this generation is hauntingly familiar.

The generals in charge, Elwell Stephen Otis (born in Frederick, Maryland, in 1838) and his second-in-command, Arthur MacArthur (born in Springfield, Massachusetts, on June 2, 1845) would issue constant assurances that the insurrection had been put down, yet it somehow never was. They continued to ask for more and more troops, and those were sent until 70,000 American soldiers were occupying the Philippines and that didn't end the rebellion either.

On March 23, 1901, after two years of the Insurrection, Aguinaldo was captured,° but that didn't end the rebellion either.

American soldiers, frustrated at the endless fleabites of an enemy they somehow couldn't defeat, turned to terror. They treated the Filipinos every bit as badly as the Spaniards had treated the Cubans and that didn't end the fighting either.

What did the job of putting an end to the Insurrection, more than anything else, was a turn to decency and honesty.

On April 7, 1900, McKinley appointed a commission to devise a civil government for the Philippines. At its head was William Howard Taft (born in Cincinnati, Ohio, on September 15, 1857). His father had been attorney general under Grant and he himself was a federal circuit judge. He was a man of integrity and in the Philippines he did his best to involve Filipinos in the government. His fairness and decency toward them probably did more to end the Insurrection than did all the toughness and cruelty of the soldiers. In the end, though, it meant the Philippines were under a colonial government.°°

° Aguinaldo lived on to see the Philippines an independent nation, however, and died in Manila on February 6, 1964, at the age of ninety-five.

°°But not forever. In less than half a century, the Philippines were released, allowed to form an independent government and be free. That was the opening event in a movement that was to see all the European overseas empires dismantled in the space of a generation.

Finally, on July 4, 1902, the Philippine Insurrection was ended—by presidential proclamation. Eventually, the fighting died down, too. In the end the Insurrection had lasted over three years and had killed 4230 Americans (along with 20,000 Filipinos).

It was much bloodier and tragic than the fleabite Spanish-American War, but in years to come whenever the wars of the United States were listed in the history books, the Spanish-American War was included but the Philippine Insurrection was not. Americans were ashamed of it, no doubt, but to pass it over in silence was dangerous. The Spanish-born philosopher, George Santayana, said, in 1905, "Those who cannot remember the past are condemned to repeat it," and that was what was in store for the United States. Had Americans learned the lessons of the Philippine Insurrection and taken it to heart, we would have been spared the much worse lesson we had to relearn in Vietnam.

Leaving the Philippine Insurrection to one side, there was the problem of how to treat the new island possessions.

Until 1898, every new piece of land acquired by the United States had become an integral part of the United States, with the promise of becoming first territories and then states. In 1898, there were still parts of the United States that were territories. There were territories in the southwest, for instance, that were someday to make up the states of Oklahoma, Arizona, and New Mexico.

To the northwest was Alaska about which nothing much had been done at first. In 1884, however, after gold had been discovered there, the first attempts to give it a formal government began, and it was clear that territorial status was on the way. And, of course, Hawaii was annexed as a territory to begin with, since that was the condition under which the Republic of Hawaii petitioned for annexation.°

But what of the new lands, taken by force, and completely out of the American cultural tradition. (Even Hawaii had had a strong American element by the time it was annexed.)

The anti-imperialists in the United States argued that any piece of land annexed to the United States became American altogether. The Constitution followed the flag, they said, and the inhabitants of Puerto

---

° And, of course, a half-century later, both Alaska and Hawaii achieved statehood.

Rico, Guam, Samoa, and the Philippines became Americans with full constitutional rights. The imperialists, on the other hand, didn't want it so. There was no fun in having colonies, unless the colonial inhabitants could be exploited, and if the colonials were Americans with full rights, such exploitation would become difficult.

The matter went to the Supreme Court in 1901 in a series of cases and that body decided in favor of the imperialists. The new islands were no longer foreign territory, but they were not automatically covered by the Constitution. Instead, it was up to Congress to decide what portions of the Constitution, if any, applied to them. (This was precisely the quarrel between the American colonies and Great Britain which resulted, at last, in the founding of the United States— and the Supreme Court had, in effect, decided in favor of George III.)

Thus, Congress could apply tariff duties to goods imported from Puerto Rico, and could make the inhabitants of that island citizens of Puerto Rico, rather than of the United States, and this they did on April 12, 1900.

7

THEODORE ROOSEVELT

THE THIRD ASSASSINATION

One thing was certain: The excitement of imperialism was, on the whole, pleasing to the American public and that boded well for the party in power—the Republicans.

The anti-imperialists might have stopped the Treaty of Paris in the Senate where they only needed one third of the senators plus one, but Bryan had urged that there be no partisan fight. He felt that the objectionable imperialist portions of the treaty could be reversed after a Democratic victory in 1900. If he believed in such a victory, however, he was living in a dreamland.

The Republican National Convention met in Philadelphia on June 19, 1900, and nominated McKinley unanimously on the first ballot. The vice-presidential nomination was less cut-and-dried since Vice-President Hobart had recently died. That fortuitious event, however, seemed a convenient one to Senator Platt of New York, the Republican boss of that state. (Platt had resigned from Congress along with Conkling in Garfield's administration but he had made a come-back.)

In 1898, the Republican party in New York had been weakened by various scandals, and Platt was reduced to the indignity of having to find someone honest to run for governor of New York. It was a difficult requirement, and Platt could not find anyone he liked who would qualify, so he was forced to take someone he didn't like. That was the Rough Rider, Theodore Roosevelt. Fresh from San Juan Hill, he was an easy winner but, as Platt had feared, he proved to be far too honest. There was absolutely no way of keeping him from being reelected in 1900 unless he could be forced into the vice-presidency, and so Platt moved heaven and earth to get him out of New York and into the nomination.

The Republicans were willing. He was the number two hero of the war and he would add military class to the ticket. Roosevelt did not want the nomination, since he considered the office a political grave-yard, but he was prevailed upon, in the end, to take it.

The Democratic National Convention met in Kansas City on July 4, 1900. For a brief while there was reason to suppose that the Demo-crats might try to counter Republican military glory by nominating Admiral Dewey, the number one hero of the war, but Dewey's wife was Catholic. To the South, the core of Democratic power and strongly Protestant, that put Dewey completely out of the running. Consequently, Bryan was nominated once more for president, and it was unanimous on the first ballot. For vice-president, Adlai Stevenson, who had been vice-president in Cleveland's second term, was nomi-nated in an effort to cast the glow of past political victory over the ticket.

There were the usual candidates for the minor parties—the Popu-lists and the Prohibitionists. A new party was added to the group when, on March 6, 1900, the Socialist party held its first convention. It nominated Eugene V. Debs, the hero of the Pullman strike.

The campaign of 1900 was remarkably like the campaign of 1896. Bryan muted the earlier free-silver speeches since that was a dead cause, anyway, and tried to rouse the conscience of the nation against imperialism. The Republicans, however, insisted on talking about free silver and acting as though Bryan was a wild-eyed fanatic.

The fortunate McKinley could conduct another front-porch campaign, while Roosevelt, dressed in Rough Rider costume, could tour the country and titillate the populace with his aura of derring-do; something he carried off well despite his high-pitched voice. The Republicans were further helped by the fact that it was a time of booming prosperity so that Roosevelt could pound away at the slogan of "A full dinnerpail for four years more."

The election, held on November 6, 1900, ended as the previous one did, but with a greater majority for the Republicans. McKinley's popular vote was 200,000 higher than in 1896, while Bryan's was 140,000 less. Bryan got the Solid South again, plus Kentucky, which he had missed the time before, but he lost six of the ten western states he had carried in 1896. The electoral vote was 292 to 155, the margin being 42 higher than in 1896. And the Republicans handily controlled both houses of the fifty-seventh Congress by increased majorities: 55 to 35 in the Senate and 197 to 151 in the House. (The only other notable election result was that Debs received 95,000 votes.)

On March 4, 1901, in the first year of the twentieth century, McKinley was reinaugurated and then his luck finally ran out.

On September 6, 1901, he attended the Pan-American Exposition being held at Buffalo. McKinley was there on purely ceremonial business. Since American presidents, aware of the democratic nature of society in the United States, pride themselves on being accessible and on shaking hands with anybody, McKinley received a line of citizens, shaking hands with each.

One of the men waiting in line was Leon Czolgosz, pronounced chol'gosh (born in Detroit, Michigan, in 1873). He was one of those who had been radicalized by the events of the 1890s and he had become an anarchist, believing all government to be evil. It seemed to him that the best way of redressing that evil was to kill the man who headed it. He therefore stood in line with a loaded revolver concealed by a handkerchief (neither of the two Secret Service men guarding the president were curious enough to take a look at what might be under the handkerchief).

Czolgosz reached the president and McKinley thrust his hand out for the shake. Czolgosz fired twice.

McKinley wasn't killed directly, but after an operation and some hope for recovery, he died on September 14. Whatever the failings of his political philosophy, McKinley was universally judged a kindly and lovable man. He was tenderly faithful to his wife, Ida, an epileptic whose malady he succeeeded in keeping from the public. His first thought on being shot was of her and the effect of the news upon her. "Be careful how you tell her," he whispered. "Oh, be careful."

Roosevelt hastened to Buffalo to be sworn in as the twenty-sixth President of the United States. He was only forty-three years old and the youngest person to sit in the White House up to that time. As for McKinley, he was the last president to have fought in the Civil War. The new century was to see a new United States.

McKinley was the third American president to have been assassinated in thirty-six years. As for Czolgosz, he was quickly tried and condemned and hanged in Auburn, New York, on October 29, 1901. His act served to jar the Golden Door a bit further shut, as immigrants came to be more closely examined in order to bar anarchists.

THE FAR EAST

Becoming a great power, the United States quickly learned, meant an increase in problems as well as in prestige. Theodore Roosevelt was the first president to find himself immersed, from the start, in matters ranging over all the world.°

Once American holdings were scattered over the oceans, the United States was affected by problems in distant corners of the globe that earlier would have meant little. Since the United States was an East Asian power due to its presence in the Philippine Islands, for instance, it was suddenly far more sharply interested in events taking place in China than it had been earlier.

American merchants had traded with China, and American missionaries had preached in China, all through the 1800s, and so had the citizens of other nations. For a while, in the early part of the century, such things had been carried through on China's terms. Since China was isolationist and was convinced of the superiority of her own

° Fortunately, Roosevelt was not fazed by this. No one had ever been president up to his time who enjoyed the job and the responsibilities as much as he did.

ancient and subtle culture over that of Europe, things were made difficult for traders from the west.

China's military might was, however, medieval, and it was only a matter of time before the nations of Europe lost patience. When China tried to restrict trade in opium (which harmed her citizens and enriched foreigners) Great Britain struck back, in the bad cause of continuing the vicious trade. The "Opium War" of 1841 ended quickly in Chinese defeat, and Great Britain forced China to open certain ports to foreign trade. She also forced China to cede to her, outright, the port of Hong Kong.

Other European powers followed the British example. Each assumed special privileges in one coastal town or another. The process of parceling China out into "spheres of influence" began, and within each one some special power was supreme and had trading privileges.

In 1854, Japan had been forcibly opened to world trade when an American fleet steamed into Tokyo harbor. Japan, however, did not merely shrink back in misery, as China did, while foreigners snarled and tore at it. Instead, Japan, in a single generation, adopted Western technology and built up an army and navy on European models. Far from becoming a target for Western exploitation, Japan was able to join the ranks of the exploiters and tear at China along with the rest.

The immediate area of confrontation between China and Japan was the peninsula of Korea that jutted out of northeastern China, just across the 180-kilometer stretch of sea, west of Japan. In 1876, Japan had opened Korea to foreign trade by force, as she herself had been opened by the United States. Since then Korea had been racked by civil war, with one side receiving support from China, the other from Japan.

In 1894, China sent troops into Korea at the invitation of one side of the civil war, and Japan promptly sent troops to aid the other. By August 1, China and Japan were at war. It was very one-sided, for Japan won every battle and destroyed the Chinese army and navy with almost no loss to herself. It was almost a preview of the situation in the Spanish-American war.

On April 17, 1895, China was forced to sign a humiliating treaty in which she ceded the island of Taiwan to Japan and acknowledged the independence of Korea.

This clear evidence of China's helplessness, even at the hands of "little Japan" (which Europeans still thought of as a quaint little land of fans and parasols), accelerated the rate at which China was being parceled out.

The United States did not participate in the dismemberment of China since until the annexation of the Philippines, it had no presence in that part of the world. But then, by the time of the Spanish-American War, it was too late to get much out of China. Everything had been pre-empted. The only thing the United States could do was to insist that it not be excluded commercially, just because it had no sphere of influence.

At the time, John Milton Hay (born in Salem, Indiana, on October 8, 1838) was secretary of state under McKinley. He had been Abraham Lincoln's private secretary during the Civil War and had become a minor poet and novelist afterward. As secretary of state, he had been an unabashed imperialist and had been a key factor in the decision to annex the Philippines. And now he had to follow up the logic of that annexation by bringing about the involvement of the United States in China.

On September 6, 1899, having persuaded McKinley of the wisdom of the course, Hay addressed identical notes to Great Britain, Germany, and Russia, and later to Italy, France, and Japan. He asked that all agree that within their spheres of influence there was to be no discrimination as to trade and investment; that all nationals be treated alike; that the Chinese themselves collect the tariffs; and that the nation possessing the sphere of influence be taxed like the rest.

This is referred to as the "Open Door" policy, since the door was to be open to all nations in each sphere of influence. The United States continued to uphold the Open Door policy for forty years, but there was no chance of its working, since if each nation in its sphere of influence treated the rest of the pack equally, what was the benefit of carving out the sphere of influence in the first place. Great Britain supported the policy since, with its great navy and merchant fleet, it was bound to get the lion's share of the trade in any free and open competition. The other nations did nothing more than pay lip service. Russia, indeed, didn't even accept it in principle.

Meanwhile, the Chinese themselves were undergoing a reaction of blind rage to the successive humiliations forced upon them by the exploiting nations. Hatred of foreigners grew, and leading the anti-foreigner reaction were the members of a secret society much given to calisthenics and to a specialized fighting technique something like that which is familiar to moviegoers today as *Kung-fu.*

The secret society called itself "I Ho Ch'uan," which is usually translated as "Righteous and Harmonious Fists." To foreigners they came to be known, more simply, as "Boxers." The Boxers felt that their expertise in their style of fighting made them invincible. The word even went out that they were impervious to bullets.

The Boxers, secretly supported by the Chinese government, turned against those foreigners it could reach and matters came to a climax when they took control of much of the countryside around the capital at Peking. On June 29, 1900, a mob of Boxers, acting on government orders, killed the German minister to China, and placed the various diplomatic legations in Peking, and the Roman Catholic Cathedral as well, under siege. This is the "Boxer Rebellion."

At once an international expedition was set up under German command and sent to China. Among its 5000 troops were soldiers from Germany, Great Britain, France, Russia, Japan, and, surprisingly enough, the United States. This was the first occasion on which American soldiers set warlike foot on the Asian continent. The international expedition had no great difficulty. It swept all before it and took Peking on August 14, looting it mercilessly.

The helpless Chinese were forced, on September 7, 1901, to accede to all Western demands. These might have been worse were it not for the fact that Hay, worried once more that most or all of China might fall beyond American reach, put out another Open Door circular in which he called for Chinese territorial integrity.

Among other humiliations, China was forced to pay an indemnity equivalent to some $740 million in gold. Of this, $25 million was to go to the United States. To the eternal credit of the United States, it only took half the money and that half was returned to China to be used as a fund for the education of young Chinese at American institutions.

Of the European nations, the most aggressive in the hunt for actual territory in China was Russia. As recently as 1858, Russia had forced the cession by China of that section of the Asian coast due west of northern Japan, and in 1860 had founded the port of Vladivostok there. In 1891, Russia had begun the construction of the trans-Siberian railroad by means of which she could supply arms and men to these far eastern provinces, which lay something like 8000 kilometers from her European center of power.

After the Sino-Japanese War, Russia took advantage of China's defeat to move into a position of domination over northern Manchuria (China's northeasternmost province) and then continued to push southward. By the time of the Boxer Rebellion, virtually all of Manchuria was under Russian control. Port Arthur on the Yellow Sea was in Russian hands, and Russian influence was felt even in northern Korea.

This Russian encroachment was a particular worry to Japan, which could see no end to it if it were allowed to go on. Japan tried to reach some sort of agreement with Russia that would protect Japan's share of the Chinese carcass, but Russia saw no reason why it should have to deal with any Oriental power. If China was so large, yet so helpless, Japan, which was tiny in comparison, was certainly to be ignored.

Japan, therefore, decided that war was the only solution and that it could be fought successfully only if Russia's superior strength was weakened sufficiently at the very start. The war began, therefore, on February 8, 1904, with a sneak attack by a Japanese torpedo boat on the Russian fleet at Port Arthur. The fleet was destroyed. (This was a curious preview of a later attack by the Japanese, and the United States might have remembered the event, but apparently she did not.)

The Japanese sneak attack laid the groundwork for a Japanese victory, for it was now possible for a Japanese army to land in Korea without the Russians being able to do anything about it. In Korea and Manchuria, Russian troops fought with their customary bravery and were defeated, as usual, by the incompetence of their command and the inefficiency of their supply. The Russians were, in fact, defeated in every land battle, and after a long siege they lost Port Arthur. When the Russian Atlantic fleet finally made it to Japanese waters after a six-month voyage around Africa, it was promptly destroyed.

In fifteen months, Japan had won an astonishing victory over the Russians. It was the first time in modern history that a non-European nation had beaten a European nation in a major war. Like the United States in the previous decade, Japan entered the world scene as a great power, the first in modern times that was not European in culture.

Russia's disastrous defeats in the Far East had brought on a revolution at home and she was anxious to end the war. As a matter of fact, so was Japan. The victories had been all very well, but on land at least, they had been bloody ones, and Japan did not have the resources with which to fight much longer. She was almost bankrupt, in fact. Russia, on the other hand, though suffering defeats, had as yet scarcely been touched as far as her total manpower and resources were involved. Her armies were intact, and if she chose to fight on, a few more Russian defeats would destroy the Japanese victor.

The United States was ready to have the war end, too. She didn't want either side to win since either nation, if totally victorious, might take over northern China and cut out all other nations.

At the start of the war, overimpressed with Russia's size on the map, Americans had cheered Japanese victories as a case of David winning out over Goliath. As Japan's victories grew numerous, however, the United States had grown uneasy. In June, 1905, therefore, Roosevelt offered to mediate an end to the hostilities, and both sides agreed at once.

Japan offered to uphold the Open Door policy, something she did not really intend to do and never did. In a secret agreement, the United States agreed to let her have a free hand in Korea, provided she agreed to leave the Philippines alone. That was kept to. In 1910, Japan annexed Korea outright and she made no move toward the Philippines—until she was ready, a generation later.

After the secret agreement had been accepted by both parties, Roosevelt was ready to begin and on August 9, 1905, Russian and Japanese representatives met in Portsmouth, New Hampshire (of all places). By September 5, the treaty was signed.

Roosevelt's influence was used to make the peace terms easier for Russia since, failing that, a desperate Russia, unable to bear too much humiliation before a small non-European power, might have renewed the war. The Japanese asked for a large indemnity and for the island of Sakhalin north of Japan; they settled for no indemnity and for half the island.

The result was an enormous personal victory for Roosevelt and, therefore, for American prestige as well. On December 10, 1906, Roosevelt was awarded the Nobel Peace Prize for what he had done.

ALASKA AND THE CANAL

There were foreign problems closer to home as the twentieth century opened.

It had been a long time since the United States proper had had to worry about its boundaries on the North American continent. Since 1853, the boundaries with Canada and with Mexico had been established and had remained unchallenged and unchanged in any significant particular way (and have continued to be so to this day).

But what about Alaska? The north-south dividing line along the 141-degree meridian was solid, but the boundary of southeastern Alaska was a wavering line from about 60 degrees north latitude to 54 degrees. It followed the coast and included the islands of the Alexander Archipelago.

These islands had been Alaskan under Russian domination prior to 1867, and there was no argument about them. The question was where the line of the mainland was to be drawn. The British held that Alaskan territory included only the islands and the immediate continental shore while the United States insisted that the line ran a good 100 kilometers inland.

There was no real conflict about this until after the discovery of the Klondike gold fields—but then it became very important. If the line were drawn according to the British contention, then some of the ocean inlets would have a Canadian shoreline at their inland edges and the gold fields could be reached by sea without having to pass through Alaskan territory.

Theodore Roosevelt was, however, adamant on the American position. On January 26, 1900, he had written to a friend, "Speak softly, and carry a big stick, and you will go far." In this case, he was willing to put the big stick on display and to speak rather loudly, too. An arbitration commission was set up consisting of three Americans, two Canadians and a Briton, and when they met in London in September 1902, Roosevelt made it quite clear that if the commission did not decide in favor of the United States, the United States would set its boundary line by force.

Though the three Americans and the two Canadians would not budge from their positions, the Briton had to consider aspects beyond Alaska. In the seven years since the argument over the Venezuelan boundary, sobering events had occurred for Great Britain. The war with the South African Boers that had then threatened had broken out in late 1899 and had continued for two and a half years, not ending till May 1902. In the course of, for Great Britain, a humiliatingly long war, it was clear that most Europeans were delighted to see the British in trouble and sympathized with the Boers. Great Britain badly felt the need of friends, especially since Germany and its new navy seemed more threatening each year.

Since Great Britain was simply not going to alienate the United States at this juncture over a minor boundary question, the British member of the commission voted with the Americans. On October 20, 1902, therefore, the Alaskan line was drawn well inland; not quite as far as the Americans claimed, but far enough so that the entire coast was American. Canada refused to sign, but that did her no good. The last American boundary dispute on the continent was settled, and nothing of any significance has been changed since.

Far to the south, meanwhile, there was another question: As soon as the United States had gained a Pacific coastline in the 1840s, it had seemed to Americans that a canal across the narrowest portion of the Central American isthmus was absolutely necessary for American welfare, especially in view of the gold that had just been discovered in California. Sea trade between the Atlantic and Pacific coasts of the United States had to go the long route around South America. A canal cut across the narrow isthmus (which was only 65 kilometers wide in spots) would reduce the length of the voyage by half.

The United States was not, however, in a position to build such a canal through land that did not belong to it. Furthermore, the British were expanding their interests in Central America and were at least as much interested in a canal as the United States was. The Monroe Doctrine would have prevented the British from doing so if that doctrine could be enforced, but in the mid-nineteenth century, the United States was not in a position to oppose the British.

The best they could do, in 1850, was to come to an agreement with the British to the effect that neither nation would try to monopolize a canal if one were built and that both would guarantee its neutrality. The result was to decrease the desire of either nation to build a canal.

In any case, the necessary technical ability to build a canal across a tropical land riddled with disease did not yet exist. A French diplomat, Ferdinand de Lesseps, who had successfully put through the construction of the Suez Canal in the 1860s, tried to build a canal across Panama, the narrowest portion of the isthmus, in 1879. The task was harder than it seemed. Too many of the workers got malaria and yellow fever, and the whole project was riddled with graft in addition. It was a fiasco and for a while it seemed there would never be a canal.

But then came the Spanish-American War, with naval battles in both oceans. That, together with Mahan's writings, which pointed out that a canal was a military necessity to the United States, brought interest in the canal to fever pitch.

By the treaty of 1850, the United States could not have exclusive control over such a canal if it were built, but the canal would be of no military use to the United States unless the control *were* exclusive. Hay therefore decided to negotiate a new treaty with the British, one that would allow the Americans full control.

At first, the British tried to refuse to come to an agreement without reciprocal American concessions in the Alaskan boundary dispute, which was going on at this time, but this the United States adamantly refused. In this case, too, Roosevelt made it plain that Great Britain must agree, or the United States would simply go ahead without that agreement.

The war with the Boers was not yet over and Great Britain could not afford to make an enemy. She gave in here, as she was soon to give in over the Alaskan boundary. On November 18, 1901, the Hay-Pauncefote Treaty was signed with the British Ambassador, Julian Pauncefote. By this treaty, the United States received a free hand to build and fortify a canal. The treaty was ratified by the Senate on December 16.

Once the United States was in a position to build the canal without interference from the only great power capable of making trouble over the matter, there remained the question of the exact site of the projected canal. It seemed logical to cut it across Panama where de

Lesseps had worked. The canal would be shortest there, but the ground was uneven and locks would have to be constructed that would raise ships some 26 meters and then lower them that distance in moving from the Atlantic to the Pacific Ocean.

Some 1700 kilometers to the northwest, there was a possible canal site across the nation of Nicaragua. It was four times the width of the canal site at Panama, but it was sea-level all the way. Besides, Lake Nicaragua could be made part of the canal, and that would take up half the distance.

The dispute over sites had already made its way into national politics immediately after the war with Spain. There were private firms angling for both the Nicaragua route and the Panama route and those representing Panama managed to reach Mark Hanna, the power behind McKinley. In the 1900 presidential campaign, then, when both parties were pledging a canal, the Republican platform specified one across Panama. The Democratic platform naturally called for one through Nicaragua.

Even though the Republicans won the election, there was still strong sentiment for the Nicaraguan route in Congress. But then, on May 8, 1902, Mount Pelée, a volcano on the western tip of the French Caribbean island of Martinique, which had been giving out slight mutterings at half-century intervals, suddenly exploded in a major eruption. It destroyed the nearby port town of Saint-Pierre and killed 30,000 people.

No volcano had ever exploded so drastically, so close to the United States in its history, and for a while Americans became very volcano-conscious. When the word went out that an active Nicaraguan volcano was located within a hundred miles of the proposed canal route, that was enough. Congress decided on the Panama route by June 28, 1902.

Panama, however, was part of the territory of the South American nation of Colombia, which was in a dilemma. The aged president of the nation knew that there were many Colombians who were anti-American and who would make a fuss over any permission granted to the United States to build a canal. This, they would claim, would be an obvious entering wedge designed to place Colombia under American domination.

On the other hand, a canal through the isthmus of Panama might bring in considerable revenue for Colombia and, in any case, with

Roosevelt in the White House, it was very likely that the United States might merely take what Colombia wouldn't give and, in that case, give nothing in return.

The Colombian president decided, finally, to make the necessary arrangement and on January 22, 1903, the Hay-Herrán treaty was signed with the Colombian representative in Washington, Tomás Herrán. By its terms, the United States took a hundred-year lease on a strip of land 10 kilometers wide across the isthmus, in return for $10,000,000 in gold and an annual rent, beginning in 1912, of $250,000.

The Senate ratified the treaty on March 17, but the Colombian Senate rejected it, and that infuriated the short-tempered Roosevelt.

He might have set about jockeying Colombian public opinion into approval of the canal plan, but there was a shorter way of getting at it. The inhabitants of the isthmus were not entirely in sympathy with Colombia. They objected to being ruled at a distance, did not feel justly treated by the Colombian government, and had rebelled on different occasions. Now they saw the possibility of revenue coming to themselves and not to the Colombians in general and they could also see that continued Colombian intransigence might push the United States to the alternate route in Nicaragua. Therefore, certain Panamanians indicated to the United States that, provided they could have American help, they would revolt again.

Roosevelt was ready to grant that help. Toward the end of October, 1903, several warships were sent into Central American waters. On November 2, they were ordered to prevent Colombian troops from landing in Panama, in case of revolt, and on November 3, right on schedule, came the revolt. On November 4, the Panamanian rebels declared Panama independent and on November 6, the United States recognized that independence, and it was all over. It was clear that Colombia would not be allowed to attempt to retake its territory.

On November 18, a new treaty was signed with the Panamanian representative, Philippe Jean Buneau-Varilla, a French engineer who had worked on the canal under de Lesseps and who had lobbied steadily toward its construction. The terms of the Hay-Buneau-Varilla Treaty, were much more favorable to the United States than had been the earlier arrangement with Colombia. The width of the strip of land to be leased by the United States was 18 kilometers rather than 10, and the lease was not for a hundred years, but in perpetuity. In return, the United States guaranteed the independence of Panama.*

The United States began construction of the 82-kilometer-long Panama Canal on May 9, 1904, and the first ships passed through it on August 15, 1914.

In the aftermath of the Spanish-American War and in the building of the canal, as it happened, the United States won victories that far transcended the kind won by bullets and shells.

Since the American casualties of the Spanish-American War had fallen mainly to disease and not to enemy action, the United States made the military surgeon Walter Reed (born in Belroi, Virginia, on September 13, 1851) head of a commission sent to Cuba to see what could be done about controlling some of the diseases.

The worst of them was yellow fever, a particularly dreaded disease which, in 1897, Reed had proved was not caused by a certain bacterium on which the blame had been placed. In Cuba, he discovered that the disease was not transmitted by bodily contact, by clothing, or by bedding and he returned to an idea that had been advanced earlier—that the germ of yellow fever was transmitted by the bite of a mosquito.

There was no way of testing this theory on animals and there followed a period of high and grisly drama in which the doctors of the commission allowed themselves to be bitten by mosquitoes to see if they would catch the disease. Some did, and one of them, Jesse William Lazear (born in Baltimore County, Maryland, on May 2, 1866), died. Reed's point was proved.

Yellow fever could be beaten, then, if breeding places for mosquitoes were destroyed, and if people slept under mosquito netting. By measures such as this, Havana and other yellow fever–prone centers were rid of the disease. With the focal points of infection in Latin America moderated, the eastern seaboard of the United States was freed of the dread of the disease which, periodically, had visited

---

* It took a long time for Colombia to forgive the United States for its sharp dealing in this matter. It was not till 1921 that the two nations were willing to make up. By that time, oil had been discovered in Colombia and the United States wanted Colombian friendship—and oil concessions—and agreed to pay Colombia $25,000,000 compensation for the canal.

such cities as New York and Philadelphia, slaying tens of thousands. The last great yellow fever epidemic in the United States struck New Orleans in July of 1905 and was brought to a halt at last by a determined anti-mosquito campaign. Incidentally, the even more widespread disease of malaria was also shown to be spread by mosquitos.

The army surgeon, William Crawford Gorgas (born in Mobile, Alabama, on October 3, 1854), was in Panama during the construction of the canal. The new antimalarial techniques proved their worth beyond any doubt. Gorgas's efforts, which held down the yellow fever and malaria that had defeated de Lesseps, did more to make the construction of the canal possible than did the work of all the engineers put together.

THE CARIBBEAN

The Spanish-American War and its aftermath witnessed the turning of the Caribbean Sea into an American lake. Some of the islands were still European colonies (Martinique was French, Jamaica was British, Curaçao was Dutch, and so on), and other areas were independent (notably Cuba), but American military forces dominated the sea. The British who, prior to the Spanish-American War, had been predominant there, were now content to leave it to the United States and to concentrate instead on areas where their chief rival, Germany, was to be feared.

Nor was the United States backward in asserting its domination. To begin with, American imperialists regretted Cuban independence and did their best to make that independence as limited as possible.

The American army was occupying Cuba in the wake of the war, of course, and conditions could be set for the removal of the soldiers. On March 2, 1901, an Army appropriations bill passed with an amendment sponsored by Senator Orville Hitchcock Platt of Connecticut (born in Washington, Connecticut, on July 26, 1827) that set such conditions.

Under the terms of the "Platt Amendment," Cuba could not make treaties with a foreign power that, in the judgment of the United

States, would impair its independence or weaken its financial stability. Moreover, the United States would have the right to intervene and even occupy the island if, in American opinion, Cuba's independence or financial stability were being impaired. The United States also received Guantánamo Bay as a naval base—which it keeps to this day.

The Cubans tried to reject the Platt Amendment, but that would scarcely work; it was clear that the American forces would not leave otherwise and that they would even welcome Cuban intransigence as a good excuse to cancel the Teller Amendment that had promised the island its independence in the first place. So Cuba accepted the Platt Amendment in the end, and, rather to the surprise of the more cynical foreign observers, the United States then actually withdrew its army on May 12, 1902.

There were occasions, even as early as 1906, when the United States sent its army back into Cuba to maintain order, but each time the soldiers were eventually withdrawn. On the whole, while Cuba could not be considered as fully independent, it did manage to govern itself within the limits set by the United States. Nor did the United States abuse the Platt Amendment very much; and the time was to come when it was given up by the United States, voluntarily. Considering the level of morality among nations, the United States did not, on the whole, do too badly by Cuba.

By the Platt Amendment, the United States had virtually taken over responsibility for Cuba's financial arrangements with other powers, since the new nation was forbidden to pile up more debts than she could pay. This was not necessarily true for other Latin American countries, which frequently borrowed too much and which then had to default. What happened then was that the governments to whose nationals the money was owed were all too likely to land troops and collect customs duties until the debt was paid off.

In doing this, the creditor nations were not entirely innocent. Those who lent the money were perfectly willing to humor corrupt Latin American rulers with more money than the nation could repay, knowing that they would get it back in the end at the point of a gun—and probably with considerably more interest than they could charge in any other way. The only losers were the Latin American people, who were victimized alike by their corrupt rulers and by their greedy creditors.

In Venezuela, for instance, an army general, Cipriano Castro, had seized power in 1899. He ruled as a despotic dictator and borrowed money without any thought as to repayment. By 1902, the two nations chiefly concerned, Germany and Great Britain, thought it was time to collect.

Both nations were careful not to run afoul of the Monroe Doctrine. They informed the American government of their intentions and explained that, though they intended to collect money due their nationals, they did not intend to annex territory. The Monroe Doctrine forbade territorial annexations, but it certainly didn't say that Europeans must be forced to swallow financial loss.

At first, this seemed correct to the United States, and the European powers were given the go-ahead. This they did with injudicious vigor, however, capturing gunboats, bombing forts, and blockading ports. American public opinion, quite accustomed by now to thinking of the Western Hemisphere as entirely American, grew restless, and Roosevelt thought it would be better to push arbitration.

There now existed an international organization for just such a purpose. A "Permanent Court of Arbitration" was set up by a disarmament conference held at the Hague, the Netherlands, in 1899, and since the court sat in that city it is commonly called the Hague Court. The Hague Court set up procedures for establishing arbitration boards to sit in review over certain cases, and the United States suggested that the European nations and Venezuela place their case before it.

Oddly enough, this did not please the Latin American governments, who did not particularly want such disputes arbitrated since they were almost always clearly in the financial wrong. What they wanted was for the United States to use the Monroe Doctrine to declare that European powers could not use armed force to collect money owed them.

It seemed to Roosevelt that there was something to this. As long as force could be used, there would always be the chance of violence in American waters, with American public anger being unnecessarily aroused, and with the chance of unpleasant incidents involving the United States, or its citizens, always present.

On the other hand, debts had to be paid. The Monroe Doctrine could not be used for the purpose of condoning theft. Therefore, if

European nations were to be debarred from using force to collect debts, the United States would have to perform that service for them. The United States therefore applied a kind of Platt Amendment to the rest of Latin America, whereby the United States would move in to collect the money out of customs and then hand it over to the creditor.

This "Roosevelt Corollary" to the Monroe Doctrine made the United States the policeman of the Western Hemisphere, and the first case in which the president successfully applied that corollary was in the Dominican Republic in 1905.

8

PROGRESSIVISM

POLITICAL REFORM

While the position of the United States in the world was undergoing a revolution in the opening years of the twentieth century, an equally remarkable change was taking place at home in the style of American politics.

Throughout the nineteenth century, the power of the political machines had been growing. With hordes of immigrants filling the cities and with the immigrants unskilled in the political arts and inexperienced at handling democracy (always excepting the Irish), the city bosses could rule as they wished.

And as long as the American government felt it need merely be an impartial observer in the struggle between employers and laborers, the latter were condemned to a life that was little different from slavery.

There were movements, however, in the direction of making the government take over the business of protecting its weaker classes, and of making it more responsive to the citizens generally rather than to only those individuals and organizations wealthy enough to afford sizable campaign contributions.

It was the Populists who had first put real steam behind a number of changes designed to increase the participation of citizens in government. Since the Populist movement was strong in the rural areas, the first changes in the direction of more intensive democracy came in the west. Because these changes seemed progressive to those in favor of them, the movement came to be called "Progressivism."

As prime examples of the Progressive movement, there were the "initiative," "referendum," and "recall," devices that had been long practiced in the much smaller republic of Switzerland.

By "initiative" is meant the right of citizens to initiate a new law by preparing a draft of it and then getting a certain number of signatures backing it. The properly signed draft can then be presented to the legislature for a vote. If the legislature turns it down, it might be placed before the citizens directly in a general vote, and this would be a "referendum." A bill, initiated by the legislature itself, can also be put before the voters as a referendum. In this way, the citizen body generally can act as a legislature on occasion, bypassing the regular representatives.

Both initiative and referendum were put through on a state level here and there. North Dakota was the first to adopt the initiative, in 1898, while South Dakota, that same year, adopted the referendum. The first state to adopt both initiative and referendum was Oregon on June 2, 1902. Over the next twenty years a number of other states adopted the initiative and referendum.

"Recall" is a more direct attack on the legislature, since it makes it possible to remove a legislator, or any public official, from office, by an appropriate petition signed by a sufficient number of people, which can then be voted on by the general population. On a citywide basis, the recall was first adopted by Los Angeles in 1903 and on a statewide basis by Oregon in 1908.

None of these devices is particularly easy, but they exist and will occasionally work. More important, just the threat of any of these, the mere existence of the possibility of their being invoked, has tended to make legislatures, if not a band of angels, at least somewhat more responsive to the public will.

Another way of bringing the political process closer to the voter is by allowing the nominations for office to be subject to election as well as the offices themselves. There would thus be a first or "primary" election for nomination to be followed by a second election for office.

To many Americans there seemed little point in voting if one could only vote for candidates whose nomination had been decided on by a few party bosses through the machinery of a convention. The result, too often, was a choice between two political hacks. If the populace themselves, divided into parties, elected able men, then the following election would have meaning.

The first statewide primary law was put through in Wisconsin in 1903, and many other states followed eventually. Unfortunately, primaries generally proved useless. Too often, the voters showed so little interest in the primaries that political hacks were in any case assured nomination, with the added legitimacy of a vote. And yet, through the primaries, nominees have occasionally emerged who would never have passed the hackish test of regular politics.

Primaries have also come to be used in presidential campaigns. The results do not necessarily confine the convention delegates so that they are often merely "beauty contests," but unexpected victories or defeats in the primaries have, on occasion, had decisive effect on the candidacies of different individuals.

BLACKS AND WOMEN

The trend toward citizen participation in government was, however, limited, even in the minds of the most militant of the Populists.

One group of Americans who did not share in the liberalizing trend of Progressivism were the Blacks, whose lot, indeed, grew steadily worse as the nineteenth century drew to its close. In the states that had once seceded from the Union, the civil rights of the Blacks were steadily withdrawn.

This was done through a variety of devices, such as the imposition of difficult literacy tests to which any Black daring enough to try to vote would be subjected, though equally uneducated Whites were not. Then, too, there were the primaries in which Blacks were simply and flatly refused the vote, since, after all, the Fifteenth Amendment said nothing about primaries.

Blacks were further excluded from any hope of a fair chance in the pursuit of happiness by a policy of systematic terror. The police and the courts openly and sometimes violently discriminated against Blacks, and when even this was not enough, they were liable to be killed in race riots, or individually lynched (that is, put to death without any legal procedure at all). Moreover, even if Whites were put on trial in connection with the murder of a Black, by however cruel a method or with however frivolous a motive, there was no way of getting a White jury (Blacks were, of course, excluded) to convict them. Between 1890 and 1900, an average of 166 Blacks were lynched each year, with impunity, in the ex-Confederate States.

Most of the people of the north and west were unconcerned about the plight of the Blacks. They had done their part by ending slavery in the Civil War and that seemed enough for them. To be sure, there was no pressure to take violent measures against the Blacks outside the ex-Confederate states, but that was because the Blacks in the rest of the nation were still few enough in proportion to the Whites to pose no political threat even when they were allowed to vote.

Socially, they were discriminated against as much in the north and west as in the south, and economically, too—but it was not part of official state policy outside the south, and it was not confirmed by laws, and that did make a difference. It meant the Black could attempt to better himself, and, however slim his chances, there was rarely a penalty by lynching visited upon him.*

The most prominent black leader at this low point in the post-Civil War history of the Blacks was Booker Taliaferro Washington (born in Hale's Ford, Virginia, on April 5, 1856, of a slave woman). He obtained an education, thanks to the strong-willed determination of his mother to see that he got one, and worked in menial occupations to support himself while studying.

---

* Sometimes there was, however. On August 14, 1908, an accusation of rape by a white woman against a black man (an accusation later proved false) led to two days of rioting in Springfield, Illinois—Lincoln's home town—in which eight Blacks, guilty of no crime, were killed.

In 1881, he was chosen to head a school for Blacks in Tuskegee, Alabama. It grew steadily from a single building and no money, to 100 buildings, 200 teachers, 1500 students and an endowment of $2,000,-000 (mostly by donations from northern industrialists who were moved by Washington's eloquence) by the time of his death at Tuskegee on November 14, 1915.

Washington emphasized vocational education. He was a practical man who knew what could not be done. It seemed to him that the Blacks could not rise in rebellion without being slaughtered, that they could not try to defy the social customs of the South even passively without inviting beatings and killings. Nor did Washington feel that the more ambitious Blacks ought to leave the South and abandon their less daring brothers to their misery.

To Washington, it seemed that the best thing the Blacks could do was to accept their lot, abandon their hope for civil rights, do their best to better themselves through education into such less prestigious work as would be permitted them, and try to make economic gains by allying themselves with those southern Whites who were relatively merciful.

It was a heartbreaking policy that meant asking for small concessions by promising to keep the Black "in his place." It meant the endless swallowing of resentment, the endless acceptance of injustice, and the endless putting off of any hope of gaining those ordinary human rights supposedly guaranteed all Americans. Yet cautiously minimal though his goals were, Washington gave the Blacks a rallying point that would carry them through the time of greatest horror to a better time when more positive policies would gradually become possible.°

Those more positive policies were coming to the fore even in Washington's lifetime, however, advocated by those Blacks who saw Washington's policies as insuring permanent serfdom and who were not willing to wait indefinitely for civil rights. Most prominent among these more militant Blacks was William Edward Burghardt Du Bois (born in Great Barrington, Massachusetts, on February 23, 1868), a

---

° The time was to come when Booker T. Washington was to be elected to the Hall of Fame (in 1945) and when his birthplace was to be established by Congress as a national monument (in 1957).

Black whose northern background made it possible for him to obtain a Ph.D. in history from Harvard in 1895. He was one of the founders of the National Association for the Advancement of Colored People (NAACP) on May 31, 1909, and he fought steadily for civil rights for Blacks.°

Oddly enough one other group that was deprived of all political and most economic rights everywhere in the United States included millions of Whites and, indeed, many wealthy and upper-class Whites. They were deprived only because they were women and for no other reason.

In the Declaration of Independence, for instance, Thomas Jefferson stated that "all men were created equal." It is doubtful if it even occurred to him to include women in that sentence. Indeed, through most of history, women have been considered as intermediate beings, higher than the four-legged animals, perhaps, but surely considerably lower than men.

Not only were women not permitted to vote, usually denied any but the most elementary education, and kept out of most jobs, but even when they did manage to work, they would get something like one third of the pay men got for the same work.

Yet occasionally there were theorists who did think of women's rights. There were one or two among those who, before the Civil War, fought ardently against Black slavery, and who occasionally gave a thought to the matter of Feminine slavery.

What was more important was that some women did. On July 19 and 20, 1848, a group of women and men got together in Seneca Falls, New York, and issued a declaration stating that "all men and women are created equal." It demanded the right of women to teach, preach, and earn a living, as well as the right to an equal education with men. In order to attain all this they demanded the right to vote so that this represented the birth of the "Women's Suffrage" movement.

One of those active in initiating this meeting was Elizabeth Cady Stanton (born in Johnstown, New York, on November 12, 1815). She

° He lived to see great advances made, but he grew steadily more radical until he became an avowed communist in 1961, and emigrated to Africa. He died in Accra, Ghana, on August 27, 1963, at the age of ninety-five.

managed to get an advanced education despite the fact that no college would teach women. She also studied law though the law would not permit her to practice.

An abolitionist before the Civil War and an atheist from childhood, she not only demanded woman's suffrage, but also advocated the right of women not to be treated as property in marriage. She wanted women to control their own property and to have the right to get a divorce when marital conditions were intolerable, as, for instance, when she was beaten by her husband or when her husband was an alcoholic. (Stanton was a prohibitionist.)

Despite her anger against unhappy marriages and women's helplessness in the face of it, she was not afraid to chance it herself. She married happily and had seven children. Nevertheless, her influence was limited because her uncompromising views caused her to be treated as a dangerous radical and as an advocate of "free love," that is, as believing in sexual relations between any two people who wish it.

Stanton's most influential act, however, may have been the conversion of Susan Brownell Anthony (born in Adams, Massachusetts, February 15, 1820) to the cause in 1851.

Anthony, more conservative and with more winning ways than Stanton, made women's rights a bit more respectable. She was, however, militant enough. She fought for women's rights by lecturing, by writing, by registering to vote in 1872 in defiance of the law and then refusing to pay the $100 fine (and getting away with it). She withstood heckling and ridicule and lived to become the grand old lady of the movement. She was respected by everyone, even those who didn't agree with her and she died in Rochester, New York, on March 13, 1906, at the age of eighty-six, active and determined to the end.

Lucy Stone (born in West Brookfield, Massachusetts, on August 13, 1818) gained her chief fame, not in the ardent work she did for women's rights, but because after she married Henry B. Blackwell (an abolitionist from Ohio) in 1855, she retained her maiden name, and called herself Mrs. Stone, as a blow for equal rights. To this day, any married woman who uses her maiden name* is called a "Lucy Stoner."

* As my wife does, for instance.

A younger member of the group who was to carry on the fight after the death of the first generation of women's rights advocates was Carrie Chapman Catt (born in Ripon, Wisconsin, on January 9, 1859). She worked in a variety of occupations ordinarily felt, in those days, to be fit only for men. She was a school superintendent, a newspaper reporter, and a newspaper editor, for instance.

When she married in 1890, her husband agreed to let her have four months a year that she might devote exclusively to the cause. He supported her cause financially and when he died in 1905 left her enough money to assure her continued independence so that she might freely continue the fight.

The first clear results of the movement came in the western states where women were fewer and, perhaps, valued the more for that reason. The Territory of Wyoming allowed women to vote in territorial elections in 1869, and when the territory became a state in 1890, women's suffrage was written into its constitution, so that women might vote in local and state elections at least. Colorado allowed women's suffrage in 1893 and Utah and Idaho followed in 1896.

It was a while before any other states followed, but in any case, the fighters for suffrage did not intend to win one state at a time, but to bring about a constitutional amendment that would allow women to vote everywhere in the United States, on every occasion on which men could vote.

Anthony fought for such an amendment and one was actually introduced in the Senate as early as 1878. It was voted down, of course, and the older generation of women's rights activitists did not live to see the suffragist victory. Catt did, however, living to a good old age and dying in New Rochelle, New York, on March 9, 1947, at the age of eighty-eight.

PROHIBITION AND CONSERVATION

Many of the women's rights advocates were also ardently in favor of the legal prohibition of the sale of alcoholic beverages and the

"Prohibition" movement was, at the turn of the century, considered a facet of Progressivism.

There was no question that the drinking of alcoholic beverages can cause a serious addiction and that alcoholism produced enormous misery both for those so afflicted and those who were related to them or who had to deal with them socially or professionally. As early as the 1840s there were crusaders against liquor who felt that the only answer was governmental force. In 1846, the first statewide prohibition law in American history went into effect when Maine passed a law controlling the manufacture and sale of alcoholic beverages.

After the Civil War, the federal government found that taxes on alcoholic beverage were a lucrative source of revenue. This rather dampened the prohibition movement for a while, but taxation produced new abuses. In the rural area, people would make cheap whiskey by secretly distilling fermented liquor in hidden places by night. These were "moonshiners" since they worked their still by moonshine. When federal revenue agents tracked them down to collect taxes or put them out of business, violence sometimes occurred.

Then, too, the more orthodox liquor producers began to be involved in local and state politics, paying less in bribes in order to save more in taxes, with nobody losing but the public. In fact, one of the major scandals of the Grant administration involved the so-called Whiskey Ring.

In 1869, therefore, the Prohibition party was founded, a party whose prime purpose was to encourage laws against the manufacture and sale of liquor. The conventions of the Prohibition party were the first to allow women delegates to attend on equal terms with men; something that was only natural since women, far more than men, were the backbone of the party.

In 1872, the Prohibition party nominated a candidate for the presidency for the first time. He received only 5600 votes, but the party did better in later years. In 1892, in the second Cleveland-Harrison campaign, John Bidwell of California (born in Chatauqua County, New York, on August 5, 1819) was the candidate of the Prohibition party on a platform that favored women's suffrage as well as prohibition. He received 271,000 votes, 2.25 percent of the total, the best the Prohibition party was ever to do.

Thereafter, the Prohibition party's power to attract votes declined. In 1896, when Bryan ran on the Democratic side, he attracted many of the Prohibitionist voters since he himself was a Prohibitionist.

The political power of the Prohibitionists was far greater, however, than the numbers they could draw in an election. Many who would not vote for a one-issue party were nevertheless sympathetic to its goals, and large numbers of ardent women who were prohibitionists could not vote.

Much of the prohibitionists' strength was organized not by the party but by social organizations. One of them was the Women's Christian Temperance Union (the WCTU). It was founded in Ohio in 1874 and in 1879 came under the leadership of the charismatic Frances Elizabeth Caroline Willard (born in Churchville, New York, September 28, 1839). By the time she died in New York City, on February 18, 1898, the WCTU had grown to a membership of 250,000 and was involved in all manner of humane and progressive causes other than prohibition. It was, in fact, a powerful influence for women's rights.

A still broader group was the Anti-Saloon League, which was founded in 1893. In 1902, it came under the dynamic leadership of a Methodist clergyman, James Cannon (born in Salisbury, Maryland, on November 13, 1864).

The result was that beginning in the 1880s, there was a steady increase in the number of states that either had prohibition laws and were "dry," or permitted its constituent counties or towns to vote themselves dry ("local option") if they wanted to.

Still another Progressive cause that came into prominence at the turn of the century was that of the conservation of natural resources and this found an ardent champion in the president himself.

Theodore Roosevelt was a Progressive. He could even find it within his heart to make some gesture toward the Blacks. On October 16, 1901, just a month after he became president, he entertained Booker T. Washington at dinner in the White House. The symbolic value of the gesture was enormous, for the social acceptability of at least one Black was thus demonstrated at the very peak. (A storm of protest broke over this and Blacks in the South had to withstand reprisals from those who felt that Roosevelt's humanity would give the Blacks dangerous ideas.)

Oddly enough, conservation of natural resources—something that should be as obviously useful to all as air and food—was scarcely less controversial. The vastness of the American land and the apparent richness of its resources had made it seem to Americans during all the first century of the existence of the nation, that it was all infinite. Forests were cut down, for instance, with no thought that trees had any uses but as instant-wood, and by the 1880s some people woke to the realization that the continental sweep of American timber was almost gone.

Roosevelt was particularly involved with conservation for, as an outdoors man who valued the strenuous life, he could see that the wilderness was rapidly being destroyed. At the very outset of his administration, then, he announced that it was vitally important to conserve the forest and water resources of the nation. While he was president, tens of millions of acres of forest land, mineral-bearing regions, and water-power sites were withdrawn from private exploitation.

Prominent in the beginnings of the conservation movement was Gifford Pinchot (born in Simsbury, Connecticut, on August 11, 1865). He studied forestry in Europe and was the first expert in the field in the United States. From 1898 to 1910, he was chief of the Bureau of Forestry and, more than anyone else, labored to make the United States conservation-conscious.

LABOR AND IMMIGRATION

Roosevelt took up a progressive stand in economics, too, recognizing that the government must not be neutral but must place its weight on the side of the weak. One way of doing this was to enforce such anti-trust laws as existed.

Not much could be done in view of the weakness of the laws, and of the conservative beliefs of those who controlled the legislatures and the courts, so that the "trust-busting" activities of Roosevelt were limited. He did, however, encourage a new attitude in the nation against the arrogance of the magnates. In a speech at Provincetown, Massachusetts, on August 20, 1907, he coined the phrase "malefactors of great wealth," which rang impressively through the minds of Americans.

Roosevelt's sympathy for labor showed up specifically in connection with a strike by the anthracite coal miners, which was called by the United Mine Workers trade union on May 12, 1902. The leader of the union was John Mitchell (born in Braidwood, Illinois, on February 4, 1870), who was a vice-president of the American Federation of Labor.

The strike, as was usual in those days, was in response to the fearsome conditions imposed on labor by employers who were confident of government support. Wages were dreadfully low, and the dangers of mining were enormously high; but the mineowners showed no interest in promoting higher pay or safer conditions. Nor did they show such interest when the strike was called. They refused to negotiate in any way or to submit to arbitration. The mineowners were convinced that the government would, if necessary, use the army to drive the miners back to work, as Cleveland had done in the case of the Pullman strikers in the previous decade.

One of the mineowners, George Frederick Baer (born near Lavansville, Pennsylvania, on September 25, 1842), was so confident that on July 17, 1902, he reached an incredible height of arrogance when he announced, "The rights and interests of the laboring man will be protected and cared for, not by the labor agitators, but by the Christian men to whom God in His infinite wisdom has given the control of the property interests of this country."

Apparently, he believed in the divine right of mineownership so that it must have seemed to him that to question any decision of a mineowner was flat blasphemy. George III might have taken a similar stand against the rebelling colonials and made a similar remark—but he wouldn't have had the nerve to do so since he was only a king and not a mineowner.

Roosevelt waited until October, by which time the mineowners had, by their arrogance, placed themselves in pretty bad odor with the country generally. He then put the pressure on for arbitration and kept the pressure on, not scrupling to use the threat of a governmental takeover of the mines. The mineowners buckled, the arbitration took place, and by October 21, the strike was at an end. The miners got a 10-percent wage increase (which still left them far from affluent), but the union was not recognized as a legitimate bargaining agent.

But this time, at least, the government did not intervene on the side of the strong against the weak. It was a new century. And on February 14, 1903, a new department with cabinet rank was established: the Department of Commerce and Labor. The federal government in this way made it clear that it was going to stay interested in the problem.

One of labor's problems was the unrestricted immigration into the United States, the beckoning call of the Golden Door, which had the unfortunate side effect of keeping the supply of unskilled labor high. For the most part, employers could freely throw out employees on trivial grounds since there were always plenty of hungry newcomers eager to take jobs on the employers' terms.

George Mitchell, the leader of the mine strikers saw that the solution was to unionize the immigrants but the law did everything it could to make unionization difficult so that labor generally turned to the simpler solution of calling for the restriction of immigration. In this they were aided by racist feelings, so that the more different particular groups of immigrants might be from the dominant white American population and culture, the easier it was to bar them.

There was no question of Black immigration at all, for instance, now that they were no longer brought, in chains, as slaves. Then, too, the Chinese Exclusion Act of 1882, which was to be in effect for ten years, was renewed for an additional ten years in 1892, and then renewed a second time in 1902, without a terminal date. Apparently, no Chinese were ever to be allowed into the United States.

The Japanese were a more ticklish problem. There was no significant Japanese immigration until the 1890s, but in that decade about 26,000 entered and Americans on the Pacific coast (where the immigrants arrived) were beginning to feel their racism stirring. Yet the situation had to be approached cautiously. China was a feeble power that could be insulted with impunity. Japan was stronger, surprisingly strong as the Sino-Japanese War had shown, and must not be humiliated too openly.

In August, 1900, about the time of the Boxer Rebellion, there was a "gentleman's agreement" carried through between Japan and the United States whereby the United States would not insultingly bar Japanese immigration, but Japan would see to it that not too many of her nationals would head for the United States.

The agreement did not work well enough, however; the Japanese continued to arrive, and the response in California was increasingly racist. "Exclusion Leagues" were formed, Asian schoolchildren were segregated in San Francisco, and the Hearst newspapers pounded hard at what they called "the Yellow Peril."

Roosevelt did his best to stop the more extreme examples of anti-Oriental prejudice, but he also strengthened the gentleman's agreement in the wake of his arbitration of the Russo-Japanese War.

Even the white immigrants were not very popular. Increasingly, they were the "New Immigrants" from Russia, Poland, Austria-Hungary, the Balkans, Italy, Spain—largely non-Protestant. Between 1901 and 1905, nearly a million immigrants came from Italy, nearly another million from Austria-Hungary, and nearly seven hundred thousand from Russia. The total number of "Old Immigrants" from northwestern Europe was only a little over half a million.

Immigration was, in fact, reaching its peak. Over a million immigrants entered the United States in each of three successive years: 1905, 1906, and 1907. The three-year total of 3,400,000 was a record never to be exceeded.

Through the opening decades of the twentieth century, then, more and more Americans began to feel that the influx of unfamiliar peoples produced a danger to themselves that outweighed the benefits of keeping up a cheap labor supply. The movement to limit immigration began to gather strength.

MUCKRAKING AND TECHNOLOGY

Progressivism was aided by a new development in the literary field. The sensationalism of the yellow press moved onto more socially useful forms, as writers began to probe into the corruption that littered the American scene and to publish exposés.

Roosevelt realized the value of these exposures but grew irritated when they seemed to go farther than he was willing to have them go. In 1906, Roosevelt referred to the literary exposés in connection with a passage in John Bunyan's *Pilgrim's Progress,* in which a man is described as having a muckrake in his hands, in order to rake through mud and filth to locate anything of value that might be hidden there. The muckraker could look no way but downward so that he didn't see a celestial crown over his head.

The name has stuck and this literary movement from 1900 to 1920 is referred to as "muckraking." (There was lots of muck, remember.)

The first of the muckrakers was Joseph Lincoln Steffens (born in San Francisco, California, on April 6, 1866). As managing editor of *McClure's Magazine* he began, in October, 1902, a series of articles on corruption in city government. These were eventually published as *The Shame of the Cities* in 1904 and *The Struggle for Self-Government* in 1906. He presented evidence to show that men of wealth routinely bought the officials of the city government and that the cities were thereupon run for the benefit of the wealthy and powerful.

Ida Minerva Tarbell (born in Erie County, Pennsylvania, on November 5, 1857) was the daughter of a small businessman who worked on the fringes of the oil industry. She believed that he was ruined by the machinations of the growing monopoly of Standard Oil, controlled by John Davison Rockefeller (born in Richford, New York, on July 8, 1839). She spent five years investigating Standard Oil, published articles on the subject in *McClure's* beginning in November 1902, and then, in 1904, published *History of the Standard Oil Company*, an unsympathetic view of the methods used by Rockefeller in his drive to monopoly.

The most successful of the muckrakers was Upton Beall Sinclair (born in Baltimore, Maryland, on September 20, 1878). His exposé took the form of a novel, *The Jungle*, published in 1906. It was his sixth novel and proved an unexpected success. It was set against the background of the Chicago stockyards and was intended to arouse sympathy for the suffering workers, but the description of conditions in the stockyard and the filth that was rampant, so horrified and nauseated the readers that it gave rise to a wave of vegetarianism.

Sinclair had lived in the stockyard district for seven weeks, and he was not making up the horrors. Actual investigations of the matter supported his descriptions and since even the wealthy and powerful had to eat the same filthy meat, it proved easy to take action in this case. A Pure Food and Drug Act was passed and signed on June 30, 1906, and government entered the business of trying to keep the American public from being poisoned at a profit.

Other muckrakers attacked the horrible abuses of child-labor, the crookedness of the railroads, and the shameful venality of Congress.

And yet if there were dark spots in American society, there was also a booming technology. By the turn of the century, there was no question that the United States was the technological leader of the world.

Though early work on the automobile had taken place in Europe, the United States joined with enthusiasm. The first transcontinental trip by automobile, from San Francisco to New York, took place in the summer of 1902. It took fifty-two days. And it was the American, Henry Ford, who made his name synonymous with the new vehicle. He organized the Ford Motor Company in 1903 and by 1908 was manufacturing the Model T cheaply enough to put it within the reach of millions.

On December 17, 1903, at Kitty Hawk, North Carolina, two brothers, Wilbur Wright (born in Millville, Indiana, on April 16, 1867) and Orville Wright (born in Dayton, Ohio, on August 19, 1871) built and flew the first successful heavier-than-air flying machine, or "airplane." Between the two new transportation devices, the automobile and the airplane, that king of distance, the railroad, rapidly declined from its royal eminence in the second half of the nineteenth century.

December 12, 1901, is usually considered as marking the birth of radio, for it was then that the Italian electrical engineer, Guglielmo Marconi, sent radio signals from the southwest tip of England to Newfoundland. Radio quickly caught on in the United States and a demonstration of radio operation was a big hit at the St. Louis World's Fair in 1904. The Canadian-American physicist, Reginald Aubrey Fessenden (born in East Bolton, Quebec, on October 6, 1866) made the radio an instrument for reproducing sound. In 1906, the first radio message was sent out from Massachusetts in such a way that receivers could pick up words and music.

Since 1889, Thomas Alva Edison had tried to add to his earlier great inventions of the phonograph and the electric light, the mechanics of projecting a series of photographic stills in rapid sequence so as to give the illusion of motion. He succeeded in inventing the motion picture, and, in 1903, his company produced *The Great Train Robbery*, the first motion picture to tell a story.

Radio and the motion picture were to be the dominating forms of American entertainment in the first half of the twentieth century.

In 1902, a twenty-story structure, the Flatiron Building (so-called from its triangular cross section) was erected in New York City. It was the first "sky-scraper" in New York, the first building constructed on a steel skeleton strong enough to allow many stories of brick, concrete, and masonry to be suspended from it. This new style of architecture was to become characteristic of New York and made it a city like no other that had ever existed, and it was to spread to every other large city in the world, too.

On a more ethereal level, the German-American scientist Albert Abraham Michelson (born in Strelno, Prussia, on December 19, 1852, and brought to the United States at the age of two) won the Nobel Prize for physics in 1907 for his work on light. He was the first American Nobel laureate in the science categories.

Technology could not utterly cancel man's age-old subjection to the destructive force of nature, however. On April 18, 1906, a 47-second earthquake, the most damaging in American history, destroyed San Francisco. Fire followed and before it was all over, four hundred people had died, four square miles had been burned to the ground, and half a billion dollars' worth of damage had been done.

9

ROOSEVELT AND TAFT

ROOSEVELT TRIUMPHANT

Roosevelt, in the years following the assassination of McKinley and his own accession to the presidency, was very conscious that he had not been *elected* president and that he was the beneficiary of an accident. It made him careful in his dealings with a Congress whose members *had* been elected, and it made him a little uncertain of his ground.

Before Roosevelt there had been four vice-presidents who had become president through the deaths of their predecessors. They were John Tyler, Millard Fillmore, Andrew Johnson, and Chester Alan Arthur (the tenth, thirteenth, seventeenth, and twenty-first Presidents of the United States, respectively.) None of them had been successful; none had done more than complete the term to which they had succeeded; none had even succeeded in obtaining a nomination for a presidential race of his own.

Roosevelt intended to break that string of nonachievement. He looked forward to 1904 and the chance of actually being elected to the post, and the prospects were favorable. In the 1902 congressional elections, the fifty-eighth Congress was elected and proved to be the fifth in a row in which the Republicans controlled both houses, 57 to 33 in the Senate and 208 to 178 in the House.

By the time 1904 opened, Roosevelt had behind him the successful closing of the Philippine Insurrection, the successful ending of the anthracite-miners' strike, the successful conclusion of the Alaska Boundary dispute, the successful clearing of the way for a Panama Canal. Mark Hanna, the most powerful anti-Roosevelt figure in the Republican party, died on February 15, 1904, and there was prosperity at home. How could he lose?

Even as the Republican National Convention met in Chicago on June 21, 1904, the fates gave Roosevelt a remarkable chance to tickle American pride. A Moroccan bandit, Ahmed ben Muhammad Raisuli, had kidnapped a Greek-American, Ion Perdicaris, on May 18, 1904. As an immigrant of Greek extraction, he was undoubtedly beyond the pale to most Americans, but a principle was involved. Roosevelt ordered warships to Morocco and on June 22, with the Republican convention newly met, Secretary of State Hay, aware of the fame-value of a staccato phrase, sent a cable to the Moroccan government that said, "We want Perdicaris alive, or Raisuli dead." Perdicaris was released two days later—alive.

The Republicans nominated Roosevelt unanimously on the first ballot. For vice-president they selected the conservative Indiana Senator, Charles Warren Fairbanks (born near Unionville Center, Ohio, on May 11, 1852), in the hope that his presence on the ticket would pacify those Republicans who found Roosevelt's progressive views indigestible.

The Democrats met on July 6 in St. Louis. They had no real hope. Having lost twice with the colorful, progressive Bryan, they nominated a colorless conservative, Alton Brooks Parker (born in Cortland, New York, on May 14, 1852). He was an honest and capable lawyer and judge, who promptly announced himself to be a Gold Democrat. For vice-president, the choice was an eighty-one-year-old West Virginia businessman, Henry Gassaway David (born in Woodstock, Maryland, on November 16, 1823).

It was an election that carried with it no suspense at all. On November 8, 1904, the election was held and Roosevelt took it by 7,600,000 to 5,000,000. Roosevelt had 56.4 percent of the popular vote, the largest percentage of victory since popular votes had begun to be counted eighty years before. In the electoral college, Roosevelt had 336 votes to Parker's 140, the latter representing the Solid South plus Kentucky, just about the irreducible minimum for a Democratic candidate in those days. With Roosevelt came in the fifty-ninth Congress, the sixth to be Republican in both houses. The Republican margin was unchanged in the Senate but moved up, 250 to 136, in the House.

Roosevelt's election did produce one puzzle. Ever since the time of Washington and Jefferson, it had been a solid tradition that no man serve as president for more than two terms. Only Grant had even tried for a third and he had failed to be nominated. Did that, however, mean two *elected* presidencies? Roosevelt's preelection period in office by nonelective succession had been for only half a year less than a full term. Did that count?

Roosevelt decided that that *did* count, and on the night of his election he announced, "Under no circumstances will I be a candidate for, or accept, another nomination." This was something he would regret eventually.

Once elected in his own right, Roosevelt could march on to the implementation of his policies at home and abroad with more vigor and self-confidence (though it is hard to believe that Roosevelt needed more self-confidence than he had).

He felt strong enough, in fact, to do something unprecedented in American history. He interfered in European affairs in a matter that was of no direct concern to the United States.

This intervention came about through European rivalries in Africa. In the course of the nineteenth century, Great Britain had carved out vast chunks in the east and south of that continent, and France had taken equally large pieces in the north and west. Even Belgium had managed to take over a large portion of the center, while Spain and Portugal held on to a few remnants of an older day.

Germany, which achieved nationhood late, found itself left behind. It was only in the 1880s that Germany began to move, occupying a few

African lands that Great Britain and France had not yet had time to take over. On the east-central coast, they established German East Africa and on the southwest coast, German Southwest Africa.

Under the new and aggressive Kaiser Wilhelm II, who came to the throne in 1888, Germany felt a certain humiliation at not having its proper "place in the sun." She therefore pushed forward wherever she could and did so rather loudly and tactlessly.

Germany, especially after she began to build up a navy, threatened the position of Great Britain particularly. Great Britain therefore followed a new course of friendship with the United States. And, as a result of the Spanish-American War, when the United States suddenly found itself a colonial power, there began to be a feeling that there was an "Anglo-Saxon mission" to civilize the world.

The result was that with the opening of the twentieth century there began a new tradition of British-American Friendship (which did not always run smoothly) and, in consequence, and despite the absence of any particular direct friction, a German-American enmity.

The whole thing came to a head over a dispute over one of the few remaining corners of Africa that still remained nominally independent in the first decade of the twentieth century—Morocco, where Hay had demanded Perdicaris alive or Raisuli dead.

In 1894, a thirteen-year-old boy, Abdul Azis, had succeeded to the Moroccan throne and by 1900, the land had fallen into complete anarchy. That suited the European powers since that was the opportunity of one or another of them to take over.

France, controlling Algeria, which lay to the east of Morocco, as well as the desert regions to the south, had the best chance. Between 1900 and 1904, France busily made agreements with Italy, Great Britain, and Spain and then, toward the end of 1904, began to move into it.

Germany, however, had not been consulted and she was furious. She tried to get the United States to join her in a declaration of an open-door policy for Morocco, similar to the one that the United States had pushed for in China, but Roosevelt cautiously avoided that.

Then, since France's chief ally, Russia, was involved in its losing war with Japan, Germany decided on the bold move of going it alone. Kaiser Wilhelm II made a spectacular visit to the Moroccan town of Tangier on March 31, 1905, delivered the kind of bombastic speech that was a specialty of his, and for a moment it looked as though there might be a European war.

France, which had been badly defeated by German armies, and which could not, at the moment, count on the military help of Russia, moved away from a direct confrontation. Germany, pushing its advantage, maneuvered for an international conference at which, it hoped, its own interest in Morocco would be confirmed. To attain this, she worked through Roosevelt.

Roosevelt, fearful of a European War and conscious of his own role as peacemaker in the war between Russia and Japan, agreed to put pressure on Great Britain and France to bring about such a conference. He succeeded, and the conference opened on January 16, 1906, at Algeciras, a Spanish town just across the Strait of Gibraltar from Morocco. The conference was attended by thirteen European powers, by Morocco *and* by the United States.

It quickly turned out that Germany had blundered egregiously in her estimate of the situation. She found herself isolated, except for her satellite, Austria-Hungary. All the rest of the nations, including the United States, supported the French position. Morocco was declared independent, but in actuality was placed under a French-Spanish protectorate.

Germany at first made signs of refusing to agree, but Roosevelt suggested some face-saving adjustments, and the conference ended on April 7, 1906, with Germany the loser.

TAFT AS SUCCESSOR

The Algeciras Conference was another triumph for Roosevelt and his stock seemed higher than ever. The 1906 congressional election had produced a sixtieth congress which, for the seventh time in a row, was controlled by Republicans in both houses. In the Senate the Republican lead had strengthened to 61 to 31, while in the House it had slipped only moderately and stood at 222 to 164.

Under the magic of McKinley and Roosevelt, the Democratic party seemed to be withering into a permanent minority that existed at all only because of the Solid South and some of the big city machines.

In 1908, there is no question that Roosevelt would have been nominated again, had he breathed the merest hint of acquiescence. However, he had promised, four years before, that he would not run again, and he kept that promise. Instead, he meant to run someone he could count on to carry on the Roosevelt policies in an appropriate fashion.

The man Roosevelt chose was William Howard Taft, who in every administrative position he had held had proved himself capable and honest. Taft had first received national attention when he was sent to the Philippines to pacify that land and he had done wonders in reconciling the Filipinos to American rule. Then, in 1904, Roosevelt had appointed Taft as the secretary of war and he had been a loyal and capable worker in that post.

The Republicans met in Chicago on June 16, 1908, and Roosevelt's word was enough. Taft was nominated on the first ballot. For vice-president, the convention nominated New York Congressman, James Schoolcraft Sherman (born in Utica, New York, on October 24, 1855), a loyal party wheel horse.

The Democrats met in Denver, Colorado, on July 8, 1908. Bryan, who had shied away from confronting Roosevelt in 1904, felt he might have a chance if that magic name were not before the voters, so he allowed himself to be nominated once more on the first ballot, to make his third try for the presidency. For vice-president, the convention chose John W. Kern of Indiana.

It was a dull election, with the chief campaign issue being the tariff. The Democrats promised they would reduce the tariff, and the Republicans said they would revise it (implying a reduction). There was no point in the Democrats raising the free silver issue or the anti-imperialist issue for gold, and colonies had proved too successful to be argued with, so that the Democrats really had nothing much to say.

The election was held on November 3, 1908, and Bryan had lost for the third time. He was the only person in either the Republican or Democratic party who ever led his side to three presidential losses. Bryan had done somewhat better than Parker had done four years before, with 6,400,000 votes to Taft's 7,700,000, but not as well as he had himself done in his first two tries. Bryan carried only the Solid South plus four western states.

Taft obtained 51.6 percent of the popular vote and won 321 votes to 162 votes in the electoral college. The sixty-first Congress, which was also elected, was the eighth in a row to have a Republican majority in both houses, 61 to 32 in the Senate and 219 to 172 in the House.

On March 4, 1909, William Howard Taft was inaugurated the twenty-seventh President of the United States.

Any man who followed Theodore Roosevelt was bound to suffer by comparison, but Taft was a particular letdown. After Roosevelt, with his grinning and his dynamism and his outdoors heartiness, it was hard to get used to a fat man who sometimes fell asleep in public. (Taft, with a weight of 325 pounds, was the fattest president the United States ever had, and when he entered the White House an outside bathtub had to be installed for him.)

He was similar to John Quincy Adams in having two different and distinguished careers in government, with an unsuccessful presidency in between. Truth to tell, Taft did not particularly wish to be nominated, but Roosevelt's determination and the ambitions of Taft's wife, Nellie, overcame his reluctance. (Nellie's pleasure in the nomination and election was short-lived. In the first year of Taft's incumbency, Nellie suffered a severe stroke and had to be slowly and patiently nursed to recovery, including having to be taught to talk once more. She lived on for twenty-four more years.)

At the very start of his administration, Taft called Congress into session to deal with the tariff, and there was general expectation that the result would be a marked decrease in duties. The measure, as prepared in the House by New York Congressman Sereno Elisha Payne (born in Hamilton, New York, on June 26, 1843) might have been satisfactory, but in the Senate, the tariff was turned upward by the wealthy, conservative Senator of Rhode Island, Nelson Wilmarth Aldrich (born in Foster, Rhode Island, on November 6, 1841).

The resulting Payne-Aldrich Tariff bill was completely unsatisfactory to the Democrats, and to many Republicans as well. Nevertheless, it was passed and Taft, who leaned strongly on Aldrich for advice throughout his administration, signed it on August 5, 1909, and praised it too, thus further infuriating a group of "Insurgent Republicans," mostly from the Middle West.

The Insurgents were ardently pro-Roosevelt and supported progressive measures. They grew increasingly anti-Taft, even bitterly so, and this presaged a party split of dire consequences for them.

Among the leaders of the Insurgent movement was the Wisconsin senator, Robert Marion La Follette (born in Primrose, Wisconsin, on June 14, 1855). As congressman and as governor of Wisconsin, he had supported Progressive ideas strongly. As governor, he turned to professors of the University of Wisconsin for the preparation of bills and for the administration of state regulatory agencies—the first case in which the intellectual community was called upon to help in governing. He entered the Senate in 1906 and there quickly emerged as a spokesman for the Progressives. Once Roosevelt retired as president, La Follette became their outstanding leader.

It was Taft's tragedy that his colorlessness and lack of ability to handle Congress made everything he did seem unsatisfactory even when he did what in Roosevelt would have been hailed. Under Taft, twice as many trust-busting actions were carried through as there were under Roosevelt, but whereas Roosevelt knew how to get credit for such procedures, Taft did not.

Again, Taft continued Roosevelt's Open Door policy not only in the Far East but in Latin America, and labored to see to it that American business interests had a fair share of the markets, in competition with the European powers. Taft said, in a message to Congress, that "this policy has been characterized as substituting dollars for bullets."

This was an unfortunate way of putting it. Certainly, dollars would seem to be better than bullets in dealings between nations. National pride, however, equated winning through force with "manliness" and "strength" and "courage." Winning by bribery or purchase, on the other hand, seemed sneaky and underhanded. The Taft policy came to be called "Dollar Diplomacy," and it was reviled.

Then, too, it seemed that the United States was placing its power at the service of American business and this appeared, to the Progressives, to be one more way in which the American government favored the rich and powerful at the expense of the poor and weak.

And when the Taft administration turned from money to force, that didn't seem to be good, either. It came about over a new canal problem.

Roosevelt had secured control over the Panama Canal route but there was still the chance of a second canal across Nicaragua, and it was important to the United States that this possible passage be prevented from falling into foreign hands.

Such an undesirable event was far from impossible. Nicaragua's dictator, José Santos Zelaya, was anti-American to begin with and he borrowed heavily from European powers. It was quite possible that one or another of the creditor powers might try to take over the potential canal route in return for getting the dictator out of debt.

Therefore, when a rebellion (financed by American firms) broke out against Zelaya in November, 1909, the United States promptly sided with the rebels. Zelaya fled, and a new government was formed under a strongly pro-American ruler.

Taft's secretary of state, Philander Chase Knox (born in Brownsville, Pennsylvania, on May 6, 1853), the architect of Dollar Diplomacy, now negotiated an agreement with the new Nicaraguan government that placed that nation as much under the control of the United States as Cuba was. The United States was to take care of the Nicaraguan debt and was thereafter to control Nicaraguan finances. Moreover, the route for a possible canal was to be reserved to the United States.

The Senate, more independent than it would have been under Roosevelt, refused to approve this agreement, but Nicaragua remained under American control unofficially. In 1912, when a new rebellion broke out against the pro-American regime, the United States acted on the side of the status quo this time. Twenty-five hundred marines and sailors were sent into Nicaragua, and the rebellion was crushed. Some American marines remained in Nicaragua for twenty years thereafter.

Taft did no more in Nicaragua than Roosevelt had done in Panama or McKinley in Cuba, but Taft did it without style and he brought upon himself widespread antagonism among the Latin-Americans abroad and among the Progressives and anti-imperialists at home.

Still another example of Taft's misfortunes lay in the field of conservation. Taft, who took himself seriously as Roosevelt's successor and who tried to follow his patron's policies faithfully, continued to uphold the principle of the conservation of natural resources.

Taft's secretary of interior, Richard Achilles Ballinger (born in Boonesboro, Iowa, on July 9, 1858), thought that some land held back in the previous administration could, legally and reasonably, be offered for sale to private firms and proceeded on that basis.

The irascible Pinchot attacked Ballinger and accused him of kowtowing to business interests. Taft tried to make peace, but Pinchot would not retreat an inch. Taft then felt he had to support his Cabinet officer and on January 7, 1910, fired Pinchot. Ballinger was exonerated of wrongdoing by a congressional committee, but the Republican Insurgents had been so offended by the treatment of Pinchot that Ballinger's usefulness was at an end. He had to resign on March 6, 1911.

And, of course, this, too, helped fix Taft in the minds of the Progressives as an enemy of conservation and as a betrayer of Roosevelt's policies.

GROWTH

One achievement of the Taft administration could not, however, be viewed by Americans generally as anything but a happy climax. It was during his stay in the White House that the continental area of the United States, as it had been before 1867, was finally filled with states.

One new state had come in during Roosevelt's tenure. This was the area between Texas and Kansas, which, since 1834, had been called "Indian Territory" and which was, supposedly, reserved in perpetuity, for Indian occupation. It was the last bit of territory reserved to the Indians without that territory being part of a state of the Union and this last bit, too, was placed under relentless pressure from white settlers.

Little by little, parts of it were opened to settlement and, after 1890, the western portion was called "Oklahoma Territory" from a Choctaw word for "red people." As each part was opened to settlement, as many as a hundred thousand settlers would rush in to grab land on a first-come-first-served basis.

Finally, on November 16, 1907, the Indian Territory came to an official end, and the entire area entered the Union as Oklahoma, the forty-sixth state. From then on, the only territory reserved to the Indians, to whom the entire nation had once belonged, were individual patches of land here and there, carefully chosen because no white men in their right minds would want them.

That left only the area south of Utah and Colorado as two territories that were not yet states. The eastern part was New Mexico and the western, Arizona (from the Spanish for "dry region"). At first there was a congressional move to admit the area as a single state, but the inhabitants of the territories turned that down.

On January 6, 1912, New Mexico entered the Union as the forty-seventh state. Arizona was not admitted at first because in the Arizonian proposed constitution it would have been permitted to remove state judges by popular vote. Congress felt this violated the principle of the independence of the judiciary. Arizona therefore repealed that law and entered the Union on February 14, 1912, as the forty-eighth state. Once a state, the Arizonians reinstated their law. Congress could not tell a state what to do about its internal affairs.

With the entrance of New Mexico and Arizona, the entire stretch of territory from the Atlantic to the Pacific ("the contiguous United States") was filled with states in a process that had begun a century and a quarter before. The process of turning land into territories and then into states seemed over, and the American flag, with forty-eight stars, seemed to be the final one. Not many Americans thought of conquering Canada and Mexico and carving new states out of those lands, and not many thought of forming states in territory separated from the forty-eight by sea or by foreign lands. And, actually, it was to be nearly half a century before new states were added.

In 1910, the population of the United States stood at 92,000,000. Its fleet rivaled that of Germany in the race for second place. (Great Britain was as yet unchallenged in first place.) It produced twice as much steel as Germany and four times as much as Great Britain.

A new 100-inch telescope, completed in California, was the largest in the world. An American explorer, Robert Edwin Peary (born in Cresson, Pennsylvania, on May 6, 1856), was the first human being to reach the North Pole on April 6, 1909. New York City extended its subways through tunnels under the East River and the Hudson River in 1908. A seventh transcontinental railroad was completed in 1909. The airplane was now an accepted part of the human scene and in the fall of 1911, an airplane was flown from the Atlantic to the Pacific in an actual flying time of three and a half days.

Labor was growing too. In 1905, William Dudley ("Big Bill") Haywood (born in Salt Lake City, Utah, on February 4, 1869), head of a miners' union, helped found the Industrial Workers of the World (I.W.W. or "Wobblies" as they were nicknamed for some reason), in opposition to the American Federation of Labor. Where the A.F. of L. was a confederation of separate unions involving skilled workers for the most part, the I.W.W. aimed at being all-inclusive, or "One Big Union for All."

In 1906, Haywood was arrested on the charge of the bombing murder of Frank R. Steunenberg, a former governor of Idaho who had used troops to break up a miner's strike. The result was a long drawn out dramatic case in which Clarence Seward Darrow (born in Kinsman, Ohio, on April 18, 1857), America's foremost lawyer for the underdog, represented Haywood and won his acquittal.

This did not hurt the cause of the I.W.W. which, by 1912, reached a peak membership of 100,000 and was able in that year to carry out and win a spectacular strike against the textile mills of Lawrence, Massachusetts. The I.W.W. was an outspokenly socialist force and, in the eyes of the conservatives, was the most shockingly radical group the United States had yet seen.

In humanity's contest with nature, however, nature was sometimes victorious. On April 14, 1912, the largest and most luxurious ocean liner ever built up to that time, the British ship, *Titanic*, was on its maiden voyage from Southampton to New York. It had a double-bottomed hull divided into sixteen separate watertight compartments. Four of these could be flooded and the remaining twelve would still keep the ship afloat, so that the *Titanic* was proclaimed unsinkable.

Shortly before midnight, however, the *Titanic* struck an iceberg, and five of the compartments were slashed open. In two and a half hours it sank, with a loss of 1513 lives, including many prominent Americans. Many errors were involved: the ship was going too fast in an effort to make a record run; there were only enough lifeboat spaces for half the people aboard; there were no lifeboat drills; a ship that was close enough to help in time had no radio operator on duty.

As a result, new regulations were established for lifeboats and lifeboat drills. It was also arranged that radio watch be maintained on all ships on a 24-hour basis. Most important of all, an International Ice Patrol was established to report, continually, on the location of all icebergs within a certain area of the North Atlantic. Since then, there have been no iceberg tragedies; not one.

THE DEMOCRATS RESURGENT

The Republicans, so powerful under Roosevelt, were now clearly splitting. The Insurgents were out for Taft's hide and they were joined by a mighty ally, Roosevelt himself.

Theodore Roosevelt, after he had left the White House, had also left the country and had gone on a ten-month hunting trip in Africa. When he returned in June 1910, to great adulation, he found himself at loose ends. He did not like retirement, he did like applause, and he was sympathetic with the Insurgents.

He tried to avoid contributing to an open split in the Republican party, but found himself personally offended by the Taft administration. The administration acted against U.S. Steel, alleging that that corporation's manipulations had brought on a stock market crash on March 13, 1907, and a short-lived "Panic of 1907." It was further alleged that U.S. Steel had managed to hoodwink Roosevelt into permitting those manipulations.

Roosevelt was infuriated at the suggestion that he could be hoodwinked (all the more so in that the charge may have been true) and moved openly into the opposition. On August 31, 1910, he delivered a speech in Osawatomie, Kansas, favoring what he called the "New Nationalism." He attacked the conservative record of the Supreme Court, denounced the power of wealth, urged a "square deal" for all. In general, he put himself firmly on the Insurgent side.

With the Republicans thus in disarray, the results of the 1910 congressional elections, not surprisingly, brought forth a Democratic victory. A string of eight consecutive all-Republican congresses came to an end, as the Democrats won control of the House of Representatives of the sixty-second Congress, 228 to 161. It was the first time since 1892 that the Democrats controlled the House. The Senate remained Republican by a majority of 10 seats compared to a majority of 29 in the previous Congress, but even so, the Insurgent Republicans, allied to the Democrats, controlled the new Senate. Taft faced a hostile Congress.

The Democrats won new governorships, too. The most significant new name appeared in New Jersey. This was Woodrow Wilson (born in Staunton, Virginia, on December 28, 1856). After an initial venture into law, he became known as a scholar. His field was government and history and he obtained a Ph.D. at Johns Hopkins in 1886. He held a seat as professor of history and political economy at several institutions, and finally came to Princeton University where, in 1902, he was chosen president of the university.

At Princeton University, he tried to democratize the life of the undergraduates and to weaken the snobbery and power of the fraternities. Here he showed two aspects of his personality that were to be influential in American history afterwards; first, his intense desire to do what was moral, and second, his inability to handle opposition, so that in the end he was defeated.

His activity at the university, however, and his speeches and writings on political questions had made him prominent and to the Democratic party bosses of New Jersey it seemed a good idea to run this unworldly man for governor in a year in which Progressives were bound to win. They had no doubt they could control him once he was in the governor's chair. Wilson agreed, campaigned vigorously, was elected, and promptly showed he could not be controlled.

Another new political face was that of Theodore Roosevelt's distant cousin Franklin Delano Roosevelt (born in Hyde Park, New York, on January 30, 1882). He had married Theodore Roosevelt's niece Anna Eleanor Roosevelt, on March 17, 1905.

Franklin's branch of the family was Democratic and in 1910, he was asked by the Democrats to run for the State Assembly, the lower house of the New York legislature. Franklin Roosevelt made sure that Cousin Theodore would not come out against him and then agreed to run. It seemed a hopeless race, but it was a Progressive year, and he was elected, thus beginning what was to prove the most successful political career in American history.

The 1910 elections were, of course, only the preliminary bout. The Insurgents wanted the total defeat of Taft. They wanted to deny him the renomination and to place one of their own at the head of the Republican ticket in 1912.

On January 21, 1911, the "National Progressive Republican League" was founded under the leadership of La Follette. The new league came out for the entire body of Progressive aims: initiative, referendum, recall, direct primaries, direct election of delegates to conventions, direct election of senators, abolition of monopolies, recognition of unions, and conservation of national resources. On October 16, 1911, the League met in convention in Chicago and endorsed La Follette for the Republican nomination.

La Follette, however, did not have the kind of national following that was needed. What is more, he had a kind of mental collapse in public during a speech he made on February 6, 1912, and that badly shocked many of his followers. The pressure mounted therefore to place Theodore Roosevelt in La Follette's place, and Roosevelt was willing to let himself be talked into it.

He announced his decision in a newspaper interview by assuming the stance of a challenger in the prize-fight ring. (In those days, when a fighter challenged one and all at a county fair, anyone accepting the challenge signified that by tossing his hat into the ring.) So Roosevelt said, "My hat's in the ring. The fight is on and I'm stripped to the buff." Since then, to throw one's hat in the ring has become standard political slang for entering a political contest.

Roosevelt went about the fight in his usual energetic way. This was the first election in which the direct primary was a factor. Several states had them, and Roosevelt entered every one to contest the nomination with Taft—and won every one of them, too. By the time, the Republican National Convention met in Chicago on June 18, 1912, Roosevelt had 278 delegates pledged to him against only 46 for Taft. La Follette, who stubbornly remained in the race, refusing to yield to Roosevelt, attacked the latter so wildly and bitterly as to damage his own cause and collected only 36 convention votes.

None of that mattered. When the convention met, the organization Republicans were in complete control and it was clear that wherever possible only those convention delegates committed to Taft were going to be accepted. So the Roosevelt delegates walked out.

After that, Taft and Sherman were quickly renominated as the Republican candidates for president and vice-president. As it happened, though, Sherman died at Utica, New York, on October 30, 1912, six days before the election and he had to be replaced, very hastily, with Nicholas Murray Butler (born in Elizabeth, New Jersey, on April 2, 1862), who was president of Columbia University, and an active political worker among conservative Republicans.

The Roosevelt delegations met separately in Chicago on June 22, the day of Taft's nomination and launched the Progressive party, making it clear it was their intention to nominate Roosevelt. They held a formal convention in Chicago on August 5, and Roosevelt was nominated after putting on a terrific show. He said, "We stand at Armageddon and we battle for the Lord!" (This was a reference to the biblical prediction of a last battle between the forces of God and of Satan.) He had, in 1900, described himself to party leaders as follows: "I am as strong as a bull moose and you can use me to the limit." Now the bull moose became the symbol of the Progressive party.

For vice-president, the Progressives nominated the Progressive Republican governor of California, Hiram Warren Johnson (born in Sacramento, California, on September 2, 1866).

This was the most serious split of any major party since 1860, when, just prior to the Civil War, the Democratic party had split down the middle. That had made it possible for Abraham Lincoln, the Republican candidate, to win the presidency with considerably less than a majority of the votes. Unless the Republican split were healed, it looked very much as though it would be the Democrats who would now benefit.

The Democratic National Convention met in Baltimore on June 25, 1912, in a state of high excitement. The leading candidate was James Beauchamp Clark (born near Lawrenceburg, Kentucky, on March 7, 1850). Usually known as Champ Clark, he was a congressman from Missouri and, in 1910, had led the fight to curtail the powers of the Speaker of the House, a conservative Republican who ruled it with a rod of iron—and had won.

There were others in the field, however, including Wilson, who had defied the political bosses who had worked for his election, and had conducted a reform administration that won the admiration of the progressives in both parties.

Wilson himself might not have thought of the presidency but there was a Mark Hanna in the field who thought of it for him. This was Edward Mandell House (born in Houston, Texas, on July 26, 1858). He was usually known as Colonel House from the honorary title he had received from a Texas governor in 1892. He felt too frail to fight in the political wars directly and he preferred to work behind the scenes through others. He was a Progressive Democrat and his eye fell on Wilson, whom he began maneuvering toward the presidency.

The balloting began and Champ Clark gradually strengthened his position. By the tenth ballot, he gained the majority and in any sensible nominating procedure he would have been nominated. However, ever since Andrew Jackson's time, the Democratic party had insisted on a two-thirds vote for nomination, and this had caused no end of trouble.

Now it meant that balloting had to continue and Clark gradually lost his lead. For a while, it looked as though no one could possibly make the two-thirds requirement and that the Democrats would break up in bickering that would lose them the great chance of that year. But then Bryan (who could not hope to run a fourth time, but who could still be a president-maker) sensed the danger and came out for Wilson at the decisive moment. On the forty-sixth ballot, Wilson had his two-thirds and was the Democratic candidate for the presidency.

For vice-president, the Democrats nominated the Progressive Democratic governor of Indiana, Thomas Riley Marshall (born in North Manchester, Indiana, on March 14, 1854).°

If Roosevelt had been running on the Republican ticket, he would probably have won. If Taft had been running without Roosevelt in the field he just might have won. With both of them running, neither could possibly win.

The Solid South stayed firmly behind Virginia-born Wilson. (He was the first major-party candidate for the presidency born in one of the ex-Confederate states since the Civil War, though of course he had lived his professional life in the north.) The Democratic city-bosses held firm, too, and La Follette, more bitter than ever, came out for Wilson and pulled some Progressive votes with him.

The result was that on November 5, Woodrow Wilson had a plurality, 6,300,000 votes to 4,100,000 for Roosevelt and 3,500,000 for Taft. Wilson had only 41.9 percent of the total vote, less than that of any winning candidate since Lincoln's 39.8 percent in 1860, and less

---

° He is best known today for an irreverent comment intended as a joke. When the Senate was debating the needs of the country, he said, wryly, "What this country really needs is a good five-cent cigar."

than any losing Democratic candidate since the Civil War, except for Parker in 1904.

Nevertheless, because of the Republican split, he won 435 electoral votes, representing forty states, the largest number any presidential candidate had ever won up to that point. Roosevelt carried six states for 88 electoral votes. As for Taft, with only one quarter of the total vote, he carried only Utah and Vermont for 8 electoral votes. It was an unprecedented humiliation for an incumbent president running for reelection. Taft is the only one who ever ran third.

The sixty-third Congress, elected with Wilson, was Democratic in both houses for the first time since the fifty-third Congress of 1892. The Democratic margin was 51 to 44 in the Senate and 291 to 127 in the House.

Eugene Debs ran on the Socialist ticket for the fourth time in a row. In 1900, 1904, and 1908, he had failed to garner more than 1 to 2 percent of the total vote. In 1912, he won over 900,000 votes for some 6 percent of the total vote, the most successful run a Socialist was ever to have.

10

WOODROW WILSON

THE NEW PROGRESSIVE

Woodrow Wilson was inaugurated as the twenty-eighth President of the United States on March 4, 1913, and once again there was a Progressive in the White House.

As an omen for the new liberal presidency, an important change had come into being shortly before, in the shape of a new amendment to the Constitution, the first since the Fifteenth Amendment had been passed in 1870. It involved the income tax.

Through most of history, taxes have tended to be applied on a per capita basis; so much per person, or so much on some transaction or other, regardless of who was involved in the transaction. In general, therefore, taxes tended to fall in equal amounts on the poor and the rich alike.

This seemed inequitable to many people since the rich could well afford to pay more than the poor. Besides which, such taxes sharply limit what a government can collect to meet its expenses. After all, you can only tax a poor man so much and if you cannot tax a rich man any more than that, the total tax receipts are small.

A poor government cannot afford to do much for its poor and weak and must confine itself to exhortation, which usually does no good. Therefore any method for raising taxes by getting more from the well-to-do than from the impoverished was considered a progressive measure.

An "income tax" is designed to take a certain fraction of each person's income in taxes and since this fraction comes to a higher sum for a person of high income than for a person of low, more money is collected altogether. A greater amount of money would be collected in the case of a "graduated income tax," where the fraction is made higher as incomes are higher.

The difficulty with income taxes, however, is that people with good incomes are naturally opposed to them and it is precisely they who have political clout. As a result, income taxes could only begin as purely temporary measures designed to meet extraordinary emergencies—usually a dangerous war—and were then repealed once the emergency was over. The first country to enact a general income tax was Great Britain, in 1799, to meet the needs of the wars against Napoleon.

The United States adopted an income tax in 1862 to meet the needs of the Civil War. It was a graduated one. The minimum rate was 3 percent on annual incomes over $600, and it was 5 percent for that part of the income that was past the $10,000 mark. It was repealed in 1872.

In 1894, an income tax was introduced by Cleveland, as a substitute for the revenue lost when the tariff was lowered. It was, however, declared unconstitutional by the Supreme Court in 1895. In order to make it possible for the United States to impose income taxes on individuals after that, a special amendment to the Constitution would have had to be passed.

In 1909, Congress passed such an amendment and it went to the states where the favorable votes of three fourths of them (thirty-six after New Mexico and Arizona joined the union) were required. On February 25, 1913, the thirty-sixth state voted its acquiescence, and the Sixteenth Amendment, legalizing a national income tax on individuals was ratified. That happened just one week before Wilson became president.

The first income tax imposed wasn't much by present standards and only reached 6 percent on that portion of a person's annual income over $100,000. Nevertheless, the ability to impose such a tax was all important. It could be, and was, rapidly increased in times of emergency, pouring vast sums into the federal Treasury and making it possible for the government to undertake all sorts of tasks it could not have afforded previously. What is more, those tasks, as they tended to grow more expensive, imposed pressures for raising the income tax still further.

Another Progressive cause that required an amendment to the Constitution was the direct election of senators. The Constitution provided for the selection of senators by state legislatures, in order (the theory was) to free those senators from the ever-shifting winds of public opinion and enable them to serve as a wise and stabilizing force on government.

In practice, state legislatures were often under the control of political machines, sometimes conservative, sometimes corrupt, often both. Would-be senators found it easier to corrupt a few key legislators than to win the electorate as a whole, and since the easiest method of corruption involved the use of money, the Senate became a rich man's club dedicated to the protection of rich men generally and utterly indifferent to a public opinion that could neither elect nor remove them.

In 1906, a muckraking writer, David Graham Phillips, wrote *The Treason of the Senate*, a book that helped mobilize indignation against the senatorial corruption that the system made possible.

Congress passed an amendment requiring direct election of senators in 1912, and the necessary number of states had voted for it by May 31, 1913, making it the Seventeenth Amendment to the Constitution.

In the 1914 elections for the sixty-fourth Congress, the first to make use of direct elections of senators, the Democratic hold on the Senate was strengthened to a margin of 56 to 40. The Democrats also retained their hold on the House, albeit in reduced strength, 230 to 196.

Once in the presidency, Wilson set about trying to carry through his campaign promises. On April 8, 1913, only a month after his inauguration, Wilson broke precedent by appearing before Congress in person to ask for a lowered tariff. (It had been well over a century since any president had appeared before Congress to read a presidential message. The last president to do so had been John Adams in 1800.)

Congress responded to presidential urgings, and thus Wilson demonstrated the value of forceful leadership. In this, and in the other measures he took, he restored to the presidency the power it had held temporarily under Lincoln, and paved the way for its still further growth to new and unprecedented heights in the decades to come.

Alabama congressman Oscar Wilder Underwood (born in Louisville, Kentucky, on May 6, 1862) sponsored a tariff measure that reduced rates to their lowest levels since the Civil War, and this "Underwood Tariff " became law on October 3, 1913. The loss in revenue resulting from the lowered rates was now unimportant, thanks to the Sixteenth Amendment, since the same bill that lowered the rates could adjust the income tax to make up for it.

The next step was to put the nation's banks under some sort of central control. Unlike the case in the powerful European nations, there was a kind of anarchy in American banking circles. Each private bank had its own policy and there was never sufficient cooperation among them to prevent panics or to control the nation's paper currency.

A Federal Reserve System was therefore set up in a bill sponsored by Virginia Congressman Carter Glass (born in Lynchburg, Virginia, on January 4, 1858) and Oklahoma Senator Robert Latham Owen (born in Lynchburg, Virginia, on February 6, 1856). The Federal Reserve System, composed of twelve regional banks, did not bank directly for the public, but was a kind of bank for banks. It could lend money to banks and it could control interest rates. In general, it could serve to coordinate the financial structure of the country. It became law on December 23, 1913.

Wilson was particularly interested in weakening the hold of the giant corporations on the economic life of the country. He therefore pushed for laws that would strengthen and extend the Sherman Antitrust Act, which had proven totally inadequate for the purpose.

The necessary bill was sponsored by Alabama Congressman, Henry De Lamar Clayton (born in Barbour County, Alabama, on February

10, 1857). The Clayton Antitrust Act became law on October 15, 1914. Not only did it go much farther than the Sherman Antitrust Act in preventing those practices that created monopolies, but it specifically exempted labor unions from its terms. For the first time, it described conditions under which strikes, peaceful picketing, and boycotts could be legal and it limited the use of the courts in preventing and in breaking strikes. Gompers of the A. F. of L. hailed it as "labor's charter of freedom," but in actual fact court interpretations weakened the act considerably, and the large corporations learned ways of getting around the provisions; ways that were particularly effective under administrations sympathetic to business rather than to labor.

Despite these examples, together with other lesser laws that represented progressive Wilsonian ideas triumphant within the nation, Wilson's presidency was to become much more noted for affairs abroad; so much so that his domestic program is an almost disregarded aspect of his term in office.

MEXICO

Wilson's first serious problem in foreign relations involved Mexico. After the United States had forced France out of Mexico, immediately after the Civil War, Mexico had fallen under the dictatorship of Porfirio Díaz. From 1876 to 1910, he retained absolute control of the nation, imposing order and developing the nation's industries and resources. Along with order, however, was a total lack of civil liberty, while the wealth that came with development accrued for the most part to Díaz himself and to foreign investors (most of them Americans).

Unrest grew as Díaz's grip loosened with age. A young Mexican idealist, Francisco Indalecio Madero, worked with the downtrodden Mexican peasants (or "peons") and clamored for social reforms. He tried to run against Díaz for the presidency in 1910, when Díaz was already eighty years old—but Díaz simply had him imprisoned.

Madero managed to escape, fled to Texas, and there roused enough

Mexicans and obtained enough money to begin a revolution. He set up a rebel government in Mexico in May 1911, and Díaz was forced to resign.

Unfortunately, once the Díaz dictatorship was broken, the fight for control of the nation became a free-for-all among generals, whom Madero could not control. One of them, Victoriano Huerta, who had supported Madero, now turned against him, had him arrested and then, on February 22, 1913, had him killed. He then announced himself President of Mexico, just as Wilson was becoming President of the United States.

It is customary for any government that is in effective control of a nation to be recognized by other nations. This makes it possible for diplomacy and trade to continue as little-disturbed as possible. As long as a government keeps the peace, allows trade, and does not endanger law-abiding foreigners, the nations of the world usually do not inquire too closely into questions of how that government came into power or what its internal policies are.

Thus, the major European powers, Great Britain, France, and Germany quickly recognized Huerta's government and would as quickly have recognized any successor who killed Huerta, as Huerta had killed Madero. This sort of recognition of reality had also been American policy, and Wilson was urged to recognize the Huerta government by his foreign policy experts.

Wilson refused. He had admired Madero and he was indignant at his murder. He felt Huerta was a butcher and he did not think the United States should recognize governments that ruled over people against their will. He therefore initiated a new American policy of withholding recognition on moral grounds.

This policy has been followed by the United States ever since and has proved thoroughly useless. In the first place, it placed the United States in the position of preaching a high morality that often irritated even our friends and that sometimes left us particularly vulnerable when we were forced into immorality itself. Such immorality always looked worse in the United States than in other nations, and was considered worse—even by Americans.

Then, again, the policy virtually never worked. American nonrecognition always added a note of heroism to the government we opposed, since the people who were being ruled often chose not to oppose the government, however evil it might be, if that looked as though they were falling in with the wishes of a foreign power.

Huerta refused to yield to Wilson and all the huffing and puffing by the United States but served to strengthen his hold on Mexico. Wilson was forced to do what he originally said he would not do—and that was to use force.

At first, he tried to do this indirectly by supporting those generals who opposed Huerta, notably Venustiano Carranza, another of Madero's supporters who, unlike Huerta, had remained faithful to Madero's ideals. By 1914, Wilson's support of Carranza became a virtual alliance, and American arms flowed to the Mexican rebel. But that, too, strengthened Huerta who could rally the nation behind him by appealing to their anti-American feelings.

But Wilson could not back down. He was displaying here, as he was to do in later cases, his inability to compromise. He was now forced to make outright use of direct American force and he needed only an excuse.

What happened to give that excuse involved seven sailors and an officer on a warship that was stationed near the Mexican port of Tampico. They went ashore without permission and tried to buy gasoline. They were arrested by some of Huerta's men, but when the matter was reported to a higher Mexican official, the American sailors were immediately released unharmed, and with an apology.

Nevertheless, the admiral in charge of the American ships at Tampico demanded more elaborate apologies, thus converting this altogether trivial event into an international incident.

It came at a very ticklish time, for a German ship laden with munitions for Huerta was approaching the Mexican port of Vera Cruz. This was a matter of peaceful commerce between Germany and the Mexican government that was recognized by Germany. There was no state of war between the United States and Mexico, and the United States had no right to interfere with peaceful trade even under the most liberal interpretation of the Monroe Doctrine. Nevertheless, it was clear that the weapons would be used by Huerta against troops supported by the United States and there was considerable excitement over the matter among the American public.

Wilson was awakened at 2:30 A.M. in the early morning hours of April 21, 1914, to be told of the arrest of the sailors in Tampico. Going off half-cocked, he ordered the occupation of Vera Cruz. The American fleet was quite ready and carried out the occupation at once, the day before Congress granted permission. Some four hundred Mexicans were killed in the course of the takeover. The Americans lost four dead and twenty wounded.

This action roused tremendous anger all over Latin America, since it seemed like a case of arrogant American imperialism—which it was. Even Carranza on whose behalf Vera Cruz had been taken had to denounce it.

Wilson found himself forced to accept an offer of arbitration by the South American nations of Argentina, Brazil, and Chile. On June 24, 1914, the conference, which was held at Niagara Falls, Canada, and which included the arbitrating "ABC powers" plus the United States and Mexico, agreed that Huerta should retire. Huerta tried to refuse, but the United States still controlled Vera Cruz, and without Latin American support, Huerta could expect to be helpless to prevent further American inroads. On July 15, 1914, Huerta resigned, and in due time, American forces were withdrawn from Vera Cruz. Carranza became President of Mexico and his government was recognized by the nations of the world and by the United States, too.

That might have seemed like a happy ending for Wilson, but it wasn't. The battle of the generals went on and Carranza, like Huerta and Madero and Díaz before him had to face revolt. Two generals who opposed Carranza were Emiliano Zapata and Francisco ("Pancho") Villa.

Carranza, who could draw on American supplies freely, defeated Zapata and Villa, and forced them to flee into the northern hills.

Wilson had grown weary of the endless Mexican quarreling and now, belatedly, he was trying to stick to a "hands off" policy, and that did not suit Villa. It occurred to him that if he could force the United States to invade Mexico on the side of Carranza, the Mexicans would, out of patriotism, flock to his own side. He therefore set about deliberately embroiling the United States.

On January 10, 1916, Villa stopped a train in northern Mexico, took off seventeen American engineers and had sixteen of them shot without even pretending to have a reason. On March 9, he did far worse. He sent four hundred raiders across the American line into the border-town of Columbus, New Mexico. They burned the town and killed nineteen Americans.

This could not be ignored. Wilson wrung out of Carranza a reluctant permission to allow an American army contingent to enter Mexico.

On March 15, 1916, about six thousand American soldiers under General John Joseph ("Black Jack") Pershing (born near Laclede, Missouri, on September 13, 1860), who had served in Cuba during the Spanish-American War, and in the Philippines afterward, invaded Mexico.

It was a lot easier to chase Villa, however, than to catch him. Villa's men knew every corner of the mountains and the Americans did not. Villa's men had the sympathy of the local population and the Americans did not. After four weeks, Pershing's column was some three hundred miles into Mexico. They had scattered Villa's men and left Villa nothing but a few faithful followers—but Villa remained at large just the same.

What's more, Carranza was very disturbed. He didn't expect so many Americans, so persistent a pursuit, or so deep an invasion. At two different places, there were outright battles between Americans and Mexican government forces. For a while, it looked as though there might be a formal war between the two nations.

If all were well elsewhere, that is exactly what might have happened, but all was not well, and Wilson had to disentangle himself from the Mexican venture. On February 5, 1917, he recalled Pershing and the American expeditionary force left Mexico with Villa still at large. (Villa eventually made his peace with the Mexican government and retired—but was assassinated on June 20, 1923, by those who felt he could only be trusted after he was a corpse.)

Other interferences in the Caribbean area by the United States also took place, though none was anywhere nearly as troublesome as the Mexican affair. United States marines landed in Haiti and in Santo Domingo, for instance. About the only pleasant event was the opening of the Panama Canal on August 15, 1914.

WAR IN EUROPE

And what was it that was going on elsewhere and that prevented Wilson from exerting all possible American force in Mexico in response to Villa's deliberate provocations?

It was war in Europe, the first general European War since the end of Napoleon at Waterloo, almost exactly a century before.

On June 28, 1914, while the arbitration conference over the American occupation of Vera Cruz was moving toward its conclusion at Niagara Falls, the heir to the Austro-Hungarian throne was assassinated in the small Austro-Hungarian town of Sarajevo.

It was a tragic event, but at the time no one dreamed it could lead to war. Unfortunately, however, over the preceding thirty years, the European powers had divided into two hostile groups: Germany and Austria-Hungary on the one side (the "Central Powers") and Great Britain, France, and Russia (the "Allies") on the other. Both groups had painted themselves into corners during a series of crises until neither side felt it could afford to back down when one more crisis arose, however minor that crisis might be.

During the month of July 1914, diplomatic stupidity piled on diplomatic stupidity as each nation feared to make any move that would betray weakness. Finally, on July 28, Austria-Hungary declared war on the small Balkan nation of Serbia, for the assassins were accused of working in the interests of Serbia.

Even that might have been a small war of no great account, but Russia backed Serbia, Germany backed Austria-Hungary, and by August 4, all the European great powers were at war. What followed was called "the Great War" or "the World War" but nowadays it is known as "World War I."

Wilson at once declared the United States to be neutral. "We must be impartial in thought as well as in action," he said.

That was impossible, however. Few Americans were impartial in thought. Those who were of German descent were pro-German almost as a matter of course. Those who were of Irish descent were often so anti-English as to be pro-German, too. Most other Americans were, however, sympathetic to the cause of the Allies.

Americans tended to be pro-French, to begin with, because of the help France had given us in the course of the Revolutionary War, something that was never forgotten. The name of the French volunteer, Marquis de LaFayette was exceeded only by Washington himself in reverence. Besides, France was the only other great power to be a republic. As for Great Britain, her assiduous cultivation of American friendship in the three decades since the Venezuela border dispute now paid off.

On the other side, Germany was unfortunate in its ruler, Kaiser Wilhelm II, who had an irritating habit of striking arrogant attitudes that seemed to please the Germans, but no one else. Furthermore, the first month of the war saw immense German victories in the west and east and the Allies began to look like underdogs, and there is always something sympathetic about underdogs.

This was especially true in the case of Belgium, a small, neutral nation that Germany casually passed through on its way to the French border, in defiance of her treaty obligations and with no apparent remorse. There was enormous American sympathy for "poor little Belgium." The Germans began to seem like pitiless and sadistic bullies.

In one of Wilhelm II's less-inspired remarks, he had urged the German soldiers leaving for China at the time of the Boxer Rebellion to make themselves feared by the Chinese as the barbaric Huns had made themselves feared by the Romans. As a result, the Germans were now called "Huns" with all the evil connotations of the term.

And if Americans could not be neutral in thought, neither could they be neutral in action. The war was being fought totally and each side wanted to blockade the other into submission, and the United States, the most important neutral power, cooperated with Allied efforts in this respect far more than with those of the Central Powers.

The United States, being neutral, wished to trade with both sides, in accordance with the rules of "freedom of the sea" that had been set up in past years. Naturally, there was no expectation that the United States would be allowed to carry arms or ammunition to either side. What about food and other nonwar materials, however?

The trouble was that in the kind of war now being fought, food was as much a tool of war as cannon was, and each side was doing its level best to starve the other into surrender. Each was trying to stop all trade with the other.

In theory, both sides were equally opposed to the kind of neutral rights the United States tried to uphold, and both sides were therefore equally offensive to the United States. It was Great Britain, however, that had the largest fleet in the world and that dominated the sea. It was therefore Great Britain that patrolled the sea lanes and interfered with American trade. As for Germany, which lacked the capacity to do the same, she readily agreed to the kind of conditions the United States tried to impose, knowing well that Great Britain would not agree and hoping in this way to gain sympathy for herself while rousing anger against Great Britain.

If the United States were truly neutral, this would have been exactly what would have happened. The United States, however, was not really neutral. When Great Britain violated American rights, the United States softened its notes of protests, as it would not have done for Germany; and the United States was satisfied with British answers that would have been unsatisfactory had they been German answers.

Furthermore, although the United States was, in theory, opposed to loans to any of the warring nations, since that would be a nonneutral act, this position was not upheld. In 1915, American banks began to lend money to France and Great Britain—money with which the embattled nation could buy supplies in the United States or elsewhere. Germany was not benefited in this way. By April, 1917, some $2300 million had been loaned to the Allies as compared to $20 million to the Central Powers. This meant that the United States was putting together a large financial stake in an Allied victory, since if the Allies were defeated, it was likely they would not be able to pay their debts.

By 1915, the war was going badly for both sides. On the map, it looked as though Germany was doing well. In the west her armies were fighting well inside France and had at one point, shortly after the beginning of the war, nearly reached Paris. In the east, Germany's armies were fighting well inside the Polish province of Russia. On both fronts, Germany's armies had inflicted more damage than they had received and the Russians, in particular, had bled heavily.

This, however, was not the kind of war that Germany had planned to fight. She had planned what in later years was to be called a "blitzkrieg," a lightning war. Her plans were to swoop down on Paris, take it, knock France out of the war; then turn the full force of her armies against the large but ill-equipped and ill-led Russian forces and destroy them. Then, as master of Europe, she could make a victor's peace with Great Britain.

That was not the way it worked. France managed to hold out against the first fierce push, more through German tactical errors than anything else, and now the war had settled down to a long, long slugfest in which everyone was bleeding to death. The Allies, however, thanks to British command of the sea, could count on endless supplies from abroad, while the Central Powers were, in the end, sure to be choked to death no matter how many victories they won.

For Germany, the only way out of that predicament was somehow to starve the British first. Great Britain, with a large population concentrated on a small island, had for years been unable to feed itself but had depended on merchant ships to bring food in. What if this were interfered with?

The British had a navy to protect those merchant ships, but the Germans had something else—submarines. The Germans called them "Unterseeboots" ("under-sea ships") and this was abbreviated to "U-boats."

Submarines, moving underwater and therefore unseen, could sneak up on merchant ships and sink them with their torpedos. It was the one way that the British lifeline might be cut without the British navy being able to interfere. On February 4, 1915, therefore, Germany declared a blockade zone all around the British Isles in which enemy ships would be sunk at sight. Neutral shipping was warned that since British ships sometimes flew neutral flags as disguise, they could not be guaranteed safety.

Submarine warfare, however, had a certain horror about it. Submarines were rather rickety vessels that could be easily put out of action if seen. This meant that a submarine attack had to be a sneak attack, which seemed cowardly and mean. Then, too, submarines were small vessels that had no room for the passengers and crew of a sinking ship, so that those people had to be left to drown, which seemed cruel and heartless.

The introduction of submarine warfare changed the character of the conflict for Americans. Earlier, it had been a matter of ships being stopped and goods confiscated, with Great Britain the chief culprit. Now it was ships being sunk and people, possibly Americans, being drowned, with Germany the chief culprit. Anti-German sentiment soared in the United States. On February 10, the United States warned that it would hold Germany strictly accountable for any American loss of life.

The matter came to a crisis on May 7, 1915, when the Cunard liner, the *Lusitania*, was torpedoed off the Irish coast. It sank in 18 minutes and 1198 people lost their lives. Of these, 128 were Americans.

The *Lusitania* was carrying some war material and the Germans had warned that she was fair game. They had actually placed advertisements in American newspapers warning Americans not to take passage in liners that carried war material. Nevertheless, the American public was furious and Wilson fired off belligerent notes to Germany.

William Jennings Bryan was secretary of state. He was a thoroughgoing pacifist, and he felt that Americans should not travel on belligerent ships; that to allow them to do so and then protest the consequences was simply asking for war. He therefore resigned on June 8, 1915, when he thought the American reaction was becoming so strong as to risk war. Replacing him was an expert in international law, Robert Lansing (born in Watertown, New York, on October 17, 1864). He was strongly pro-Allies and labored to end unnecessary American involvements in the Caribbean, in order that the nation be ready for greater tasks in Europe.

By July 21, a third note was sent to Germany on the *Lusitania* affair, over the signature of Lansing, one that was just about an ultimatum. Germany backed down, promising not to sink liners without warning and without providing for the safety of noncombatants. It was a diplomatic victory, especially since Germany eventually apologized for the sinking and offered an indemnity.

However, Germany could not really stop submarine warfare without losing the war and this was, sooner or later, bound to bring the United States into the war on the side of the Allies.

PREPAREDNESS

American anger against Germany also mounted as revelations were made concerning German plans to sabotage American plants that served as arsenals for the Allies. On July 24, 1915, Heinrich Albert, director of German propaganda within the United States carelessly left his briefcase on a New York subway train. It was picked up at once by American agents and proved to have documents relating to sabotage plans signed by Franz von Papen, a military attaché to the German embassy, and by the ambassador himself.

On November 30, there was an explosion at a du Pont powder plant in Wilmington, Delaware, and 31 people were killed. There was a widespread conviction that this was the result of German sabotage. The fact that on the next day, the United States requested the recall of von Papen lent official weight to this belief. On July 30, 1916, there was a munitions explosion on Black Tom Island, New Jersey, which did 22 million dollars worth of damage and again German sabotage was suspected.

Those Americans who felt that all this was preliminary to open American participation in the war realized that there was nothing the United States could do in its then state of military readiness. Visions of the United States being as helpless as "poor little Belgium" seemed natural.

A strong movement for "Preparedness" began, therefore. Among those who were prominent in the movement was Theodore Roosevelt who was, perhaps, the outstanding American jingo at this time. He attacked Wilson intemperately as a weakling and, by strong implication, a coward. Other interventionists of the time were Henry Cabot Lodge and the man who had been Taft's secretary of war, Henry Lewis Stimson (born in New York City on September 21, 1867).

There were also Americans who were determinedly pacifistic and who saw the European war as a great tragedy that the United States must labor to stop, rather than to join. The pacifists, however, were rather ineffectual and, sometimes, ridiculous.

The automobile magnate, Henry Ford, for instance, meaning well, chartered a ship and, on December 4, 1915, with twenty of his staff, plus sixty pacifists of various shades and fifty-seven newsmen, embarked for Europe. On December 19, the "peace ship" reached a port in neutral Norway and, of course, there was nothing it could do. The pacifists had quarreled among themselves over small matters throughout the voyage, and Henry Ford, disillusioned, secretly left for home on December 24. Those pacifists who remained toured neutral countries and made speeches, but it was all empty wind and the episode played into the hands of the jingos by making pacifism seem foolish.

On occasion, there was more direct action against the mounting war fervor. There was a preparedness parade in San Francisco on July 22, 1916, and in the course of it a bomb exploded, killing ten people and injuring forty. Nobody has ever discovered who was responsible, but somewhere in the vicinity were Thomas J. Mooney (born in 1882) and Warren K. Billings (born in 1894). They were watching the parade peaceably and had nothing to do with the bomb, but they were pacifists and radical labor leaders and that seemed crime enough.

They were seized and brought to trial in the usual atmosphere of hysteria that prevails under such conditions. Mooney and Billings, protesting their innocence, had no chance. The evidence against them was shaky and later proved to be perjured, but Mooney was condemned to death and Billings to life imprisonment. The trial was phony enough to cause Wilson to change the death sentence to life imprisonment, and the two remained in jail till 1939 before they were pardoned and released.

Wilson was himself not eager for war. Although his interventionist secretary of state, Lansing, made no secret of his feeling that Germany must be defeated, even at the cost of American intervention, Wilson hung back.

On May 10, 1915, in Philadelphia, Wilson, in the course of a speech, made the statement, "There is such a thing as a man being too proud to fight. There is such a thing as a nation being so right that it does not need to convince others by force that it is right."

This was widely ridiculed by the interventionists and, to be sure, the concept of being too proud to fight was not an easy one to get across. It was a lot easier to think of someone as being too scared to fight and that was the point that Roosevelt in particular kept making about Wilson.

Still, in the wake of the *Lusitania* crisis, and of other deaths of Americans at sea by German submarine action, Wilson had to give in. There was no way in which the United States could make increasingly belligerent noises against Germany without developing something in the way of military force. By the end of the year, Wilson was presenting a program for expansion of the military and in January, 1916, he was touring the country to advocate preparedness.

Wilson saw clearly that if the war continued the United States would sooner or later be drawn in, and he longed therefore to have the war end. Since nobody was winning the war and everyone was clearly losing, it should be possible to have all the warring nations agree to some reasonable peace.

Wilson sent his close friend and adviser Colonel House to Europe in early 1915 to sound out the warring nations and all of them had agreed peace was desirable but each wanted the other side to buy peace with concessions while it refused to make any of its own.

In January 1916, Wilson sent House to Europe a second time. This time, the United States was more clearly on the side of the Allies, and House told the British that if they agreed to a peace conference and the Germans did not, the Americans would come into the war against Germany.

Even so, the Allies wouldn't move. They feared the bluff might work too well; that Germany would accept a peace conference, that they would then demand concessions, and that the United States would put pressure on the Allies to yield in order to end the war.

So the war continued with each side fearing defeat would be intolerable and that one more push might bring victory. And the United States found herself increasingly caught in a tangle of events that was dragging her into the war willy-nilly.

And the war was growing more horrible and fearful.

In 1916, the Germans launched a great offensive against the French fortifications about the city of Verdun near the middle of the Western Front. The French were determined to hold that city to the end. Hundreds of thousands died on each side for the sake of insignificant gains of territory first one way, then the other.

Farther to the northwest, the British were fighting at the Somme

River. It was at this Battle of the Somme that the British first used armored vehicles. These were called "tanks" while they were being developed, to hide their real nature, and the name stuck. Again, hundreds of thousands died without important change in the area controlled.

In the east, Russia, which had been losing steadily but had been holding on with grim tenacity over the bodies of its soldiers, launched a counteroffensive and by the time it was stopped, she had lost an additional million men and had nearly ruined herself.

This incredibly bloody mess, fought by generals who, among all of them, showed scarcely any sign of military talent, destroyed forever the myth of the glamour of war.

The only battle of the year that proved decisive came at sea. The German fleet, second only to that of Great Britain, had, during the first two years of the war remained in port, for Germany had been reluctant to risk it.

Yet it was British control of the seas that kept Great Britain from starvation and that was slowly, in turn, strangling Germany. If the British fleet were broken, then German victory was sure. Submarine warfare might have turned the trick, but Germany had promised the United States that submarine warfare would be stopped. That meant there was nothing left but to try the gamble of breaking the British fleet by the use of the surface vessels of the German navy.

At the end of May, the German fleet came out of harbor. The watching British fleet steamed to meet it and off the Danish peninsula of Jutland, the battle was fought on May 31 and June 1, 1916. It was the last great naval battle fought between surface ships only, with neither submarines nor airplanes involved.

The German fleet was smaller but it was better handled and displayed better marksmanship. The British lost more ships, with nearly twice the tonnage of the German losses, so that viewed in itself, the Battle of Jutland was a tactical German victory.

However, the British could afford to lose more ships and those it lost it could replace more quickly. The Germans, realizing that, even while it was winning, their fleet would be destroyed, made for the safety of the ports again and never emerged again for the duration of the war. The battle was a strategic British victory, therefore, since Britain retained control of the seas.

If British standing in the eyes of Americans was improved by the result of the Battle of Jutland, it had received a bad blow in the events that took place in Ireland a month before the battle.

The Irish, so long under the British boot, saw in British difficulties opportunities for themselves. A rebellion might succeed when Great Britain's military might was so involved elsewhere, especially if help might somehow arrive from Germany.

On April 24, 1916, Easter Monday, some 2000 Irish rebels took over various strategic points in Dublin and proclaimed the Irish Republic. The British, however, had known what was going on and did not need to divert much in the way of troops to handle the poorly armed and organized rebels. In a week, the British had restored order and, eventually, hanged fourteen leaders of the rebellion.

This meant that a new thrill of hatred for Great Britain was felt by all Irish-Americans, and those who favored American neutrality were able to point out that both sides were equal sinners in their treatment of small nations.

11

WORLD WAR I

"HE KEPT US OUT OF WAR"

In the stalemate year of 1916, a new American presidential election loomed.

On June 7, the Republican party met in convention in Chicago. The leading candidate for the nomination was Charles Evans Hughes (born in Glens Falls, New York, on April 11, 1862). He had a record of intelligent and honest service, had been a two-term governor of New York between 1906 and 1910, and had then been appointed by Taft to the Supreme Court. He was willing to step down, however, in order to run for president, and on the third ballot, he was nominated.

For vice-president, the Republicans nominated Fairbanks, who had held that post under Roosevelt. It was a clear gesture of peace toward the formidable ex-President.

Roosevelt was all for that. The Progressive party met on June 7 also, and in Chicago as well. It nominated Roosevelt for president once again, of course, and Roosevelt at once declined and announced he would support Hughes. With that, the Progressive party, which had made such a brave show in 1912, simply disintegrated and disappeared. The Republican party was reunited.

On June 14, 1916, the Democratic National Convention was held in St. Louis, and Wilson and Marshall were renominated by acclamation for president and vice-president.

Things boded ill for Wilson, however. He had won the election in 1912 only because the opposition had been so badly split, and he had only received a little over 40 percent of the vote. Could he win over a united Republican party that from 1860 on had won 15 out of 18 presidential elections?

The interventionists were, for the most part, Republicans, and there was no way Wilson could win them over. He therefore had to try hard to hold on to those who did not want war. When Wilson was being seconded for the nomination, one of the speakers had listed his various diplomatic feats with the refrain, "And we did not have war." Consequently, the slogan "He kept us out of war" was coined and was widely used during the campaign. Wilson carefully refrained from promising flatly that he would continue to keep the nation out of war, but the antiwar segment of the population rallied to him.

Hughes, as it turned out, was a poor campaigner. Although he traveled round the country, as did Wilson, Hughes was a reserved man without charisma, who did not rouse his audiences with his oratory. Also, he retained the beard of an older generation and with the opening of the twentieth century, smooth-shaven faces had come into fashion, so that he seemed out of touch with the times.

Nor did Hughes have the feel for practical politics. The governor of California, Hiram Johnson, had run for vice-president on the Progressive ticket in 1912. When Hughes campaigned in California, he did not bother to call on Johnson, perhaps because he felt the defector did not deserve the honor. It was a mistake, for Johnson's feelings were hurt, and that proved to be important.

Even so, with all Hughes's failings, the traditional Republican ascendancy of half a century made it a close race.

The election was held on November 7, 1916, and as the evening progressed it became clear that Hughes was carrying every large state in the northeast, with the exception of Ohio. Wilson was only carrying the smaller states of the south and west. As the night wore on, it seemed clear that Hughes was going to make it.

Finally, it was all up to California. Minus California, the electoral votes stood at 264 for Wilson and 254 for Hughes. California's thirteen electoral votes could move the election either way, and the decision was coming in slowly, partly because California time was three hours earlier than east coast time so that the polls closed late by eastern time, and partly because the count was close.

Nevertheless, California hadn't gone for Wilson in 1912. It had gone for Roosevelt and Johnson, so it was assumed that Governor Johnson's influence would hold it in line. The Democrats virtually conceded defeat and when Hughes went to bed, he was sure he was the president-elect.

But now the snub to Johnson produced its fatal effect. Johnson's lack of ardor for the Republican ticket had resulted in a failure to get out the maximum Republican vote and toward morning it was clear that, by a margin of 4000, California was moving into the Democratic column. Wilson was reelected in one of the most thrilling squeakers Election Day had ever seen, 277 electoral votes to 254.

There is a story that a newspaperman, arriving at Hughes's headquarters to give him the news, was told by an aide, "The president-elect is sleeping." The newspaperman said, "Tell the president-elect when he wakes up that he isn't the president-elect."

Wilson's victory, despite the delay in its coming, was a solid one. In popular votes, he had 9,100,000 to Hughes's 8,500,000. Wilson did not quite get an overall majority of the votes, however. He had 49.3 percent to Hughes's 46.1 percent, because there were minor parties in the field who carried off the remaining nearly 5 percent. The Socialists got 3.2 percent and the Prohibitionists 1.2 percent.

Wilson drew in with him the sixty-fifth Congress, which was the third in a row to be Democratic in both houses. In the Senate, the margin was 53 to 42, but in the House, the Democratic hold was narrow. It was 216 to 210, with 6 Representatives belonging to neither party.

Marshall, upon being reelected vice-president, was the first man to serve a second term in that office since 1828. In the eighty-eight years since then, even when the same man had been elected to the presidency twice, as with Lincoln, Grant, Cleveland, and McKinley, it had been with a different vice-president the second time in each case.

Montana elected as its representative Jeannette Rankin. She was the first woman to serve in Congress and she did so at a time when women could not yet vote for national offices, nor, in most states, for any office.

Jews, too, broke precedent in this respect. On January 28, 1916, Wilson had named one of America's greatest lawyers, Louis Dembitz Brandeis (born in Louisville, Kentucky, on November 13, 1856), to the Supreme Court. He was the first Jew to reach so high a position in the government. There was great opposition to it, based openly on nothing more than the fact that he was Jewish and therefore had an "Oriental mind," but the Senate confirmed the appointment 47 to 22.

On March 5, 1917 (March 4 was a Sunday), Wilson was reinaugurated president and found himself governing a nation that was steadily continuing its transformation into the industrial giant of the world.

Automobile traffic was becoming a major form of transportation and the first traffic lights were set up in Cleveland on August 5, 1914. In 1915, taxicabs came into use.

Long-distance telephones now spanned the nation. On January 25, 1915, Bell, the inventor of the telephone, once again said his famous first words to his coworker, Thomas A. Watson, "Mr. Watson, come here, I want you." This time, however, they were not on separate floors; Bell was in New York and Watson was in San Francisco. What's more, radio communication could now put the United States in direct touch with Germany over oceans and battlefields.

The airplane was becoming capable of wonders and, in 1914, an American plane set an altitude record of nearly 4.8 kilometers and flew over Mount Whitney, the highest mountain in the 48 states. Overseas, it was beginning to be used in warfare.

The motion picture was increasing in popularity each year. In 1915, the first of the great movies, *The Birth of a Nation*, was released. In 1917, the nation was paying over $175,000,000 in admission to the movie theaters.

SUBMARINES AND THE ZIMMERMANN NOTE

Wilson's great problem after his reelection continued to be the European war.

At home, he cleared the decks. He recalled Pershing from his useless pursuit of Villa, and he made sure that the nation was in complete control of the Caribbean. (Now that the Panama Canal was open, the United States had to make sure that it was absolutely safe, so that it could be securely used in case of war.) And it was in complete control, for in addition to the American possession of Puerto Rico, American troops were in Cuba, Haiti, the Dominican Republic, Nicaragua, and Panama.

In fact, the only loophole possible was in connection with the Danish West Indies, three small islands that formed part of a group called the Virgin Islands lying just east of Puerto Rico. The islands had been in the possession of Denmark for two and a half centuries. Denmark was neutral in the war but its only land boundary was with Germany, and there was some fear that Denmark might be forced to cede the islands to Germany, which might then use them as her base in the Caribbean.

How Germany could do that in the face of the British and American fleets passes human understanding, but the fear existed and the United States moved first. It put the necessary pressure on Denmark and on August 4, 1916, Denmark agreed to accept $25,000,000 for the islands. On January 17, 1917, the transfer of sovereignty was made official.

Meanwhile, Germany, heartened by the election, and by the use of the "He kept us out of war" slogan, moved to take advantage of what it thought to be American eagerness to avoid war. In the west she controlled Belgium and a large section of northeastern France. In the east, she controlled Russia's westernmost provinces while that vast nation was reeling on the brink of anarchy and revolution.

Now, then, was the time for Germany. If she could force peace talks she would be bound to end up with some of the land that she now controlled outside her boundaries. Without actually saying that she intended to ask for territorial gains, Germany indicated to Wilson both before and after his reelection that she was ready to talk peace.

Wilson greeted the news gladly and assumed that such talks would be on the kind of level his own idealism would welcome. On January 22, 1917, he made a speech before the Senate in which he called for a "peace without victory"—a return, in other words, to the situation as it was when the war began.

Well, none of the warring nations wanted that. Each wanted victory and even Russia was not yet ready to concede defeat. So there was no peace conference.

The German military machine had not expected one. The military leaders had been willing to allow the government to make its try for peace, but at the first indication that Wilson's idea was "peace without victory" they moved toward their own next step.

That had to be submarine warfare again. To be sure, the Germans had promised the United States that they would not do this, but now they had no alternative. The attempt to use the German fleet to break British naval power had failed at Jutland, and Germany's only remaining chance of victory was to starve Great Britain by means of the submarine.

There was a chance that that might bring the United States into the war but the reasoning was that (1) the United States might not come in; (2) the United States might come in, but would come in regardless of what the Germans might do; (3) even if the United States came in, Germany might force victory before the Americans could ever manage to ferry an army across the ocean.

On January 31, 1917, therefore, Germany announced the resumption of unrestricted submarine warfare. Any ship, and that included American ships, that entered the various blockade zones set up by the Germans, would be subject to being torpedoed without warning.

Nor did the United States have to wait long to find out whether the Germans were serious about this. On February 3, 1917, a German submarine sank the American ship *Housatonic*. In this case, warning was given so that there was time to launch the lifeboats—but the ship was sunk. On that day, the United States broke diplomatic relations with Germany.

Wilson went on to try to get Congress to order the arming of merchantmen so that they could fight back against submarines, if possible. The House agreed at once, 403 to 13, but the Senate stalled. In the Senate there was the tradition of unlimited debate and twelve pacifists, led by La Follette, feeling that arming was merely an incitement to war and that it would make more sense to keep the merchantmen at home for the duration, proceeded to debate unlimitedly. The Senate did not act, therefore, and Wilson exploded in exasperation against what he called "a little group of willful men, representing no opinion but their own." He then went on to order the merchantmen armed, on presidential authority.

What was needed was some final act by the Germans to move American public opinion massively and irretrievably into the camp of intervention—and Germany managed to provide it.

The German Foreign Minister, Alfred Zimmermann, thought he saw a chance of immobilizing the United States by capitalizing on the recent difficulties between that nation and Mexico. On January 19, 1917, he sent a telegram to the German minister to Mexico for transmission to the Mexican government. He suggested that if the United States went to war against Germany, Mexico should seize the opportunity of declaring war on the United States. (This would occupy the United States on its own borders, Zimmermann reasoned, and prevent effective American intervention in Europe.)

What was in it for Mexico? Why, whether Mexico won or lost, a German victory would mean that Mexico would receive as the reward for its help, some of the territory it had lost in the Mexican War, seventy years before—specifically, Texas, New Mexico, and Arizona.

It was a ridiculous move. Mexico was not likely to risk such a war no matter what, since it had no military force to speak of and was still in a state of anarchy. Then, too, even if Mexico made the gesture and fought as well as it could, even a German victory in Europe would not save Mexico from American frustration and fury afterward.

What was even worse for Germany was that this foolish proposition did not even reach its destination. The British intercepted the message, finally managed to decode it and, scarcely able to believe their good fortune, turned it over to the United States on February 24, 1917. On March 1, the United States, convinced that the telegram was genuine, published the note, and a spasm of rage passed over the American people.

In the 140 years of the existence of the United States, American territory had grown steadily larger, and never had a single square centimeter of that territory ever been yielded up to foreign force. Even the suggestion that such a thing was possible raised the war cry to new and deafening heights.

At the same time, something else happened. Russia finally collapsed. The suffering of her people and the incredible inefficiency of her government finally caused the army itself to join the rebelling populace. On March 15, 1917, Tsar Nicholas II was forced to abdicate, and a new government under revolutionaries intending to set up a parliamentary democracy was set up.

This meant that the Russian resistance on the Eastern Front would weaken even further but there was a good side, too, to the news. Many Americans failed to see the advantage of fighting against autocratic Germany and Austria-Hungary, when that meant fighting on the side of a still more autocratic Russia, whose anti-Semitic pogroms held it up to the world as a model of bestiality.

If, however, Russia was now going to be a democratic republic, the battle-lines would be clearly drawn. It would truly be the democracies versus the autocracies. The United States eagerly recognized the new government on March 22—the first nation to do so—and Wilson would soon be able to say that the war was designed to "make the world safe for democracy."

The day before that recognition, on March 21, a German submarine sank the American steamer *Healdton,* this time without warning. It was the latest of several such incidents and it was the last straw. Wilson called a special session of Congress into being. It passed resolutions of war against Germany and, on April 6, 1917, Wilson made it official and the United States was at war.

AMERICA AT WAR

To the Allies, it must have seemed that American intervention had come not a moment too soon, for things looked blacker than ever for them.

In the east, the new democratic government in Russia tried to

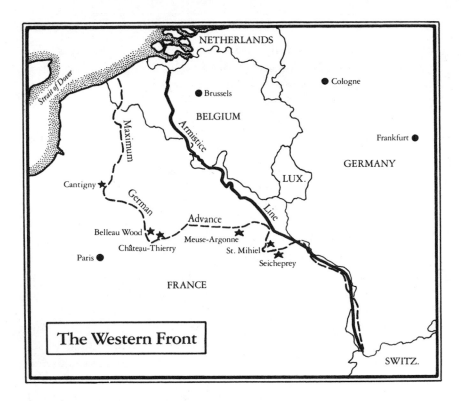

The Western Front

continue the war and actually launched an offensive in July, 1917, but the Russian people no longer wanted to fight, and the Germans had no trouble smashing the half-hearted advance and then, in their turn, advancing deeper into the land. The Eastern Front virtually disappeared.

In the west, new Allied offensives failed with new slaughter and a dangerous mood of mutiny was appearing in the French army. Furthermore, in April 1917, the month of American entry, 881,000 tons of Allied shipping were sent to the bottom. Ships were going down twice as fast as they could be replaced. It would not be long at that rate before the British would be starving. It seemed quite reasonable for Germany to hope that a decision, favorable to herself, would be reached long before American intervention could be made effective.

The United States, however, moved more rapidly than anyone in Europe expected. She threw her fleet into the war at once, carrying supplies and helping set up convoys for Allied shipping. This quickly reduced the monthly toll of loss to the submarines to about 300,000 tons and then to 200,000. That was still a fearful loss but it was not fatal. At that rate, the submarine strategy would fail.

Then, too, the United States established a draft, began training men at a great rate, and prepared to send an army to Europe, for the first time in its history, and all this much more rapidly than anyone would have thought possible.

The first skimpy contingents of the American Expeditionary Force were ordered to Europe on May 18, 1917. They embarked on June 13 and landed on June 26. At their head was Pershing, fresh from his Mexican campaign. On July 4, 1917, Pershing, at the head of these first American troops ever to fight in Europe, marched through Paris to enormous French enthusiasm. The Americans weren't many in number, but they represented a new and untouched source of vast numbers of men who would relieve a nation that had been bled white by the war.

The Americans marched five miles from the tomb of Napoleon to the tomb of LaFayette, the great French volunteer in the American Revolutionary War. Pershing deputed a friend, Colonel Charles E. Stanton, to say something appropriate, and he remarked simply, "LaFayette, we are here." No greater eloquence, at any length, was possible.

The British and French wanted to use the American troops as they came across, feeding them into British and French divisions as reinforcements. This Pershing prevented, and it was an implacable decision. He saw that Americans, a few at a time, in Allied divisions, would be used up to no purpose, with no credit. He insisted instead that the Americans would form their own divisions and go into battle as units under their own commanders and in this, he was firmly supported by Wilson.

It was not till October 23, 1917, that any American fired a shot against the Germans, and by that time, things looked even worse for the Allies. Mutinies in the French army had been quelled only by shooting various soldiers chosen by lot from the affected regiments and there were serious doubts as to how effective the French army would continue to be.

The Italians, who were fighting on the side of the Allies, were smashed at the Battle of Caporetto and were reduced to virtual helplessness. In Russia, the radical revolutionaries—Communists under Nikolai Lenin—were seizing power in the Russian capital, Petrograd, and in Moscow.

It almost seemed as though one last German push against the west would settle the entire war, and Germany let matters simmer down during the winter of 1917–1918, in order that it might prepare for that last push. Meanwhile, by that winter, there were over 100,000 Americans in France, with more pouring into the country every day.

The United States was fighting its first prolonged and deadly war since the Civil War and its very first against a foreign enemy. It was the first in which every aspect of American life was involved. There was price-fixing and military training for draftees and drives for the purchase of war bonds and government control of the railroads.

Patriotism was debased. People at home, who were not fighting an armed enemy, felt it their duty to fight anyone who might be accused of being a spy or traitor. Up to 1500 pacifists were arrested and many, including Debs and Haywood, were thrown in jail.

Americans denounced not only German civilians in the United States, but threw German books out of the libraries, German music out of the repertoire, and German food out of the menus. Beethoven and Goethe were somehow confused with the Kaiser, and sauerkraut was renamed "liberty cabbage." People actually kicked dachshunds. It was not one of the more inspiring periods of American history.

Of course, there was suffering. There were coal shortages particularly, because of the difficulty of allocating transport, and the winter of 1917–1918 was a freezing time in the north. The necessity for exporting as much food as possible abroad put Americans on short rations.

A severe propaganda blow was felt toward the end of the year when the new Communist government in Russia uncovered the records of the defunct tsarist regime and came across copies of secret treaties among the Allied powers that showed them clearly to be far more rapacious under cover than they pretended to be on the surface. The Communists promptly published these treaties and if something weren't done, there was the danger that the war would seem only a conflict among thieves so that the American people would lose heart.

Wilson was anxious to prevent this and, also, to force a new understanding in place of the secret treaties. On January 8, 1918, therefore, in a speech to Congress, he announced the various goals and war aims to which he wanted the Allies to feel dedicated. There were fourteen of these and they came to be known as the "Fourteen Points."

They were, put most simply:

1. All treaties to be arrived at in public discussion and then to be published.

2. Freedom of the seas, with all nations possessing equal access to the sea in peace and war.

3. No economic barriers so that all the world could trade freely.

4. Disarmament as far as possible.

5. Adjustment of all conflicts in colonial claims, with due consideration being given to the native populations.

6. Evacuation of Russia, and no interference with its government. (Wilson was still hoping for a democratic government there.)

7. Evacuation of Belgium.

8. Evacuation of France, and restoration of Alsace-Lorraine, which Germany had taken in 1870, to France.

9. Italy's boundaries to be readjusted to include Italian settlements just beyond its borders.

10. Freedom for the various submerged nationalities in Austria-Hungary.

11. Boundaries in the Balkans to be adjusted according to nationality, and Serbia to have access to the sea.

12. Freedom for the various submerged nationalities in the Turkish Empire (which was fighting on the side of Germany), with free access to the Dardanelles Straits at Constantinople for all nations.

13. A free Poland, with access to the sea.

14. An association of nations that would settle disputes and prevent wars in the future.

These fourteen points were mostly at the expense of Germany, Austria-Hungary, and Turkey, but the Allies were unenthusiastic. They were not delighted over freedom of the seas, free trade, disarmament, and consideration for colonial populations. They did not want to have their hands tied at the peace table, since it was possible they might want a little injustice in their own favor when the time came. However, since they could not afford to offend the United States, they accepted the Fourteen Points with what enthusiasm they could pump up.

THE FINAL OFFENSIVES

The winter (the last of the war, as it turned out) passed, and it was time to accelerate the fighting again. Germany was ready.

On the Eastern Front, the war was over. On March 3, 1918, the Communist government of Russia had been compelled to sign a drastic peace treaty at the town of Brest-Litovsk that split one third of its entire population away, and set whole provinces up as German puppet states. This meant that Germany could ship most of its eastern armies westward to the Western Front.

There, things were not so bright. Submarine warfare had definitely failed thanks to the American fleet and accelerated American supplies, and the American army was being built up in France far more quickly than Germany had anticipated.

But the German general Erich Ludendorff had worked out a new form of tactics. Until then, both sides had simply attacked all along the line and tried to push the enemy back everywhere. This had been stupid, ineffective and incredibly bloody. Ludendorff worked out a scheme of "infiltration" whereby the initial advance probed for weak spots. There was then a concentration at the weak spot and a breakthrough, leaving the strong spots behind to be disposed of at leisure. Indeed, once the breakthrough took place, the enemy might have to withdraw generally.

Ludendorff built up Germany's army with soldiers brought from the east until he had superiority in numbers. Then, on March 21, 1918, he attacked at the point of junction of the British and French armies, where the leadership, being double, might be confused. Behind a tremendous artillery barrage, he managed to break through the British lines and in a week gained over 40 kilometers.

Nothing like this had been seen in three and a half years of trench warfare and the Allies reacted with virtual panic. Great Britain and France, for the first time, agreed on a single overall generalissimo for the Western Front. They chose the French general, Ferdinand Foch. Pershing came to see him, and though he continued to insist on

Americans serving as separate units, offered to place himself under Foch and to use all his men in an attempt to stop the offensive.

The Germans kept it up, however. After a pause to regroup, they surged forward a second time, and then a third. By June 3, the Germans were at the French town of Château-Thierry, just 90 kilometers east of Paris. It was close enough for Germany's biggest guns to lob shells into the city. There were important signs that the Allies might be giving up. The French government was preparing to leave Paris and increasing numbers of French soldiers grew hopeless enough to wish to surrender.

By that time, Pershing had, under his command, 325,000 men divided into four divisions. A few thousand Americans had been under fire in the course of Ludendorff's "spring offensive," but now came the time for American soldiers to show their metal.

On June 4, American soldiers moved toward Château-Thierry and stopped the German advance even as the French were retreating around them. They then went on the offensive. West of Château-Thierry was a small wooded area, Belleau Wood, which the Germans were holding in force. On June 6, American soldiers poured into it and for the first time, Americans in force met German veterans. The fight lasted a week and over half the Americans were killed or wounded, but they took Belleau Wood.

The German advance, magnificent though it looked on the map, and though it drove the Allies to the edge of defeat, was not carried through without cost. The Germans lost heavily both in men and material, and they were exhausted. Though they had gained much ground, they had not reached Ludendorff's objectives, and he was running out of time and force. Then, on top of that, he found, at the last minute, Americans fighting in the line against him, and fighting with ferocity and determination.

Ludendorff decided he had to make one last try, but not immediately. He could squeeze nothing more out of his troops for a while, so he called a halt for three weeks. The Allies welcomed the halt for they needed it desperately to strengthen their own lines and, most of all, to bring in more Americans.

Then, on July 15, Ludendorff ordered another push at Rheims, at a point on the front about 55 kilometers east of Château-Thierry. As usual, the Germans advanced at first, but now they encountered

Americans again, 85,000 of them, and those Americans stood firm.

After three days, the Germans were played out and at this moment, Foch, judging the time precisely, sent in troops, including 270,000 Americans, in a counterattack. About 54,000 Americans were also counterattacking along with the British further south.

The Germans gave way and Ludendorff knew it was all over. There was nothing left in the German army and it could attack no more. It could only defend. As for the Allies, they could continue to attack indefinitely, since more and more Americans, fresh and eager, were pouring into the lines.

By August 10, Pershing finally extorted permission from the Allies to organize an entire independent American army for action at chosen points, and Ludendorff advised the Kaiser to make peace on any terms he could.

The German government couldn't believe that. Germany had fought for so many years, always giving better than she had received. She had smashed Russia, Rumania, and Italy, and only a few months before had all but smashed France. The government couldn't bring themselves to acknowledge defeat so the war continued till the fact of defeat was made clear even to the dullest German and, of course, at the cost of thousands of additional lives.

During the final offensive against the Germans, the American army was concentrated at St. Mihiel, near the southern end of the front where the German holdings bulged into French territory as a salient. The newly formed army, half a million strong, under Pershing's sole command, attacked on September 12.

In two days of hot fighting, the Americans took over the entire salient, capturing 16,000 prisoners and 443 guns, at a cost of only 7000 casualties to themselves.

It was Pershing's intention now to do what Ludendorff had done, and to infiltrate. He wanted to follow up the victory, which left him facing an utterly demoralized German army, by punching through into German territory, realizing that this was likely to force an immediate German surrender.

Foch, however, had not caught on to the new way of fighting war. He was a veteran of four years of trench warfare and to him it was still a matter of rolling back the German line all along the front, even if at great cost. Foch was generalissimo and Pershing had to give in. The

Americans were moved westward to the section of the front along the Meuse River and the Argonne forest.

From September 26 onward, for some six weeks, the Americans pressed forward. There were 1,200,000 American soldiers fighting in that sector now which made it the greatest battle in which American soldiers were engaged up to that time. There were some 120,000 casualties. By November 7, the Americans had reached the city of Sedan near the German border, over 50 kilometers from their starting point.

It was all over by then. Germany's two minor allies, Bulgaria and Turkey, had surrendered and on October 23, Ludendorff was relieved of his command and fled to neutral Sweden. On November 4, 1918, Austria-Hungary surrendered and Germany was left alone. On November 9, Kaiser Wilhelm II abdicated and fled Germany for the neutral Netherlands, and on November 11, 1918, Germany surrendered, and the war ground to a halt.

World War I had lasted a little over fifty-one months. On the Allied side over 42,000,000 men were engaged in fighting in one way or another as against 23,000,000 men on the side of the Central Powers. The Allies lost a total of 5,000,000 dead (mostly French and Russians) while the Central Powers suffered 3,400,000 dead (mostly German and Austro-Hungarian.) More than 21,000,000 men on both sides were wounded.

The United States got off comparatively lightly. It was in the war only nineteen months and Americans saw heavy fighting for only about six months. The United States had 4,735,000 men serving in its armed forces by the end of the war and about 2,000,000 of them were in France at the time of the Armistice.

Of these, 53,400 died (one-third as many as had died on the Union side alone in the Civil War.) An additional 63,000 died outside of battle, a good many of them of the influenza epidemic that wracked the world in 1918 and killed even more human beings than the war did. Some 204,000 Americans were wounded.

With the war over, Europe was in a shambles. Russia and Austria-Hungary were in a state of disintegration. Italy was reduced to ineffectuality. Germany was exhausted and at the mercy of her conquerors. France and Great Britain were intact but almost as exhausted as Germany.

Of the world's great powers, only the two non-European ones remained strong and essentially untouched: Japan and the United States. Of the two, the United States was clearly the stronger.

In fact, one hundred and forty-two years after thirteen raggle-taggle colonies had decided to declare their independence from powerful Great Britain, the United States had become incomparably the strongest nation in the world, something everyone could see. And its president, Woodrow Wilson, was incomparably the most powerful individual in the world.

Millions of people everywhere now looked to the United States, and to Wilson, for the establishment of a just peace and of a world without war.

And yet first Wilson and then the United States, through short-sightedness, threw it all away. Instead, the United States permitted a situation to arise that made it possible for another and even worse war to break out in only twenty years.

How that came about will have to be the story of the next volume of this history of the United States.

A TABLE OF DATES

1863 June 7 French troops occupy Mexico City

1864 June 10 Maximilian of
Austria becomes Emperor
of Mexico

1865 April 14 Lincoln assassinated; Andrew Johnson
becomes 17th President of
the United States
May 10 Capture of Con-
federate president, Jefferson Davis
December 18 13th
Amendment becomes part
of Constitution; slavery
outlawed
December 24 Ku Klux
Klan founded

1866 June 16 14th Amend-
ment becomes part of
Constitution; Blacks granted citizenship
July 24 Tennessee read-
mitted to the Union

1867 March 1 Nebraska enters
the Union as the 37th state
March 2 Reconstruction
Act passed; ten ex-Con-
federate States under military rule

March 14 Last French
troops leave Mexico under
American pressure
June 19 Maximilian ex-
ecuted in Mexico
July 1 Dominion of Cana-
da comes into being
August 5 Johnson defies
Congress and asks for res-
ignation of Secretary of
War Stanton
August 28 United States
annexes Midway Islands
October 18 United
States purchases Alaska
from Russia

1868 February 24 House of
Representatives impeach-
es President Johnson
May 26 Senate acquits
President Johnson by one
vote
June 23 Christopher I.
Sholes patents typewriter
June 25 Ex-Confederate
States begin to be read-
mitted to Union under car-
petbagger governments
November 3 Ulysses S.
Grant (R) elected presi-

dent over Horatio Sey-
mour (D)
December 25 Jefferson
Davis pardoned

1869 March 4 Grant inaugurated as 18th President of
the United States
May 10 First transconti-
nental railroad completed
September Prohibition
party founded
September 24 "Black
Friday" on Wall Street;
Gould and Fisk try to corner gold

1870 Population of the United
States, 38,558,371
March 30 15th Amend-
ment becomes part of the
Constitution; Blacks given
vote

1871 January 18 German Em-
pire founded
October 8 Great
Chicago fire

1872 February 17 United
States takes over Pago
Pago in Samoa
August 25 *Alabama*
claims dispute decided in
favor of the United States
November 5 Grant (R)
reelected president over
Horace Greeley (LR)
November 29 Death of
Horace Greeley

1873 February 12 Gold standard adopted
March 4 Grant reinau-
gurated
September 18 Jay

Cooke's firm bankrupt;
"Panic of 1873"

1874 Woman's Christian Temperance Union founded

1875 July 31 Death of Andrew
Johnson
November 22 Vice-Pres-
ident Wilson dies in office

1876 February 14 Alexander
G. Bell patents telephone
May 10 Grant opens
Centennial Exposition
June 5 James G. Blaine
reads Mulligan letters to
Congress
June 25 Battle of the Lit-
tle Big Horn. Sitting Bull
defeats George A. Custer
July 4 Centennial of the
independence of the Unit-
ed States
August 1 Colorado en-
ters the Union as the 38th
state
November 7 Disputed
election between Samuel J.
Tilden (D) and Rutherford
B. Hayes (R)

1877 March 2 1876 election
decided in favor of Hayes
March 5 Hayes inaugu-
rated as 19th President of
the United States
September 5 Crazy
Horse shot "while at-
tempting to escape"
October 5 Joseph of Nez
Perce Indian tribe surrenders

1878 Thomas A. Edison invents
phonograph

February 22 Greenback Labor party founded
February 28 Bland-Allison Silver Act passed; Gold standard rescinded
April 12 Boss Tweed dies in jail

1879 Thomas A. Edison invents electric light

1880 Population of the United States, 50,155,783
November 2 James A. Garfield (R) elected president over Winfield S. Scott (D)

1881 March 4 Garfield inaugurated as the 20th President of the United States
March 13 Tsar Alexander II assassinated; beginning of Russian Jewish immigration to the United States
May 16 Roscoe Conkling resigns from Senate
July 2 Charles Guiteau shoots Garfield
September 19 Garfield dies; Chester A. Arthur succeeds as the 21st President of the United States

1882 May 6 Chinese Exclusion Act passed
June 30 Guiteau hanged

1883 Hiram S. Maxim invents machine gun
January 16 Pendleton Act passed; beginning of civil service
May 24 Opening of Brooklyn Bridge, first of the suspension bridges

1884 October 29 Samuel D. Burchard's "Rum, Romanism and Rebellion" speech
November 4 Grover Cleveland (D) elected president over Blaine (R)

1885 March 4 Grover Cleveland inaugurated as 22nd President of the United States
July 23 Death of Ulysses S. Grant
November 25 Vice-President Thomas A. Hendricks dies in office

1886 May 4 Haymarket Square bombing
June 2 President Cleveland marries his ward, Frances Folsom
August 20 Accused Haymarket Square bombers hanged
September 4 Geronimo, Apache chief, surrenders
October 28 Statue of Liberty dedicated in New York Harbor
November 18 Death of Chester A. Arthur
December 8 American Federation of Labor founded

1887 January 20 United States leases Pearl Harbor in Hawaii
February 4 Interstate Commerce Act passed; regulates railroads

1888 November 6 Benjamin

Harrison (R) elected president over Cleveland (D)

1889 March 4 Harrison inaugurated as the 23rd President of the United States

March 16 Hurricane prevents naval battle in Samoa between United States and Germany

November 2 North Dakota and South Dakota enter the Union as the 39th and 40th states

November 8 Montana enters the Union as the 41st state

November 11 Washington enters the Union as the 42nd state

December 6 Death of Jefferson Davis

1890 Population of the United States, 62,622,250

July 2 Sherman Antitrust Act passed

July 3 Idaho enters the Union as the 43rd state

July 10 Wyoming enters the Union as the 44th state; first state to allow woman suffrage

July 14 Sherman Silver Purchase Act passed

August 6 Electric chair used for the first time in executions

October 1 McKinley Tariff passed

November 6 Mormon Church gives up polygamy

December 15 Sitting

Bull shot "while attempting to escape"

December 20 "Battle" of Wounded Knee. End of Indian resistance. "End of frontier."

1891 May 19 Populist party founded

1892 November 8 Cleveland (D) elected over Harrison (R)

1893 January 14 Queen Liliuokalani of Hawaii attempts to set up Hawaiian rule over the islands

January 17 Sanford B. Dole sets up American-dominated Republic of Hawaii

January 17 Death of Rutherford B. Hayes

March 4 Cleveland inaugurated as the 24th President of the United States

April Henry Ford builds his first automobile

June 26 John P. Altgeld pardons remaining accused Haymarket Square bombers

June 27 Stock market crash; "Panic of 1893"

September 9 Cleveland's daughter born in the White House

November 1 Sherman Silver Purchase Act repealed; Democratic party splits

1894 May 1 Coxey's Army in Washington

May 10 Pullman strike begins

July 3 Cleveland sends in troops against Pullman strikers

August 1 Sino-Japanese War begins

August 8 United States recognizes the Republic of Hawaii

1895 February 24 Cuba revolts against Spain

April 17 Sino-Japanese War ends in complete Japanese victory

July 20 Secretary of State Olney sends stiff note to Great Britain over the Venezuelan boundary dispute

December 29 Jameson Raid in South Africa; Great Britain begins to seek American friendship

1896 Gold discovered in Klondike

January 4 Utah enters the Union as the 45th state

July 8 William J. Bryan makes his "cross of gold" speech

August 30 Philippine Islands revolt against Spain

November 3 William McKinley (R) elected over Bryan (D)

1897 February 2 Great Britain and Venezuela agree to arbitration of boundary dispute

March 4 McKinley inaugurated as 25th President of the United States

July 24 Dingley Tariff enacted

1898 January 1 "Greater New York," with five boroughs, established

February 15 Battleship *Maine* blown up in Havana harbor

February 25 Theodore Roosevelt, as acting secretary of the navy, orders Pacific Fleet to Hong Kong

April 21 Spanish-American War begins

April 27 Admiral George Dewey leaves Hong Kong for Manila

May 1 Battle of Manila Bay. Dewey defeats Spanish fleet

May 19 Dewey brings Filipino insurgent Emilio Aguinaldo to Philippines to aid Americans

May 19 Spanish fleet reaches Santiago, Cuba

June 10 First American troops reach Cuba

June 20 Americans occupy Guam

July 1 Battle of San Juan Hill. Americans defeat Spanish

July 3 Battle of Santiago. Admiral Sampson defeats Spanish fleet

July 4 Americans occupy Wake Island

July 17 Americans take

Santiago

July 25 Americans occupy Puerto Rico

August 12 Hawaii becomes a territory of the United States

August 13 Americans take Manila; Spanish-American War over

October 1 Peace negotiations begin between Spain and the United States

December 10 Treaty of Paris officially concludes Spanish-American War

1899 February 4 Aguinaldo begins Philippine Insurrection against the United States

February 6 Senate accepts Treaty of Paris and denies Philippine independence

September 6 Secretary of State John Hay initiates "Open Door" Policy in China

October 3 Venezuelan boundary dispute with Great Britain settled

1900 Population of the United States, 75,994,575

March 6 Socialist party founded in the United States

March 14 Gold standard reestablished

April 7 William H. Taft sent to Philippines

June 29 Boxer Rebellion begins in China

August 14 Western troops take Peking

August "Gentleman's Agreement" limits Japanese immigration to the United States

November 6 McKinley (R) reelected over Bryan (D)

1901 February 25 United States Steel founded

March 2 Platt Amendment establishes American protectorate over Cuba

March 4 McKinley reinaugurated

March 13 Death of Benjamin Harrison

March 23 Aguinaldo captured in the Philippines

September 6 Leon Czolgosz shoots President McKinley

September 7 China bows to all Western demands

September 14 Death of President McKinley; Theodore Roosevelt becomes 26th President of the United States

October 16 Booker T. Washington entertained at White House dinner

October 29 Czolgosz hanged

November 18 Hay-Pauncefote Treaty with Great Britain gives United States a free hand to build canal across isthmus

December 12 Guglielmo Marconi sends first radio message across the Atlantic

1902 20-story "Flatiron Building" constructed in New York; beginning of the New York skyline

First transcontinental automobile trip

May 8 Volcanic eruption of Mount Pelée in Martinique

July 4 Philippine Insurrection declared over

October 20 Alaskan boundary dispute with Canada settled in favor of the United States

1903 Ford Motor Company founded

Edison produces *The Great Train Robbery;* first motion picture to tell a story

January 22 Hay-Herrán treaty with Colombia permits United States to build a Panama canal; rejected by Colombian Senate

February 14 Department of Commerce and Labor given cabinet rank

May 23 Wisconsin is first state to adopt a direct primary election

November 3 Panama rebels against Colombia with American help

November 6 United States recognizes Panamanian independence

November 18 Hay-Buneau-Varilla Treaty with Panama permits United States to build Panama Canal

December 17 First airplane flight by the Wright brothers

1904 February 8 Japan surprises Russian fleet at Port Arthur; Russo-Japanese War begins

May 9 Construction of Panama Canal begins

November 8 Roosevelt (R) reelected over Alton B. Parker (D)

December 6 "Roosevelt Corollary" to the Monroe Doctrine announced

1905 March 4 Roosevelt reinaugurated

June Industrial Workers of the World founded

September 5 Peace treaty at Portsmouth, N.H., ends Russo-Japanese War with Roosevelt mediating

1906 January 16 United States participates in Algeciras Conference on the fate of Morocco

April 18 San Francisco earthquake

December 10 Roosevelt awarded Nobel Peace Prize

1907 Immigration into the United States at a peak; 1905–1907 total 3,400,000

never surpassed
March 13 Stock market
crash; "Panic of 1907"
November 16 Oklahoma
enters the Union as the
46th state

1908 Model-T Ford produced as
the first cheap automobile
June 24 Death of Grover
Cleveland
November 8 William H.
Taft (R) elected president
over Bryan (D)

1909 March 4 Taft inaugu-
rated as the 27th President
of the United States
April 6 Robert E. Peary
reaches the North Pole
August 5 Payne-Aldrich
Tariff passed; beginning of
Republican split

1910 Population of the United
States, 91,972,266
Japan annexes Korea
November 8 Woodrow
Wilson elected governor of
New Jersey

1911 First transcontinental air-
plane flight
January 21 Progressive
party founded by Robert
M. La Follette
May 25 Dictatorship of
Porfirio Díaz overthrown
in Mexico

1912 January 6 New Mexico
enters the Union as the
47th state
February 14 Arizona en-
ters the Union as the 48th
state

April 14 *Titanic* strikes
iceberg and sinks on its
maiden voyage
November 5 Wilson (D)
elected president over
Taft (R) and Roosevelt
(Pr)

1913 February 22 Victoriano
Huerta declares himself
President of Mexico
February 25 16th
Amendment becomes part
of the Constitution; per-
mits income tax
March 4 Wilson inaugu-
rated as the 28th President
of the United States
May 31 17th Amendment
becomes part of the Con-
stitution; provides for the
direct election of senators
October 3 Underwood
Tariff passed
December 23 Federal
Reserve System founded

1914 April 21 American fleet
occupies Vera Cruz, Mex-
ico
June 24 Inter-American
arbitration conference at
Niagara Falls; resignation
of Huerta called for
June 28 Archduke Franz
Ferdinand of Austria as-
sassinated at Sarajevo
July 15 Huerta resigns;
Venustiano Carranza be-
comes President of Mexico
July 28 Austria-Hungary
declares war on Serbia;
World War I begins

August 4 Great Britain joins France and Russia (Allies) against Germany and Austria-Hungary (Central Powers)

August 15 Panama Canal open to shipping

October 25 Clayton Antitrust Act passed

1915 January 25 New York and San Francisco connected by telephone

February 4 Germany begins unrestricted submarine warfare

May 7 Sinking of the *Lusitania;* 128 Americans dead

June 8 Bryan resigns as secretary of state

July 21 American protests over *Lusitania* force Germany to abandon submarine warfare temporarily

July 24 German sabotage plans left in New York subway and picked up by American agents

November 30 du Pont explosion in Wilmington; sabotage suspected

December 4 Henry Ford's "peace ship" leaves for Europe

1916 January 10 Pancho Villa has 16 Americans shot

March 9 Villa raids Columbus, N.M.

March 15 John J. Persh-

ing leads troops into Mexico in pursuit of Villa

April 24 Irish rebellion against Great Britain

July 22 Preparedness parade bombing in San Francisco

July 30 Black Tom Island, N.J., explosion; sabotage suspected

November 7 Wilson (D) reelected over Charles E. Hughes (R)

1917 January 17 United States annexes Virgin Islands

January 22 Wilson calls for "peace without victory"

January 31 Germany resumes unrestricted submarine warfare

February 3 German submarine sinks *Housatonic*

February 5 Pershing recalled from Mexico

March 1 United States publishes Zimmermann note

March 5 Wilson reinaugurated

March 15 Tsar Nicholas II abdicates

March 21 German submarine sinks *Healdton*

March 22 United States recognizes the Russian Republic

April 6 United States declares war on Germany; enters World War I

June 26 First American

troops arrive in France under Pershing
July 4 Pershing heads a parade of American troops in Paris; "LaFayette, we are here."
October 23 American troops see combat in France for first time
November 11 Death of Liliuokalani, last native ruler of Hawaii
1918 January 8 Wilson announces the "Fourteen Points"
March 3 Russia signs Treaty of Brest-Litovsk; drops out of World War I
March 21 German troops under Ludendorff launch a huge offensive
June 4 American troops stop Germans at Château-Thierry, 90 km from Paris
June 6 American troops attack at Belleau Wood
July 15 German troops attack for last time; stopped by Americans at Rheims
September 12 American troops attack and reduce the St. Mihiel salient
September 26 American troops participate in the Meuse-Argonne offensive
October 23 Ludendorff relieved of post; flees to Sweden
November 4 Austria-Hungary surrenders
November 7 American troops reach Sedan near the German border
November 9 Kaiser Wilhelm II of Germany abdicates; flees to the Netherlands
November 11 Armistice; World War I ends

INDEX